Mathematics Olympiad

Class 07

A must have book for all Olympiads & Talent Search Exams...

by
Akash Deep

BLoOM CAP
Bloom Cap Edu Ventures Pvt. Ltd.

Bloom Cap Edu Ventures Pvt. Ltd.

卐 **Administrative & Production Office**

'Ramchhaya' 4577/15, Agarwal Road, Darya Ganj, New Delhi -110002
Tele: 011- 47630600, 43518550

卐 **ISBN :** 978-93-25519-16-9

卐 **PRICE :** ₹100.00

卐 **PO No :** TXT-XX-XXXXXXX-X-XX

For further information about the books log on to
www.bloomcap.org

Follow us on   

Preface

"Future belongs to those Who prepares for it today"

School Olympiads are National & International level competitions conducted by different Government, Non-Government & Educational Organisations with the purpose of making the children ready to face competitive exams. The challenging Questions asked in Olympiads motivate them to learn more & more and bring out the best result with improved academic performance. The Awards & Scholarship offered in Olympiads motivate children to aspire & strive for doing better and emerge out to be the best.

Maths Olympiads

Mathematics is an integral part of all competitive exams be it Aptitude or Commerce or Science. Maths Olympiads are meant to develop Mathematical aptitude in school students. They provide students with an opportunity to master their concepts and comprehend tricky questions effortlessly. Challenging Questions of Maths Olympiads encourage students to develop a logical approach to solve Mathematical Problems.

'Bloom Mathematics Olympiad Study Book Class 7' is a perfect resource to Study & Practice for Olympiad Exams and other National & State Level Talent Search Exams & Other Competitions.

Some Special Features of Bloom Maths Olympiad Study Books are;

- Chapterwise Exercises having different types of Objective Questions at par with the Olympiad Level.
- Detailed Explanation for each question.
- Olympiad Pattern Practice Sets at the end.

This book is prepared by Expert Panel with the utmost care, still if you have any suggestions regarding its improvement, then feel free to contact us at olympiads@bloomcap.org. We will try to inculcate your suggestions in the further editions.

Contents

Chapter 01

Integers

1 Mark Questions

1. Choose the greatest positive integer.
(a) $-(+100)$ (b) $-(-2)$
(c) (-48) (d) $+(-101)$

2. Opposite of going above sea level to 20 km in integer form is
(a) $+20$ km
(b) -20 km
(c) rise in 20 km
(d) descending 20 km

3. Choose the correct statement.
(a) Integers are closed under addition but not under subtraction.
(b) Integers are closed under subtraction but not under addition.
(c) Integers are closed both under addition and subtraction.
(d) None of the above

4. Which of the following is incorrect (if, $a \neq b$)?
(a) $a + b = b + a$ (b) $a - b = b - a$
(c) $a + 0 = a = 0 + a$ (d) $a - 0 = a \neq 0 - a$

5. Pick the odd one out.
(a) -4 and -7 (b) $+11$ and -22
(c) -5 and -6 (d) -2 and -10

6. The absolute value of $-28 + 12 + 42 - 63$ is
(a) 37   (b) -36
(c) 145   (d) -145

7. Fill in the box with appropriate integer.

$$\boxed{-6} \xrightarrow{+} \boxed{-24} \to \boxed{48} = \boxed{?}$$

(a) 78
(b) -78
(c) 6
(d) -6

8. The six-day forecast for the Antartica lists the low temperatures (in °C) as $-52°C, -53°C, -40°C, -58°C, -70°C, -79°C$. Which choice shows the temperatures in order from lowest to highest?
(a) $-79°C, -70°C, -52°C, -53°C, -48°C, -58°C$
(b) $-52°C, -53°C, -58°C, -70°C, -79°C, -48°C$
(c) $-79°C, -70°C, -58°C, -53°C, -52°C, -48°C$
(d) $-48°C, -52°C, -53°C, -58°C, -70°C, -79°C$

Directions (Q. Nos. 9 and 10) Study the figure given below and answer the following questions.

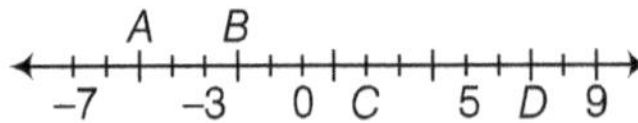

9. Find the value of $D - A$.

(a) 2   (b) −2   (c) −12   (d) 12

10. Use the correct values of C, B, D, A and fill in the box given below.
$$C + B\ \square\ D + A$$

(a) >   (b) <

(c) =   (d) Can't say

11. If we multiply −1 to itself 20 times, then what would be the answer?

(a) 1   (b) −1

(c) 0   (d) Can't say

12. "Product of a negative and a positive integers depends on the sign of the greater integer."

If the above statement is not correct, then choose the following statements to correct it.

(a) Product of a negative and a positive integers depends on the sign of the smaller integer.

(b) Product of a negative and a positive integers is always negative.

(c) Product of a negative and a positive integers is always positive.

(d) No change

13. The value of $3 \times (-7) \times (-8) \times 9 \times 0 \times 4 \times 2$ is equal to

(a) −12096   (b) 0

(c) 12096   (d) 1

14. Fill in the box with the correct option.
$$2 \times (5 + 6) = (2 \times 5)\ \square\ (2 \times 6)$$

(a) ÷   (b) ×

(c) +   (d) −

15. If '÷' is replaced by '×', then find the correct value of the following problem.
$$(-2) \div 3 \times (-4) \div 1 = ?$$

(a) 24   (b) −12

(c) 8   (d) −6

16. State which property is shown below.
$$7 \times (8 + 9) = 7 \times 8 + 7 \times 9$$

(a) Commutative

(b) Associative

(c) Closure

(d) Distributive

2 Marks Questions

17. Fill in the blanks with the help of options, given in the box.

(i) odd,	(ii) negative,
(iii) 0,	(iv) even
(v) 1,	(vi) less

P. The multiplicative identity of integers is ……

Q. If $(-1)^n$ is negative, then n is ……

R. A negative number is …… than zero.

S. −1 is between −2 and …… on the number line.

Codes

     P   Q   R   S

(a) (v)   (i)   (vi)   (iii)

(b) (vi) (ii)   (v)   (i)

(c) (ii) (iv) (iii)   (v)

(d) (v) (vi) (iv)   (ii)

18. Which of the following will give '−2' as the simplified value?

(a) $\dfrac{(-2) \times (-2) + 2 \div (-1)}{1}$ (b) $\dfrac{(-2) \times 2 - 2 + 1}{1}$

(c) $\dfrac{2 \times (-2) + 2 \div (-1)}{-1}$ (d) $\dfrac{2 \times 2 + 2 \div (-1)}{-1}$

19. Match the following.

Column A		Column B	
I.	$(-31)+30+(-31)+30$ $+...30$ terms	(i)	-15
II.	$(-7)\times5+1\times0$	(ii)	$+35$
III.	$42\times(91-91)$	(iii)	0
IV.	$21\div(5-8)$	(iv)	-35
		(v)	$+15$
		(vi)	-7

Codes

	I	II	III	IV
(a)	(v)	(iv)	(iii)	(ii)
(b)	(v)	(iii)	(vi)	(ii)
(c)	(i)	(iii)	(iv)	(ii)
(d)	(i)	(iv)	(iii)	(vi)

20. Which of the following sequences of operator will satisfy the equation given below?

$$(-3)\ \square\ (-8)\ \square\ (-4)\ \square\ 2\ \square\ (-2)=3$$

(a) $+,-,\times,\div$ 　　　(b) $\div,+,\times,-$
(c) $+,\div,-,\times$ 　　　(d) $\times,\div,+,-$

21. Find the values of $\diamondsuit$ and ∇ in the given equations.

$$100\times\nabla=\nabla+\nabla+98\times7$$
and $153\div\diamondsuit=923-230\times4$

(a) $\diamondsuit=41,\nabla=7$ 　　(b) $\nabla-7,\diamondsuit=51$
(c) $\diamondsuit=7,\nabla=41$ 　　(d) $\nabla=51,\diamondsuit=7$

22. Assertion (A) $17-\{(2+\overline{7-3})-8\}=19$

Reason (R) In simplification, it is not necessary to follow the order of operations.

(a) A is true and R is correct explanation of A
(b) A is false and R is correct explanation of A
(c) A is true and R is false
(d) Both A and R are false

23. Dr. Christian advised her patient to take three tablets A, B and C such that the patient had to take A and B in the numbers two and one respectively in a day and to take tablet C once in every two days. How many tablets in all did she advise to take in 30 days?
(a) 60 　　　　　　(b) 90
(c) 105 　　　　　(d) 120

24. $65-(-3)\{-2-\overline{8-3}\}\div3\{5+(-2)(-1)\}$ is
(a) 64 　　　　　　(b) 62
(c) 96 　　　　　　(d) 48

25. Study the below statements carefully and answer the question given below.
(i) $(-10)\times(5-2)=(-10)\times(-3)$
(ii) The successor of $0\times(-51)$ is $1\times(-51)$
(iii) $(-3)+(-10)$ is less than $(-10)-(-3)$
(iv) Integers are closed under division.

Which of the following statements is/are corrects?
(a) Only (i)
(b) Only (ii)
(c) Only (iii)
(d) All (i), (ii), (iii) and (iv)

26. Mr. Anil had a balance of ₹ 11700 in his account. He deposited amount of ₹ 1925, ₹ 3380, ₹ 4000 on different days of a month and withdraw ₹ 2500, ₹ 5850, ₹ 1000 also. What is his final balance (in ₹) at the end of the month?
(a) 11700 　　　　　(b) 11655
(c) -2000 　　　　(d) -2050

27. An elevator descends at a speed of 1 floor/sec. If Mohan takes the elevator from 24th floor of a multistoreyed building to reach to the 3rd basement of parking, then how much time will he take?
(a) 27 sec 　　　　(b) 24 sec
(c) 21 sec 　　　　(d) 18 sec

Rational Number

1 Mark Questions

1. Evaluate and choose the correct option $\dfrac{2}{5}+\left(-\dfrac{5}{6}\right)+\left(-\dfrac{7}{9}\right)$.

(a) $-\dfrac{109}{90}$

(b) $\dfrac{-14}{90}$

(c) $\dfrac{14}{9}$

(d) $\dfrac{27}{20}$

2. The sum of two rational numbers is $\dfrac{8}{9}$. If one of them is $\dfrac{2}{18}$, then the other is

(a) $\dfrac{1}{18}$

(b) $\dfrac{3}{18}$

(c) $\dfrac{7}{9}$

(d) $\dfrac{6}{9}$

3. What should be added to $\dfrac{-1}{4}$ to obtain the nearest natural number?

(a) $\dfrac{2}{4}$

(b) $\dfrac{-1}{4}$

(c) $\dfrac{-5}{4}$

(d) $\dfrac{5}{4}$

4. What should be subtracted from $\left(\dfrac{2}{3}-\dfrac{3}{4}\right)$ to get $-\dfrac{1}{6}$?

(a) $-\dfrac{1}{2}$

(b) $\dfrac{1}{12}$

(c) $\dfrac{1}{6}$

(d) $-\dfrac{1}{6}$

5. If A and B represent a rational number, then $(A-B)$ is equal to

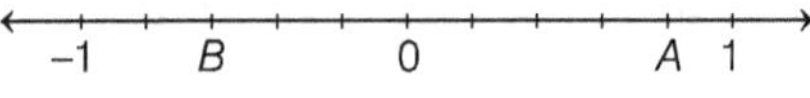

(a) $\dfrac{2}{5}$

(b) $-\dfrac{4}{5}$

(c) $\dfrac{7}{5}$

(d) -1

6. Choose the correct statement.
   (a) Rational numbers are closed under division.
   (b) Rational numbers are commutative under division.
   (c) Rational numbers are associative under division.
   (d) None of the above

7. Which of the following statements is true?

(a) $-\dfrac{3}{5}$ lies to the right of zero on number line.

(b) The rational numbers $\dfrac{-17}{-13}$ and $\dfrac{-7}{17}$ lie on the same side of zero.

(c) The rational numbers $\dfrac{-4}{-5}$ and $\dfrac{-4}{5}$ lie on opposite side of number line.

(d) None of the above

8. Which of the following rational numbers satisfies of
$$(a + b) + c = a + (b + c)?$$

(a) $a = -2,\ b = -\dfrac{2}{3},\ c = -\dfrac{3}{5}$

(b) $a = -10,\ b = -\dfrac{9}{11},\ c = -\dfrac{7}{12}$

(c) $a = -\dfrac{7}{21},\ b = -\dfrac{7}{11},\ c = \dfrac{5}{12}$

(d) All of the above

9. Chaaru simplified the number in this manner $\dfrac{-49}{-63} = \dfrac{7}{-9}$. Did she simplify correctly?

(a) Yes   (b) No

(c) Can't say   (d) None of these

10. Which is the correct sequence of numbers in ascending order?

(a) $\dfrac{1}{3} < \dfrac{3}{7} < \dfrac{2}{5}$ (b) $\dfrac{3}{7} < \dfrac{1}{3} < \dfrac{2}{5}$

(c) $\dfrac{2}{5} < \dfrac{3}{7} < \dfrac{1}{3}$ (d) $\dfrac{1}{3} < \dfrac{2}{5} < \dfrac{3}{7}$

11. If $p = -\dfrac{2}{3} + \dfrac{4}{5} + 1$ and $q = \dfrac{2}{3} - \dfrac{4}{5} + \dfrac{7}{15}$, then

(a) $p > q$

(b) $p < q$

(c) $p = q$

(d) Can't be determined

12. Which of the following rational numbers doesn't lie between $\dfrac{2}{101}$ and $\dfrac{3}{71}$?

(a) $\dfrac{150}{7171}$ (b) $\dfrac{1000}{35855}$

(c) $\dfrac{4}{914}$ (d) $\dfrac{500}{21513}$

13. Match the following.

	Column A		Column B
I.	$\left(\dfrac{-6}{25}\right) \times \dfrac{50}{36}$	(i)	$\dfrac{-10}{9}$
II.	$\dfrac{3}{11} \times \left(\dfrac{-33}{21}\right)$	(ii)	-1
III.	$\dfrac{5}{21} \times \left(\dfrac{42}{-9}\right)$	(iii)	$\dfrac{-1}{3}$
IV.	$\left(\dfrac{-7}{11}\right) \times \dfrac{77}{49}$	(iv)	$\dfrac{3}{-7}$

Codes

	I	II	III	IV
(a)	iii	i	iv	ii
(b)	ii	i	iv	iii
(c)	iii	iv	i	ii
(d)	ii	iv	i	iii

14. Pick the odd one out.

(a) $\dfrac{2}{3} \times \left(\dfrac{1}{2} - \dfrac{1}{4}\right) = \dfrac{2}{3} \times \dfrac{1}{2} - \dfrac{2}{3} \times \dfrac{1}{4}$

(b) $\dfrac{4}{5} \times \left(\dfrac{2}{3} - \dfrac{2}{7}\right) = \dfrac{4}{5} \times \dfrac{2}{3} + \dfrac{4}{5} \times \dfrac{-2}{7}$

(c) $\dfrac{7}{9} \times \left(\dfrac{-7}{11} + \dfrac{2}{11}\right) = \dfrac{7}{9} \times \dfrac{2}{11} + \dfrac{7}{9} \times \dfrac{7}{11}$

(d) $\dfrac{3}{5} \times \left(\dfrac{3}{7} - \dfrac{2}{5}\right) = \dfrac{3}{5} \times \dfrac{3}{7} + \dfrac{3}{5} \times \dfrac{2}{-5}$

15. What is the reciprocal of $\left(\dfrac{3}{2} \times \dfrac{1}{3}\right) + \left(\dfrac{1}{3} \times 9\right)$?

(a) $\dfrac{7}{2}$

(b) $\dfrac{5}{3}$

(c) $\dfrac{3}{5}$

(d) $\dfrac{2}{7}$

2 Marks Questions

16. State 'T' for true and 'F' for false.

   I. All fractions are rational numbers.

   II. The value of $\left(\dfrac{-16}{21} \div \dfrac{-4}{3}\right)$ is $\dfrac{4}{7}$.

   III. $\dfrac{9}{72}$ and $\dfrac{-3}{21}$ are equivalent rational numbers.

   IV. $\dfrac{48}{-96}$ is in standard form.

Codes

	I	II	III	IV
(a)	F	F	T	T
(b)	T	T	F	F
(c)	T	F	F	T
(d)	F	T	F	F

17. Fill in the blanks with the help of options, given in the box.

(i) opposite,	(ii) $\dfrac{-79}{30}$,
(iii) same,	(iv) $\dfrac{-20}{19}$,
(v) greater,	(vi) less,

   P. The rational number $\dfrac{120}{-114}$ when reduced to standard form is ……. .

Q. The rational numbers $\left(\dfrac{-11}{-5}\right)$ and $\left(\dfrac{7}{-26}\right)$ lie on the …… side of 0 on the number line.

R. $\dfrac{-5}{8}$ is …… than $\dfrac{-7}{-12}$.

S. $\dfrac{-4}{-9}$ is …… than $\dfrac{1}{4}$.

Codes

	P	Q	R	S
(a)	(i)	(ii)	(iii)	(iv)
(b)	(ii)	(iv)	(v)	vi
(c)	(v)	(vi)	(i)	(iv)
(d)	(iv)	(i)	(vi)	(v)

18. Shehnaz earns ₹ 25000 per month. She spends $\dfrac{1}{5}$ of her income on food, $\dfrac{3}{10}$ of the remainder on house rent and $\dfrac{9}{28}$ of remainder on the education of children. How much money is still left with her?

(a) ₹ 10000   (b) ₹ 8500

(c) ₹ 10500   (d) ₹ 9500

19. Match the following.

	Column A		Column B
I.	$\left(-7\dfrac{1}{24}\right) + \left(-3\dfrac{1}{16}\right) = \left(-3\dfrac{1}{16}\right) + \left(-7\dfrac{1}{24}\right)$	(i)	Associative property
II.	$\left(\dfrac{3}{5} \times \dfrac{12}{13}\right) \times \dfrac{7}{18} = \dfrac{3}{5} \times \left(\dfrac{12}{13} \times \dfrac{7}{18}\right)$	(ii)	Distributive property
III.	$\left(\dfrac{-12}{5}\right) \times \left\{\dfrac{4}{15} + \left(\dfrac{-16}{25}\right)\right\} = \left(\dfrac{-12}{5}\right) \times \dfrac{4}{15} + \left(\dfrac{-12}{5}\right) \times \left(\dfrac{-16}{25}\right)$	(iii)	Commutative property

Codes

	I	II	III			I	II	III			I	II	III			I	II	III
(a)	i	ii	iii		(b)	i	iii	ii		(c)	iii	i	ii		(d)	ii	i	iii

20. What is the percentage of the smallest number to the greatest number, if $\dfrac{5}{6}, \dfrac{7}{12}, \dfrac{13}{18}, \dfrac{23}{24}$ are arranged in descending or ascending order?

(a) $31\dfrac{2}{24}$

(b) $39\dfrac{3}{23}$

(c) $35\dfrac{3}{18}$

(d) None of the above

21. A train is moving at a speed of $\dfrac{2024}{15}$ km/h. How much distance will it cover in $\dfrac{25}{4}$ h?

(a) $\dfrac{2530}{3}$ km

(b) 2560 km

(c) $\dfrac{2560}{15}$ km

(d) None of the above

22. Mr Tiwari had a piece of land which he distributed among his three children. He gave $\dfrac{1}{3}$ to his eldest son and $\dfrac{2}{5}$ of the remaining to his daughter and the left amount of land to his youngest child. How much did his youngest child got, if Mr Tiwari had 25000 sq m of land?

(a) 5000 sq m

(b) 10000 sq m

(c) 15000 sq m

(d) 2000 sq m

23. Which of the given answers do we get, on evaluating the following equation?

$$\left(1-\frac{1}{2}\right)\left(1-\frac{1}{3}\right)\left(1-\frac{1}{4}\right)\left(1-\frac{1}{5}\right)\ldots\left(1-\frac{1}{100}\right)$$

(a) $\dfrac{99}{100}$

(b) $\dfrac{1}{100}$

(c) $\dfrac{1}{99}$

(d) None of the above

Fractions and Decimals

1 Mark Questions

Fractions

1. What fraction of the following figure is shaded?

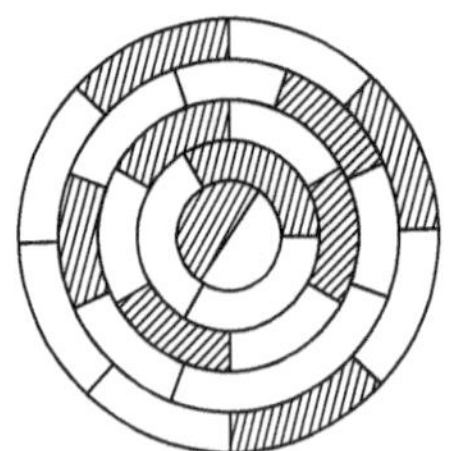

   (a) $\dfrac{14}{25}$ (b) $\dfrac{5}{13}$

   (c) $\dfrac{9}{26}$ (d) $\dfrac{10}{27}$

2. Which of the following options represents $\dfrac{3}{4}$ of 8 parts shaded?

   (a)

   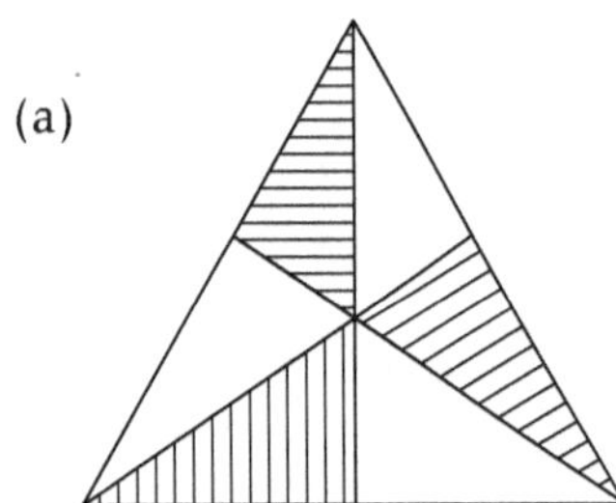

   (b)

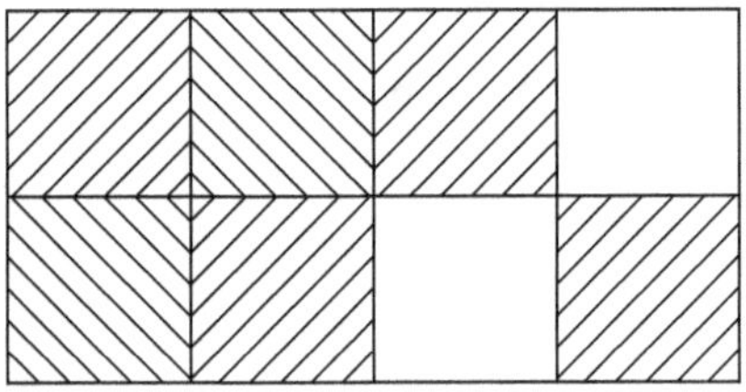

   (c)

   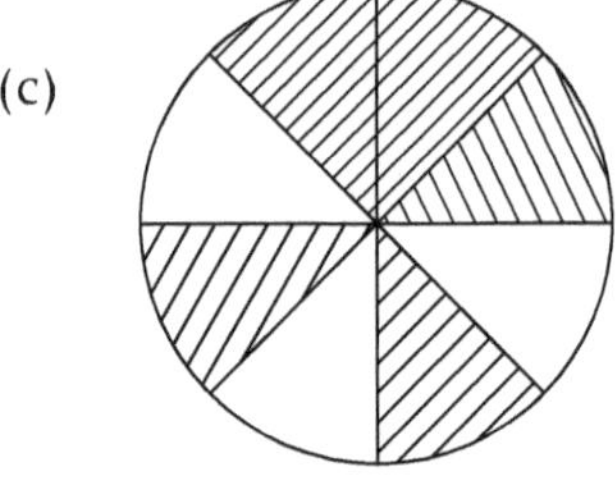

   (d) None of the above

3. Choose the correct statement.

   (a) Fractions are in the form of $\dfrac{p}{q}$, where p, q are integers and $q \neq 0$.

   (b) $\dfrac{7}{9}$ is not a fraction.

   (c) Mixed fractions can be converted into proper fractions.

   (d) Improper fractions have numerator greater than denominator.

4. Which of the following fractions is closest to zero?

(a) $\dfrac{6}{13}$ (b) $\dfrac{3}{5}$

(c) $\dfrac{5}{6}$ (d) $\dfrac{1}{4}$

5. $\dfrac{19}{\square}$ is a fraction that lies between $\dfrac{1}{9}$ and $\dfrac{1}{11}$. What will be the correct whole number to fill the box?

(a) 99   (b) 198

(c) 189   (d) 110

6. If $\square + 2\dfrac{37}{44} = 10\dfrac{9}{44}$, then missing fraction in the box is

(a) $7\dfrac{4}{11}$ (b) $2\dfrac{10}{44}$

(c) $8\dfrac{1}{44}$ (d) $4\dfrac{7}{11}$

7. If $x = \dfrac{6}{25}$ and $y = \dfrac{3}{5}$, then the value of $\dfrac{x}{y}$ is

(a) $\dfrac{6}{5}$ (b) $\dfrac{18}{125}$

(c) $\dfrac{2}{5}$ (d) None of these

8. If $a * b = \dfrac{a \times b}{a \div b}$, then what is the value of $21 * 3$?

(a) $\dfrac{21}{3}$ (b) $\dfrac{42}{7}$

(c) $\dfrac{9}{1}$ (d) $\dfrac{7}{3}$

9. One pack of cookies requires $3\dfrac{1}{2}$ cups of flour and $2\dfrac{1}{3}$ cups of sugar. Estimated total quantity of both ingredients used in 10 such packets of cookies will be

(a) less than 50 cups

(b) between 50 cups and 60 cups

(c) between 60 cups and 70 cups

(d) above 60 cups

10. A cricket team won 12 games and lost 4 in a tournament. Then, the fraction of the games they lost, is

(a) $\dfrac{4}{16}$ (b) $\dfrac{4}{12}$

(c) $\dfrac{12}{16}$ (d) $\dfrac{12}{4}$

11. State 'T' for true and 'F' for false.

  I. A fraction acts as operator 'of '.

  II. Product of a proper and improper fraction is greater than the improper fraction.

  III. $2\dfrac{2}{5} + 2\dfrac{1}{5} = 2$.

  IV. The reciprocal of $\dfrac{7}{8}$ is $\dfrac{-7}{8}$.

  V. A mixed fraction can converted to a proper fraction.

Codes

	I	II	III	IV	V			I	II	III	IV	V
(a)	T	F	F	F	F		(b)	T	T	T	T	T
(c)	F	F	F	F	T		(d)	F	F	F	F	F

Decimals

12. The decimal expression 0.321 can be expressed as

(a) $\dfrac{107}{999}$ (b) $\dfrac{329}{900}$

(c) $\dfrac{321}{1000}$ (d) $\dfrac{329}{1000}$

13. Which of the following arrangements is correct?

(a) $0.723 < 0.462 < 0.572 < 0.213$

(b) $0.512 < 0.758 < 0.831 < 0.913$

(c) $0.713 < 0.721 < 0.658 < 0.412$

(d) $0.412 < 0.712 < 0.799 < 0.099$

14. The value of $14.63 - \dfrac{1}{6} \times 0.6$ is

(a) 14.52   (b) 14.63

(c) 14.62   (d) 14.53

15. Choose the correct statement.

(a) To multiply a decimal by 10, we move the decimal point in the number to the left by one place.

(b) To multiply a decimal by 100, we move the decimal point in the number to the right by two places.

(c) Both (a) and (b)

(d) None of the above

16. If $73.47 \times 100 = 92 \times 73.47 + 8 \times \square$, then what will be the missing number in the box?

(a) 100

(b) 734.7

(c) 73.47

(d) 7.347

17. On Tuesday, Marshall put 12 L of fuel in his car for ₹ 616.8. The following Friday, he put 15 L in and paid ₹ 817.5. On which day, he gets the better price?

(a) Tuesday

(b) Friday

(c) Same on Tuesday and Friday

(d) Can't say

18. In a Mathematics class, a teacher asked Aman, Navnidh and Jaskaran to determine the decimal by giving the following clues.

Clue 1 : between $\dfrac{2}{5}$ and $\dfrac{3}{5}$

Clue 2 : greater than $\dfrac{1}{2}$

Clue 3 : multiple of 0.11

Determine who gave the correct answer.

(a) Aman → 0.55

(b) Navnidh → 0.66

(c) Jaskaran → 0.45

(d) None of the above

2 Marks Questions

19. How many more triangles in the figure must be shaded to make the fraction of shaded squares equal to $\dfrac{4}{9}$?

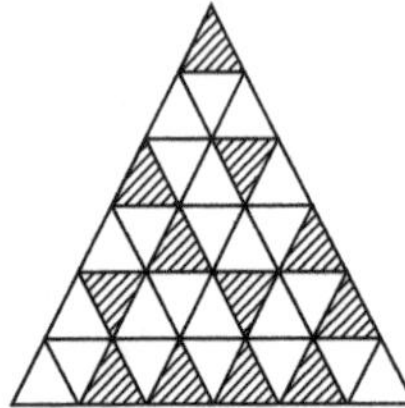

(a) 3   (b) 4   (c) 5   (d) 6

20. Evaluate and choose the correct option for $\left(1-\dfrac{2}{3}\right) \times \left(1-\dfrac{2}{5}\right) \times \left(1-\dfrac{2}{7}\right) \times$

$\left(1-\dfrac{2}{9}\right) \times \dots \times \left(1-\dfrac{2}{99}\right).$

(a) $\dfrac{2}{3}$

(b) $\dfrac{2}{99}$

(c) $\dfrac{1}{99}$

(d) $\dfrac{1}{3}$

21. $\cfrac{1}{1+\cfrac{1}{2+\cfrac{1}{3+\cfrac{1}{2}}}} = ?$

(a) $\dfrac{11}{23}$

(b) $\dfrac{16}{23}$

(c) $\dfrac{13}{23}$

(d) $\dfrac{17}{23}$

22. Mihir was asked to solve the fraction
$$\dfrac{\dfrac{5}{3}+1\dfrac{1}{2}\text{ of }\dfrac{7}{3}}{2+2\dfrac{2}{3}}$$
and his answer was $\dfrac{1}{7}$. By how much times was his answer wrong?

(a) $\dfrac{7}{10}$ (b) $\dfrac{29}{3}$

(c) $\dfrac{31}{4}$ (d) None of these

23. Fill in the blanks with the help of options, given in the box.

(i) 10,	(ii) 100,
(iii) multiplying,	(iv) 16.92,
(v) 0.07,	(vi) Dividing,
(vii) 0.25,	(viii) 172.4

I. $64.008 \times \square = 6400.8$

II. .... by 10 shifts the decimal one place to left side.

III. $16.92 \times 100 = 16.92 \times 93 + \square \times 7$

IV. $(0.4) \times (0.4) - (0.3) \times (0.3)$ is ....

Codes

	I	II	III	IV
(a)	ii	iii	v	viii
(b)	i	iii	iv	vi
(c)	ii	vi	iv	v
(d)	i	vii	v	viii

24. State 'T' for true and 'F' for false.

I. To multiply a number by 1000, we move the decimal point to the right by one place.

II. $4.7 \div 10 = 47$

III. $4.06 \times 100 = 406$

IV. If cost of 5 apples is ₹ 2.15, then 40 apples can be bought for ₹ 20.

Codes

	I	II	III	IV
(a)	F	F	F	F
(b)	T	T	T	T
(c)	F	F	T	F
(d)	T	F	F	T

Directions (Q. Nos. 25-27) Barack and Ben go shopping to a mall. They each planning on buying one pair of jeans and 2 shirts. They each brought ₹ 1000.

Store A	Store B	Store C
One pair of jeans A ₹ 399.7	One pair of jeans B ₹ 449.9	One pair of jeans C ₹ 499.5
2 shirts A ₹ 444.8	1 shirt B ₹ 224.8	1 shirt C ₹ 204.6

25. At which store should Barack and Ben shop to spend the least amount of money?

(a) A   (b) B

(c) C   (d) Can't say

26. Ben really likes the jeans from store C, a shirt from store A and another shirt from store B. Does he has enough money to buy these clothes? If so, how much money would he get back?

(a) No   (b) Yes, ₹ 50.32

(c) Yes, ₹ 53.3   (d) Can't say

27. Ben decides that he really wants to get 2 pairs of jeans and 1 shirt. Is it possible for him to do this, if he shops at different stores? If so, how much more money is required?

(a) Yes   (b) No, ₹ 4

(c) No, ₹ 50   (d) Can't say

Exponents and Powers

1 Mark Questions

1. Express (-2187) as power of (-3).
   (a) $(-3)^7$
   (b) $(-3)^4$
   (c) $(-3)^{-7}$
   (d) $(-3)^8$

2. On solving $\dfrac{2^0 + 3^0 + 4^0}{2^0 \times (3^0 + 4^0)}$, we get
   (a) 0
   (b) 1
   (c) 2/3
   (d) $\dfrac{3}{2}$

3. If $x = 1$ and $y = 2$, then $x^y + y^x$ is equal to
   (a) 3
   (b) 4
   (c) 5
   (d) 6

4. Find the value of b, if $\left(\dfrac{4}{5}\right)^3 \times \left(\dfrac{4}{5}\right)^{b+8}$
   $= \left(\dfrac{5}{4}\right)^{-11}$
   (a) 0
   (b) 1
   (c) 12
   (d) 11

5. If $2^x = 4^y = 8^z = 64$, then find the value of $x + y + z$.
   (a) 10
   (b) 11
   (c) 13
   (d) Can't be determined

6. If $5^x = 999$, then the value of 5^{x-3} is
   (a) $\dfrac{999}{5}$
   (b) $\dfrac{1000}{27}$
   (c) $\dfrac{999}{125}$
   (d) $\dfrac{1000}{125}$

7. Evaluate and choose the correct option for $\dfrac{(a^2 b^3 c)^2}{a^4 b^6 c^2}$.
   (a) 0
   (b) 1
   (c) abc
   (d) $\dfrac{1}{abc}$

8. Simplify and choose the correct option for $\left(\dfrac{169}{225}\right)^{\frac{1}{2}} \times \left(\dfrac{125}{27}\right)^{\frac{2}{3}} \times \left(\dfrac{81}{4}\right)^{\frac{1}{2}}$.
   (a) 0
   (b) 1
   (c) $\dfrac{65}{6}$
   (d) $\dfrac{75}{3}$

9. The simplified value of $\dfrac{\left(\dfrac{-1}{3}\right)^6}{\left(\dfrac{-1}{3}\right)^5} \div \dfrac{\left(\dfrac{-1}{27}\right)}{\left(\dfrac{-1}{9}\right)}$ is
   (a) 0
   (b) 1
   (c) -1
   (d) 3

10. The simplified value of $\dfrac{2x^2y}{3x} \cdot \dfrac{9xy^2}{y^4}$ will be equal to

    (a) $\dfrac{2}{3}xy^2$　　　　　(b) $\dfrac{2}{3}xy$

    (c) $\dfrac{2x}{3y}$　　　　　(d) $\dfrac{6x^2}{y}$

11. Simplify and choose the correct option.
    $$\left(\dfrac{m^3p^5}{n^7}\right)^6 \times \left(\dfrac{m^2n^0p^3}{m^4n^2}\right)^3$$

    (a) $\dfrac{m^{12}p^{39}}{n^{48}}$　　　　(b) $\dfrac{m^{12}p^{40}}{n^{36}}$

    (c) 0　　　　　　(d) 1

12. Find the value of
    $$(5x^7y^3z^{-1})^2 \times (2xy^{-5})^3 \times (2y^{-3}z^2)^3$$

    (a) $20x^9y^{10}z^4$　　　　(b) $400x^8y^{-9}z^2$

    (c) $800x^{17}y^{18}z^4$　　　(d) $\dfrac{1600x^{17}z^4}{y^{18}}$

13. Which of the following is the equivalent to 9.9×10^{-6}?

    (a) 0.00000099　　　(b) 0.0000099

    (c) 0.000099　　　　(d) 0.00099

14. The equivalent form of 0.000000748 is

    (a) 748×10^{-6}　　　(b) 74.8×10^{-7}

    (c) 7.48×10^{-7}　　　(d) 0.748×10^{-9}

15. Choose the correct signs.

    I. $(2^2)^3 \square 2^{2^3}$

    II. $(4^4)^{\frac{1}{2}} \square 2^4$

III. $\left(3^{\frac{1}{3}}\right)^9 \square \left(81^{\frac{1}{4}}\right)^2$

Codes

	I	II	III			I	II	III
(a)	>	<	=		(b)	<	=	>
(c)	=	<	>		(d)	<	>	<

16. Mr. Xen asked two of his students to solve the expression $\left(\dfrac{24a^3b^{-8}}{6a^{-5}b^2}\right)^{\frac{-1}{2}}$ and write the answer on blackboard. Andy wrote the answer as $4a^{-4}b^5$, whereas Zuck wrote the answer as $\dfrac{4b^5}{a^4}$. Who wrote the correct answer?

    (a) Andy　　　　　(b) Zuck
    (c) Both of them　　(d) None of the above

17. A rectangular piece of land is to be sold off is smaller pieces. The total area of the land is 2^{17} sq miles. The pieces to be cut out are 16^2 sq miles in size. How many smaller pieces of the land can be sold at the given size?

    (a) 2^{15}　　　　　(b) 16^4

    (c) 2^9　　　　　(d) None of these

18. The average household spends about ₹ 40000 each month. If there are about 1×10^8 households, what is the total amount of money spent by the households in one month?

    (a) ₹ (40×10^8)　　(b) ₹ 40000

    (c) ₹ (4.0×10^{14})　　(d) ₹ (4×10^{12})

2 Marks Questions

19. The correct value of

$(-1)^{101} + (-1)^{102} + (-1)^{103} + \ldots + (-1)^{200}$ is

(a) 0   (b) 1

(c) −1   (d) −2

20. Find the value of

$$7^4 \left[\left(\frac{6}{7}\right)^2 + \left(\frac{6}{7}\right) - \left(\frac{6}{7}\right)^3\right] + (-7)^3$$

$$\left[\left(\frac{6}{7}\right) + 1 - \left(\frac{6}{7}\right)^2\right] \times 6$$

(a) 0   (b) 1

(c) $\dfrac{7}{6}$ (d) $\dfrac{6}{7}$

21. Match the following.

	Column A		Column B
(I)	$\dfrac{6^3 \times 9^2 \times 25^2}{3^2 \times 4^2 \times 15^4}$	(i)	$5^2 \times 3^4$
(II)	$\dfrac{3^8 \times 16^2 \times 7^5}{81^2 \times 2^5 \times 49^2}$	(ii)	$\dfrac{3}{2}$
(III)	$\dfrac{15^4 \times 21^3}{3^3 \times 5^2 \times 7^3}$	(iii)	56

Codes

	I	II	III			I	II	III
(a)	i	ii	iii		(b)	ii	i	iii
(c)	ii	iii	i		(d)	i	iii	ii

22. Simplify and choose the correct option.

$$\left(\frac{a^{5b-3} \times a^{3-2b}}{a^{4b-6} \times a^{2b-9}}\right)^{\frac{-8}{6}}$$

(a) a^{3b+15} (b) a^{13-3b}

(c) a^{4b-20} (d) a^{4b+18}

23. The mass of Earth is 5.9×10^{24} kg. The mass of Pluto is 1.3×10^{22} kg. How much greater is Earth's mass?

(a) 5.887×10^{24} (b) 5.792×10^{25}

(c) 58.87×10^{24} (d) None of the above

24. $\left(\dfrac{p^{a^4}}{p^{b^4}}\right)^{\frac{1}{a^2+b^2}} \times \left(\dfrac{p^{b^4}}{p^{c^4}}\right)^{\frac{1}{b^2+c^2}} \times \left(\dfrac{p^{c^4}}{p^{a^4}}\right)^{\frac{1}{c^2+a^2}}$

is equal to

(a) 1   (b) 2

(c) 3   (d) 4

25. If $xyz = 1$, then find the value of

$$\frac{1}{(1+x+y^{-1})} + \frac{1}{(1+y+z^{-1})} + \frac{1}{(1+z+x^{-1})}$$

(a) 1   (b) 2

(c) 3   (d) 4

26. If $a^x = b^y = c^z$ and $abc = 1$, then what is the value of $xy + yz + zx$?

(a) 1   (b) 3

(c) 0   (d) 5

Ratio and Proportion

1 Mark Questions

1. In the ratio 3 : 4 if the antecedent is 75, then what is the consequent?
   (a) 45   (b) 50   (c) 100   (d) 120

2. If $p : q = 5 : 7$, then $\dfrac{5p + 3q}{2p - q} = ?$
   (a) 40 : 7   (b) 50 : 11
   (c) 17 : 5   (d) 46 : 3

3. If $p : 5 :: 12 : 20$, find the value of p.
   (a) 3   (b) 5   (c) 6   (d) 2

4. If $p : q = 3 : 4$ and $q : r = 2 : 3$, then $P : r = ?$
   (a) 1 : 2   (b) 2 : 3   (c) 4 : 5   (d) 5 : 3

5. What is the fourth proportional to 72, 168 and 150?
   (a) 450   (b) 300   (c) 350   (d) 400

6. Which fraction in equivalent to the ratio 105 : 135?
   (a) $\dfrac{7}{5}$ (b) $\dfrac{7}{9}$ (c) $\dfrac{3}{7}$ (d) $\dfrac{4}{3}$

7. A bag contains ₹ 360 in the form of ₹ 1, ₹ 2 and ₹ 5 coins in the ratio of 3 : 4 : 5. Then find the number of each type of coins.
   (a) 30, 40, 50   (b) 40, 50, 30
   (c) 50, 40, 30   (d) 30, 50, 40

8. Arun divides ₹10000 betwen his sons, Anil and Ajay in the ratio 5 : 3. Find the share of each of them.
   (a) ₹ 2560 and ₹ 8440
   (b) ₹ 6250 and ₹ 3750
   (c) ₹ 5000 and ₹ 5000
   (d) ₹ 4000 and ₹ 6000

9. The ratio of the income and saving of a family in 8 : 3. Find the expenditure, if the saving is ₹ 1332.
   (a) ₹ 3000   (b) ₹ 2220
   (c) ₹ 2000   (d) ₹ 4200

10. The ratio of age of Aman and her mother is 3 : 11. The difference of their ages is 24 yr. What will be the ratio of their ages after 3 yr?
    (a) 1 : 3   (b) 2 : 3   (c) 4 : 5   (d) 5 : 7

11. A certain amount was divided between A and B in the ratio 7 : 9, if B's share was ₹ 7200, then find total amount.
    (a) ₹ 92070   (b) ₹ 6280
    (c) ₹ 12800   (d) ₹ 7200

12. If $6A = 4B = 9C$ what is $A : B : C$?
    (a) 6 : 4 : 9   (b) 9 : 4 : 6
    (c) 4 : 9 : 6   (d) 6 : 9 : 4

13. If $x : y = 3 : 1$, then $x^3 - y^3 : x^3 + y^3 = ?$
    (a) 13 : 14   (b) 14 : 13
    (c) 10 : 11   (d) 11 : 10

14. Two numbers are in the ratio 3 : 4 and their LCM is 180. The first number is
    (a) 15   (b) 60   (c) 36   (d) 45

15. Ram got twice as many marks in English as in Science. His total marks in English, Science and Maths are 180. If the ratio of his marks in English and maths is 2 : 3, what is his marks in Science?
    (a) 30   (b) 60   (c) 72   (d) 90

16. The product of two positive integers is 1575 and their ratio is 9 : 7. The smaller integer is
    (a) 25   (b) 35   (c) 45   (d) 70

17. The ratio between two numbers is 3 : 4. If each number is increased by 6, the ratio becomes 4 : 5. The difference between the numbers is
    (a) 1   (b) 3
    (c) 6   (d) 8

18. If 5 kg wheat costs ₹ 825. What is the cost of 12 kg wheat?
    (a) ₹ 2000   (b) ₹ 1980
    (c) ₹ 2100   (d) ₹ 2250

19. A mixture contains milk and water in the ratio 4 : 3. If 5 litres of water is added to the mixture, the ratio becomes 4 : 5. Find the quantity of milk in the given mixture.
    (a) 10 litres   (b) 10.5 litres
    (c) 20 litres   (d) 15 litres

2 Marks Questions

20. If A and B are in the ratio 4 : 5 and the difference of their squares is 81. Then, find the value of A?
    (a) 36   (b) 15   (c) 45   (d) 12

21. Divide ₹ 2600 among A, B, C in the ratio $\dfrac{1}{2} : \dfrac{1}{3} : \dfrac{1}{4}$. Find the share of each.
    (a) ₹ 1200, ₹ 600, ₹ 800
    (b) ₹ 1200, ₹ 800, ₹ 600
    (c) ₹ 900, ₹ 200, ₹ 1500
    (d) ₹ 1300, ₹ 800, ₹ 600

22. What number should be added to each of the numbers 94, 24, 100 and 26, so that the resulting numbers are in continued proportion?
    (a) 10   (b) 11   (c) 9   (d) 8

23. The smallest integer, which when subtracted from both the terms of 6 : 7 gives a ratio less then 16 : 21 is
    (a) 5   (b) 4   (c) 3   (d) 2

24. The ratio of the ages of a father to that of his son is 5 : 2. If the product of their ages (in years) is 1000, then find the father's age after 10 yr.
    (a) 50 yr   (b) 60 yr
    (c) 80 yr   (d) 100 yr

25. Divide ₹ 990 into 3 parts in such a way that half of the first part, one-third of the second part and one fifth of the third part are equal.
    (a) 198, 494, 298
    (b) 198, 297, 495
    (c) 200, 300, 490
    (d) 196, 298, 496

26. Weekly incomes of two persons are in the ratio of 7 : 3 and their weekly expenses are in the ratio of 5 : 2. If each of them saves ₹ 300 per week, then the weekly income of the first person is
    (a) ₹ 7500   (b) ₹ 4500
    (c) ₹ 6300   (d) ₹ 5400

Chapter 06

Percentage

1 Mark Questions

1. The sum of 40% of 70 and 70% of 40 is equal to
(a) 28   (b) 36
(c) 48   (d) 56

2. What percent of 7500 is 4500?
(a) 75%   (b) 60%
(c) 45%   (d) None of these

3. If 45% of $x + 30\%$ of $90 = 30\%$ of 210, then what is the value of x?
(a) 36   (b) 48
(c) 72   (d) 80

4. If 25% of a number is added to 30, then the result is the number itself. Find the number.
(a) 30   (b) 40
(c) 60   (d) 80

5. 1600 pupils attended a concert. 5% of the pupils were late for the concert. How many pupils were punctual for the concert?
(a) 1220   (b) 1440
(c) 1520   (d) 80

6. Chee Hong has 30 goats on his farm. How many goats must he buy to increase the number of goats on his farm by 20%?
(a) 36   (b) 30
(c) 12   (d) 6

7. Mr. Brown uses 3 grey tiles for every 5 white tiles. What is the percentage of grey tiles used out of the total number of tiles, if 45 white tiles are used?
(a) 37.5%   (b) 45.5%
(c) 56.5%   (d) 60%

8. A school's population increased by 42 students. This was a 3% increase. About how many students attended before increase?
(a) 2100   (b) 1600
(c) 1400   (d) 1200

9. Out of 600 students of a school, 126 go for a picnic. The percentage of students that did not go for the picnic is
(a) 60%   (b) 45%
(c) 79%   (d) 75%

10. In a club, 40% of the members are men. If 20% of the males and 30% of the females are married, then what percentage of members are married?
(a) 26%   (b) 20%
(c) 44%   (d) 74%

11. The price of gasoline drops from ₹ 2.00 per gallon to ₹ 1.90 per gallon. What is the percent of decrease in price?
(a) 1%   (b) 3%
(b) 5%   (d) 7%

12. A salesman is on a commission rate of 5%. How much commission does he make on sales worth ₹ 15000?
(a) ₹ 750   (b) ₹ 1500
(c) ₹ 250   (d) None of these

13. Meenakshi scored 97 out of 100 in Mathematics, 94 out of 100 in English and 46 out of 100 in Hindi. In order to have an aggregate of 80% in his overall marks, how much should she score in Science?
(a) 93   (b) 73
(c) 83   (d) 63

14. Rohit and Deepak appeared at an examination. Rohit secured 9 marks more than Deepak and his marks were 56% of the sum of their marks. The marks obtained by them are:
(a) 40, 50
(b) 42, 33
(c) 30, 70
(d) 65, 42

15. The length and breadth of rectangle are 40 cm and 30 cm. If the length is decreased by 20%, then what will be the new area of the rectangle?
(a) 1200 sq unit
(b) 960 sq unit
(c) 720 sq unit
(d) 1440 sq unit

16. There are 180 apples in a basket. 40% of them are red and the rest are green. 25% of the green apples are bad in quality. How many green apples are not bad in quality?
(a) 51   (b) 72
(b) 81   (d) 92

17. The city of Delhi spends 15% of its annual budget on its maintenance of bus stands. If Delhi spent ₹ 30 lakh on it this year, then what was its annual budget this year?
(a) ₹ 4000000
(b) ₹ 50000000
(c) ₹ 20000000
(d) ₹ 10000000

18. In a dance competition, 20% of the children are below 10 yr. 22 of them were girls and the remaining $\frac{2}{3}$ were boys. How many children participated in the competition?
(a) 200   (b) 250
(c) 330   (d) 460

2 Marks Questions

19. Aniket has to score of 30% marks to get throughout. If he gets 30 marks and fails by 30 marks, then find the maximum marks set for the examination.
(a) 250
(b) 100
(c) 200
(d) 300

20. In an office, 40% of the staff is female. 40% of the female and 60% of the male voted for me. The percentage of votes I got was
(a) 40%
(b) 50%
(c) 60%
(d) 52%

21. Which of the following statements is true?

Statement - I The price of a certain article is ₹ 15000. But due to slump in the market, its price decreases by 8%. The new price of the article is ₹ 13800.

Statement - II If due to 10% decrease in the price of rice. Rahul can buy 5 kg more rice in ₹ 100, then the actual price of rice is ₹ $2\dfrac{2}{9}$.

(a) Only Statement I is true
(b) Only Statement II is true
(c) Both Statements I and II are true
(d) Neither Statement I nor II is true

22. Two students appeared for an examination. One of them secured 10 marks more than the other and his marks were 75% of the sum of their marks. The marks obtained by them are
(a) 52 and 42
(b) 68 and 58
(c) 63 and 53
(d) 15 and 5

23. If the mean age of combined group of boys and girls is 18 yr and the mean of age of boys is 20 and that of girls is 16, then what is the percentage of boys in the group?
(a) 60%
(b) 50%
(c) 45%
(d) 40%

24. Fill in the blanks with the help of options, given in the box.

(i) 10	(ii) 12%
(iii) 200	(iv) 2.4,
(v) 2.5%	(vi) 5

I. 10% of 2 km is ……… m.

II. ……… % of 20 min is 144 sec.

III. $\dfrac{7}{5}$ of 200 cm is equal to ….. % of 28 m.

IV. 25% of ……… kg is 600 gm.

	I	II	III	IV		I	II	III	IV
(a)	i	ii	iii	iv	(b)	iv	iii	ii	vi
(c)	iii	ii	i	iv	(d)	vi	v	ii	iv

25. Match the following.

	Column A		Column B
I.	400% is equal to	(i)	2%
II.	$\dfrac{1}{4}$ is equal to	(ii)	$\dfrac{1}{10}$
III.	0.02 is equal to	(iii)	$\dfrac{25}{4}\%$
IV.	$6\dfrac{1}{4}\%$ is equal to	(iv)	4
V.	10% is equal to	(v)	25%

Codes

	I	II	III	IV	V
(a)	v	iii	ii	iv	i
(b)	iv	v	i	iii	ii
(c)	iii	i	v	ii	iv
(d)	i	ii	iii	iv	v

Profit and Loss

1 Mark Questions

1. The cost price of a TV set is ₹ 48000. It was sold at a profit of 15%. What is the profit earned?
   - (a) ₹ 4800
   - (b) ₹ 3600
   - (c) ₹ 6000
   - (d) ₹ 7200

2. Mr. Ben bought 100 batteries at a cost of ₹ 2 each. He sold them at 4 for ₹ 10, then what is percentage of profit he made?
   - (a) 100%
   - (b) 125%
   - (c) 25%
   - (d) 50%

3. The usual price of a play station game pack is ₹ 7000. It is sold for ₹ 6090. What is the percentage of loss suffered?
   - (a) 1%
   - (b) 13%
   - (c) $14\dfrac{20}{7}\%$
   - (d) 15%

4. The cost price of a scooter is ₹ 20000 and the profit percentage is 12%. What is the selling price?
   - (a) ₹ 22000
   - (b) ₹ 22400
   - (c) ₹ 10000
   - (d) ₹ 32000

5. An article is sold for ₹ 1980 at 10% profit. What is the cost price?
   - (a) ₹ 1900
   - (b) ₹ 2000
   - (c) ₹ 1800
   - (d) ₹ 1700

6. Suresh sells apples at 10 for ₹ 1, gaining 40%. How many apples did he buy for ₹ 1?
   - (a) 15
   - (b) 10
   - (c) 14
   - (d) 20

7. Amisha bought 4 dozen eggs at ₹ 10.80 per dozen and sold them for 80 paise each. Find her loss percent.
   - (a) $\dfrac{100}{3}\%$
   - (b) $\dfrac{100}{11}\%$
   - (c) $\dfrac{100}{7}\%$
   - (d) $\dfrac{100}{8}\%$

8. If the selling price of a toy is ₹ 750 and shopkeeper sold it at a profit of 20%. Then, what is the cost price of the toy?
   - (a) ₹ 625
   - (b) ₹ 650
   - (c) ₹ 725
   - (d) ₹ 500

9. Find the loss percentage when the cost price and selling price of an article are in the ratio of 5 : 3.
   - (a) 40%
   - (b) 30%
   - (c) 50%
   - (d) 45%

10. If a shopkeeper purchases almonds at ₹ 250 per kg and sells it at ₹ 10 per 50 gm, then he we will have?
    - (a) 20% profit
    - (b) 25% profit
    - (c) 20% loss
    - (d) 25% loss

11. A man bought an old typewriter for ₹ 1200 and spend ₹ 200 on its repair. He sold it for ₹ 1680. His profit percent is
    - (a) 20%
    - (b) 10%
    - (c) 8%
    - (d) 16%

12. If the cost price is 95% of the selling price, what is the profit percent?
    - (a) 4%
    - (b) 4.75%
    - (c) 5%
    - (d) 5.26%

13. If selling price is doubled, the profit triples. Find the profit percent.
(a) 66%   (b) 100%
(c) 110%   (d) 90%

14. By selling 36 pencils, a shopkeeper loses the selling price of 4 pencils. What will be his loss percent.
(a) $12\dfrac{1}{2}\%$ (b) $10\dfrac{1}{2}\%$
(c) 10%   (d) 11%

15. Ankit sold his watch for ₹ 75 and got a profit percentage equal to the cost price. The cost price of the watch is
(a) ₹ 40   (b) ₹ 45
(c) ₹ 50   (d) ₹ 55

16. The profit made on the sale of a product is 25%. What is the loss percentage incurred on the sale if the cost price and selling price are interchanged?
(a) 35%   (b) 60%   (c) 20%   (d) 16%

2 Marks Questions

17. A man purchases a certain number of apples at 3 per rupee and the same number of apples at 4 per rupee. He mixes them together and sells them at 3 per rupee. What is his gain or loss percent?
(a) Gain%, $14\dfrac{2}{7}\%$ (b) Loss%, 15%

(c) Gain%, 20%   (d) Loss%, $14\dfrac{2}{7}\%$

18. Pragati buys lemons at 4 for ₹ 3 and sells them at 5 for ₹ 4. How much percent loss or gain does she make?
(a) 5%   (b) 40%
(c) $13\dfrac{1}{3}\%$ (d) $6\dfrac{2}{3}\%$

19. Which of the following statement is correct?

Statement-I Profit after selling a commodity for ₹ 524 is the same as loss after selling it for ₹ 452. The cost price of the commodity is 485.

Statement-II By selling 25 m of cloth a trader gains the selling price of 5 m of cloth. The gain percent of the trader in % is 25%
(a) Only Statement I is true
(b) Only Statement II is true
(c) Both Statements I and II are true
(d) Neither Statement I nor II is true

20. A merchant finds his profit as 20% of the selling price. What is his actual profit percent?
(a) 20%   (b) 22%
(c) 25%   (d) 30%

21. A tea merchant blends green tea and lemon tea in the ratio of 5 : 4, introducing a new variety of tea which is mix green herbal and lemon. The cost of green tea is ₹ 200 per kg and that of lemon tea is ₹ 300 per kg. If he sells the blended tea at the rate of ₹ 275 per kg, find out the percentage of his profit or loss.
(a) 12.5%   (b) 22%
(c) 24%   (d) 27%

22. Sangeeta bought a VCD player at 20% discount during a sale. The price of the VCD player is ₹ 5500. After 6 months, she sold the VCD player to a friend and made a profit. What was here buying price of the VCD player? If she wants to make a profit of 10%, at what price should she sell the VCD player?
(a) ₹ 5000, ₹ 4000
(b) ₹ 4400, ₹ 4840
(c) ₹ 3460, ₹ 3600
(d) ₹ 4200, ₹ 4620

Simple Interest

1 Mark Questions

1. A sum of money at simple interest amounts to ₹ 840 in 2 yr and 920 in 4 yr. The sum is
(a) ₹ 700   (b) ₹ 640
(c) ₹ 760   (d) ₹ 820

2. What sum of money must be given as simple interest for 6 months at 4% per annum in order to earn ₹ 150 interest?
(a) ₹ 5000   (b) ₹ 7500
(c) ₹ 10000   (d) ₹ 15000

3. In how many year will a sum of ₹ 3000 yield a simple interest of ₹ 1080 at 12% per annum?
(a) 3 yr   (b) $2\frac{1}{2}$ yr   (c) 2 yr   (d) $3\frac{1}{2}$ yr

4. In what time will the simple interest be $\frac{2}{5}$ of the principal at 8% per annum?
(a) 8 yr   (b) 7 yr   (c) 5 yr   (d) 6 yr

5. Simple interest on a sum of money at 8% per annum for 4 yr is $\frac{1}{3}$ of the sum invested. What is the sum of money invested?
(a) ₹ 6000   (b) ₹ 4000
(c) ₹ 2000   (d) Data inadequate

6. Priyanka deposited ₹ 5000 which amount to ₹ 7000 after 3 yr at simple interest. Had the interest been 2% more. She would get how much?
(a) ₹ 10000   (b) ₹ 5300
(c) ₹ 7300   (d) ₹ 10300

7. What will be the ratio of simple interest earned by certain amount at the same rate of interest for 12 yr and that for 20 yr?
(a) 1 : 3   (b) 2 : 4   (c) 3 : 5   (d) 1 : 9

8. Seema took a loan of ₹ 1200 with simple interest for as many years as the rate of interest. If she paid ₹ 432 as interest at the end of the loan period. Then, what was the rate of interest?
(a) 10%   (b) 6%   (c) 16%   (d) 4%

9. A sum of money triple itself in 5 yr. What will be the rate of Interest?
(a) 10%   (b) 20%   (c) 40%   (d) 60%

10. ₹ 6400 were lent to Feroz and Rashmi at 15% per annum for $3\frac{1}{2}$ yr and 5 yr respectively. What is the difference in the interest paid by them?
(a) ₹ 570   (b) ₹ 1000
(c) ₹ 1200   (d) ₹ 1440

11. Sara deposits ₹ 8000 at 6% p.a for 5 yr while Alisha deposits ₹ 12000 at 8% p.a for 2.5 yr. Who get more Interest?
(a) Sara (b) Alisha
(c) Both get equal (d) Can't get

12. Rishu borrowed ₹ 8000 from a bank at 8% per annum. Find the amount he has to pay for 9/2 yr.

(a) ₹ 5080 (b) ₹ 70880
(c) ₹ 10880 (d) ₹ 8000

13. Simple interest for a sum of ₹ 1550 for 2 yr is ₹ 20 more than the simple interest for ₹ 1450 for the same duration. Find the rate of interest.
(a) 5% (b) 10%
(c) 20% (d) 2%

2 Marks Questions

14. In 4 yr, ₹ 6000 amounts to ₹ 8000. In what time at the same rate, will ₹ 525 amount to ₹ 700?

(a) 2 yr (b) 3 yr (c) 4 yr (d) 5 yr

15. A man lent ₹ 60000, partly at 5% and the rest at 4% simple interest. If the total annual interest is ₹ 2560, the money lent at 4% was
(a) ₹ 40000 (b) ₹ 44000
(c) ₹ 30000 (d) ₹ 45000

16. Aru lent some money at the rate of simple interest of 6% for 8 yr. He received ₹ 312 less than its principal is
(a) ₹ 300 (b) ₹ 350 (c) ₹ 600 (d) ₹ 425

17. Match the following

	Column A	Column B (SI)
I.	$P = ₹1000$ $R = 2\%$ $T = 1\,yr$	(i) ₹ 30
II.	$P = ₹500$ $R = 3\%$ $T = 2\,yr$	(ii) ₹ 20
III.	$P = ₹250$ $R = 4\%$ $T = 4\,yr$	(iii) ₹ 40

	I	II	III			I	II	III
(a)	ii	i	iii		(b)	i	ii	iii
(c)	iii	i	ii		(d)	i	iii	ii

18. Divide ₹ 10000 in 2 parts, so that the simple interest on the 1st part for 4 yr at 12% per annum may be equal to the simple interest on the 2nd part for 4.5 yr at 16% per annum.
(a) ₹ 7000 and ₹ 3000
(b) ₹ 6000 and ₹ 4000
(c) ₹ 2500 and ₹ 7500
(d) ₹ 6400 and ₹ 3600

19. Mr. Ajay divided a sum of ₹ 20000 among his two sons Anish and Anuj. Anish invested the amount at the rate of 12% for 2 yr, whereas Anuj invested the amount at the rate of 8% for 2 yr. Both got same interest after 2 yr.

Find the amount each one of them got.
(a) Anish = ₹ 10000 and Anuj = ₹ 10000
(b) Anish = ₹ 12000 and Anuj = ₹ 8000
(c) Anish = ₹ 8000 and Anuj = ₹ 12000
(d) Anish = ₹ 6000 and Anuj = ₹ 14000

20. Harsha lends ₹ 300 to Supriya at 4% and ₹ 600 to Rashmi at 6% for the same time. If the total amount she gets at the end is ₹ 1092. What is the time?
(a) 12 yr (b) 7 yr
(c) 3 yr (d) 4 yr

Algebraic Expression

1 Mark Questions

1. Which is the correct pair of like terms in the given expressions $9a(2b-a)$ and $-6b(4a-2b)$?
(a) $9a, -9a^2$ (b) $2b, 2b^2$
(c) $18ab, -24ab$ (d) None of these

2. $\left(3m + \dfrac{1}{2n}\right)^2 - \left(3m - \dfrac{1}{2n}\right)^2 = ?$
(a) $\dfrac{4m}{3n}$ (b) $\dfrac{6m}{n}$
(c) $2\left(4m^2 + \dfrac{1}{9n^2}\right)$ (d) $\dfrac{8m}{3n}$

3. $[(2a^3b)^3][(4a^2b^2)]$ is equivalent to which of the following?
(a) $32a^{11}b^5$ (b) $8a^{11}b^5$
(c) $32a^{18}b^6$ (d) $8a^{18}b^6$

4. If $3y = 15$ and $2x = 16$, then $3x + 2y$ is equal to
(a) 20   (b) 18
(c) 24   (d) 34

5. If $h = 10$, then find the value of $3h + 45 - 12 + (3 \times 5)h$.
(a) 213   (b) 243
(c) 200   (d) 273

6. If $C = \dfrac{5}{9}(F - 32)$ gives the formula for temperature, then find the value of C, where $F = 32$.
(a) 49   (b) $\dfrac{5}{9}$
(c) 1   (d) 0

7. Meera has $4q$ skirts. Tara has $12q$ skirts and Lara has $2q$ skirts. If $q = 5$, then how many more skirts does Tara have both Meera and Lara?
(a) 10   (b) 20
(c) 30   (d) 40

8. What should be subtracted from $(-2x^3 + 5x^2 - x + 8)$ to get $5x^2 - 4x + 12$?
(a) $2x^3 + 3x - 4$ (b) $-2x^3 - 3x + 4$
(c) $-2x^3 + 3x - 4$ (d) $2x^3 - 3x + 4$

9. What should be added to $x + x^2 + 6$ to get $3x^2 + 2x + 1$?
(a) $2x^2 + x - 5$
(b) $2x^2 - 2x + 5$
(c) $x^2 + 2x - 5$
(d) None of the above

10. Which of the following expression is correct?

(a) $\dfrac{pq+r}{q}=p+r$ (b) $\dfrac{p+r}{q+r}=\dfrac{q}{r}$

(c) $\dfrac{pq+pr}{ps}=\dfrac{q+r}{s}$ (d) $\dfrac{p(q+r)}{p+s}=\dfrac{q+r}{s}$

11. Simplify the expression by combining the like terms.

$12a+14b-3b-11c+8.5a$

(a) $4.5a+13b-11c$ (b) $20.5a+11b-11c$

(c) $26a+14b-8.5c$ (d) None of these

12. Simplified value of expression

$$\left(\dfrac{2}{5}a^4-2a+7\right)-\left(-\dfrac{3}{10}a^4+6a^3\right)$$

$-\left(2a^2-7\right)$ is

(a) $\dfrac{7}{10}a^4-6a^3-2a^2-2a+14$

(b) $\dfrac{-5}{10}a^4+8a^3-2a^2+2a$

(c) $\dfrac{-5}{15}a^4+6a^3+2a^2-2a+7$

(d) None of the above

13. What is the missing term in the following product?

$(2a^3-3)(5a^3-2)=10a^6+\ldots+6$?

(a) $19a^3$ (b) $-19a^3$ (c) $16a^3$ (d) $-16a^3$

14. If $A=10w^3+20w^2-55w+60,$

$B=-25w^2+15w-10$ and

$C=5w^2-10w+20,$

then $A+B-C$ is equal to

(a) $10w^3+10w^2+30w+30$

(b) $10w^3+10w^2-30w-30$

(c) $10w^3-10w^2-30w+30$

(d) None of the above

15. The area of the given figure is

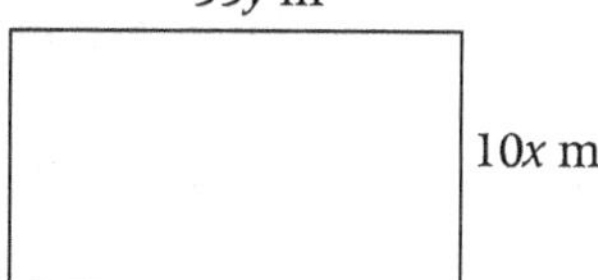

(a) $(33y+10x)\text{m}^2$ (b) $(66y+10x)\text{m}^2$

(c) $(66y+20x)\text{m}^2$ (d) $(330xy)\text{m}^2$

16. The perimeter of the regular pentagon having sides equal to $(3x+1)$ inch, is

(a) $(15x+1)$ inch   (b) $(15x+5)$ inch

(c) $(5x+5)$ inch   (d) $(3x+1)$ inch

17. If sum of 'n' natural numbers is given by $\dfrac{n(n+1)}{2}$, then the value of sum of first 20 natural numbers is

(a) 210   (b) 200   (c) 220   (d) 190

2 Marks Questions

18. Match the following expressions at $x=1$ and $y=-2$.

	Column A	Column B
I.	x^2+y^2+3xy	(i) 7
II.	$x^2+x^2y+xy^2+y^2$	(ii) -3
III.	x^2+y^2-3xy	(iii) -1
IV.	(x^2-y^2)	(iv) 11

	I	II	III	IV		I	II	III	IV
(a)	i	ii	iii	iv	(b)	iv	iii	i	ii
(c)	iii	i	iv	ii	(d)	ii	iv	iii	i

19. Fill in the blanks with the help of options, given in the box.

(i)	Like terms	(ii)	$7y-4x$
(iii)	Unlike terms	(iv)	4
(v)	Monomial	(vi)	$4x-7y$
(vii)	Trinomial	(viii)	5

I. ……… is an algebraic expression containing three terms.

II. The degree of the expression $4x^2y - 12xy^2 + 4z^2x + 5xy$ is ………

III. The subtraction of 4 times of x from 7 times of y is ………

IV. $10xy$ and $10x^2y^2$ are ………

	I	II	III	IV		I	II	III	IV
(a)	vii	iv	ii	iii	(b)	i	iii	v	viii
(c)	iv	ii	vii	iii	(d)	i	ii	iv	v

20. Projected from 2018 to 2019, the total population P and the male population M of United Kingdom (in thousand) can be expressed by the following equations, where 't' is the number of years since 2018.

Total population, $P = 2387.74t + 155211.46$

Male population, $M = 116416t + 75622.43$

Which expression represents the female population F of the United Kingdom from 2000 to 2019?

(a) $1421.21t + 7001.46$

(b) $1421.46\ t + 72942.04\ t$

(c) $1227.59\ t + 72589.03$

(d) $1223.58\ t + 79589.03$

21. Kaira buys one dozen eggs worth ₹ a, three breads where price of one bread is ₹ b and five bottles of juice worth ₹ c each. What is the total money (in ₹) she has to pay, if the price of the items are not given?

(a) ₹ $(a + 3b + 5c)$ (b) ₹ $(a + b + c)$

(c) ₹ $(3a + b + 3c)$ (d) Can't be determined

22. Gargi plans to build a house that is 1.5 times as long as it is wide. She wants the land around the house to be 20 ft wider than the width of the house and twice as long as the length of the house, as shown below. Write the expression for remaining area of land and find the area of it, if $x = 30$.

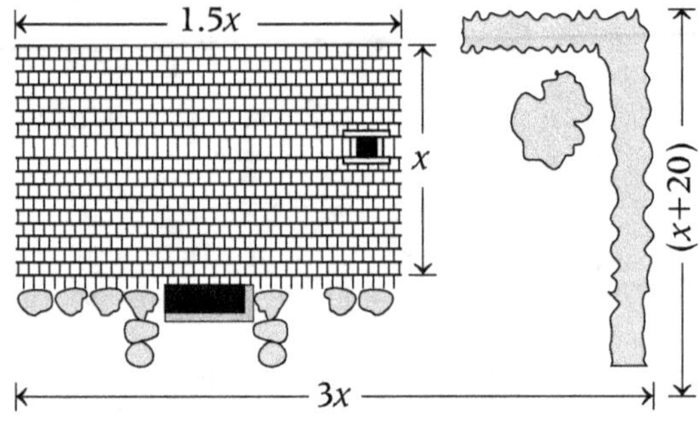

(a) $2x^2 + 60x, 3200$ sq units

(b) $3x^2 + 60x, 3050$ sq units

(c) $3x^2 + 60x, 3150$ sq units

(d) $1.5x^2 + 60x, 3150$ sq units

23. Max's monthly salary was ₹ 5445 q. He saved 30% of it and gave $\dfrac{1}{2}$ of the remaining to his parents. If Max used $\dfrac{3}{4}$ of the amount of money, he had left to buy a guitar, then how much money would be have left after buying the guitar, if $q = 8$?

(a) ₹ 11400.5   (b) ₹ 11434.5

(c) ₹ 11079.5   (d) ₹ 3811.50

24. A vacuum cleaner set costs ₹ 154.25 K. Additional pipe costs ₹ 15.2 K.

What is the total cost of 3 vacuum sets and 5 additional pipes?

(a) ₹ 400   (b) ₹ 530.75 K

(c) ₹ 538.75 K (d) ₹ 600

Chapter 10

Simple Equation

1 Mark Questions

1. Choose the correct statement which justifies the following equation.

$$\frac{x}{3} = x - 10$$

(a) One-third of a number is 10 more than the number itself.

(b) One-third of a number is 10 less than the number itself.

(c) Difference between one-third of a number and the number itself is less than 10.

(d) All the statements are correct.

2. 9 exceeds two-third of a number by 10, is represented by

(a) 2   (b) 3

(c) −2   (d) None of these

3. The equation which can be solved in integers is

(a) $5y + 3 = 12$ (b) $\frac{4}{5}x - 2 = 2$

(c) $7x + 4 = x + 8$ (d) None of these

4. To solve $7x + 3 + 9x - 5 = 18x - 3$ following steps are involved:

Step I $16x + 3 - 5 = 18x - 3$

Step II $16x - 2 = 18x - 3$

Step III $16x - 2 + 2 = 18x - 3 + 2$

Step IV $16x = 18x - 1$

Step V $\dfrac{16x}{16} = \dfrac{18x - 1}{16}$

Step VI $x = \dfrac{1}{2}$

Which of the step(s) is/are wrong?

(a) Step III   (b) Step IV

(c) Step V   (d) All are correct

5. Which of the given equations does not have −4 as the solution?

(a) $5 - x = 9$ (b) $14 + x = 10$

(c) $\dfrac{20}{(-x)} = 4$ (d) $9x = -36$

6. If two supplementry angles difference by 74°, then one of the angle is

(a) 127°   (b) 73°

(c) 117°   (d) 63°

7. The sum of two consecutive odd numbers is 184. What is the value of greater number?

(a) 91   (b) 93   (c) 101   (d) 97

8. Solve for $x : \dfrac{4x - 5}{7} + \dfrac{x + 11}{21} = \dfrac{1}{3}$

(a) $\dfrac{7}{13}$ (b) $\dfrac{7}{9}$ (c) $\dfrac{11}{9}$ (d) $\dfrac{11}{13}$

9. Hari father's age is 7 yr more than four times Hari's age. Hari father's age is 47 yr old. Form an equation to find Hari's age, if Hari age is x yr old.
(a) $4x+7=47$ (b) $2x+7=47$
(c) $3x+1=47$ (d) $4x+47=7$

10. Which of the following equation has $x=3\dfrac{1}{4}$ as a solution?
(a) $7x+\dfrac{5}{3}=\dfrac{47}{3}+\dfrac{5x}{3}$ (b) $7x-\dfrac{5}{3}=\dfrac{47}{3}+\dfrac{5x}{3}$
(c) $7x-\dfrac{5}{3}=\dfrac{47}{3}-\dfrac{5x}{3}$ (d) None of these

11. One-fourth of a pole is painted blue, two- fifth is painted red and remaining 21 m is painted green. What is the height of two pole?
(a) 90 m (b) 60 m
(c) 80 m (d) 40 m

12. Aryan says that he has 8 pens more than four times the number of pens Rakesh has. If Aryan has 48 pens, then how many pens does Rakesh have?
(a) 8 (b) 9
(c) 10 (d) 12

13. In any triangle, the sum of the measures of the angles is 180°. In $\triangle ABC$, if $\angle A$ is 3 times as large as $\angle B$. $\angle C$ measures 20° less than $\angle B$. Then, the measure of $\angle B$ is
(a) 30° (b) 40° (c) 50° (d) 60°

14. Subramaniam and Naidu donate some money in a Relief Fund. The amount paid by Naidu is ₹ 125 more than that of Subramaniam. If the total money paid by them is ₹ 975, then find the amount of money donated by Subramaniam.
(a) ₹ 500 (b) ₹ 725
(c) ₹ 425 (d) ₹ 800

15. In a school, the number of girls is 50 more than the number of boys. The total number of students is 1070. Find the number of girls.
(a) 1000 (b) 560 (c) 1020 (d) 510

16. A girl is 28 yr younger than her father. The sum of their ages is 50 yr. Find the ages of the girl and her father respectively.
(a) 12 yr and 48 yr (b) 14 yr and 36 yr
(c) 20 yr and 30 yr (d) 11 yr and 39 yr

17. In a bag, the number of ₹ 1 coins is 3 times the number of ₹ 2 coins. If the worth of the coins is ₹ 120, find the number of ₹ 1 coins.
(a) 24 (b) 72 (c) 25 (d) 52

2 Marks Questions

18. Match the following.

	Column A		Column B
I.	Twice a number is 3 less than thrice of it. Then, number is	(i)	$x=12$
II.	3 subtracted from two-third of a number is 5. Then, number is	(ii)	$x=9$
III.	8 times a number subtracted from 72 is zero. Then, number is	(iii)	$x=3$

    I   II   III   I   II   III
(a) i   ii   iii   (b) i   iii   ii
(c) ii   i   iii   (d) iii   i   ii

19. State 'T' for true and 'F' for false.
I. If $5x-6=8x-4$, then $x=-\dfrac{2}{3}$.

II. One-fifth of a number is 5 more than one-tenth of the number, then the number is -10.

III. An equation remains the same, if the LHS and RHS are interchanged.

IV. Any term of an equation may be transposed from one side of the equation to the other side of the equation by changing the sign of the term.

$$\begin{array}{cccc} & I & II & III & IV \end{array}$$

(a) T T F F
(b) T F F T
(c) T F T F
(d) T F T T

20. In a Science quiz, 40 prizes consisting of 1st and 2nd prizes, only are to be given. 1st and 2nd prizes are worth ₹ 3000 and ₹ 2000, respectively. If the total prize money is ₹ 90000, then match the following.

	Column A		Column B
I.	If 1st prize are x in numbers. Then, the numbers of 2nd prize are	(i)	$3000x + 2000(40 - x)$
II.	The total value of prizes in terms of x is	(ii)	$1000x + 80000 = 90000$
III.	The equation formed is	(iii)	$40 - x$

$$\begin{array}{cccc} & I & II & III \end{array}$$

(a) iii ii i
(b) i ii iii
(c) iii i ii
(d) ii iii i

21. There are some toys to be distributed to a group of children. Let one toy will be given to one child, then one child will be left. If two children will be given a toy to share, then one toy will be left extra, then the numbers of toys and children are, respectively

(a) 3 and 4   (b) 4 and 3
(c) 2 and 3   (d) 3 and 2

22. Which of the following is/are not solved correctly?

(a) $2(x - 3) = 5$

$$2x - 3 = 5$$
$$2x = 8$$
$$x = 4$$

(b) $5 - 3x = 10$

$$2x = 10$$
$$x = 5$$

(c) $\dfrac{1}{4}x - 2 = 7$

$$x - 2 = 28$$
$$x = 30$$

(d) All of the above

23. The temperature within Earth's crust increases about 30°C for each km of depth beneath the surface. If the temperature at Earth's surface is 20°C, at what depth would you expect the temperature to be 110°C?
Write the correct equation to solve the above.

(a) $110 = 20 + 30\,d$ then, $d = 3$
(b) $110 = 20d + 30$ then, $d = 4$
(c) Both (a) and (b)
(d) None of the above

24. Study the following statements carefully and select the correct option.

I. If $\dfrac{3}{4}(7x - 1) - \left(2x - \dfrac{1 - x}{2}\right) = x + \dfrac{3}{2}$, then

$$x = 1$$

II. If $\left\{\left(y - \dfrac{1}{2}\right) \times 4 + 25\right\} \div 3 = 10,$ then

$$y = 7$$

(a) Only Statement I is true
(b) Only Statement II is true
(c) Both Statements I and II are true
(d) Neither Statement I nor Statement II are true

Lines and Angles

1 Mark Questions

1. An angle exceeds 3 times its supplement by 40°. The measure of the angle is
   (a) 100°   (b) 125°   (c) 145°   (d) 160°

2. At 6 O'clock, the angle formed between the two hands of a clock is
   (a) right   (b) straight
   (c) obtuse   (d) acute

3. What is the value of S in the given figure?

   (a) 100°   (b) 80°   (c) 50°   (d) 30°

4. In the given figure, find the value of $\angle y$.

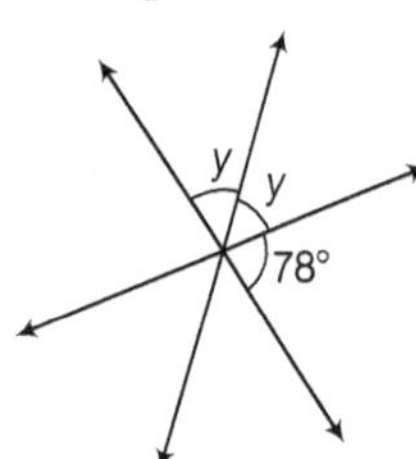

   (a) 102°   (b) 78°   (c) 51°   (d) 144°

5. In the given figure, if PQ and RS are parallel lines. Then, the value of $\angle x$ is

   (a) 120°
   (b) 140°
   (c) 160°
   (d) None of the above

6. What are the values of x and y in the given figure?

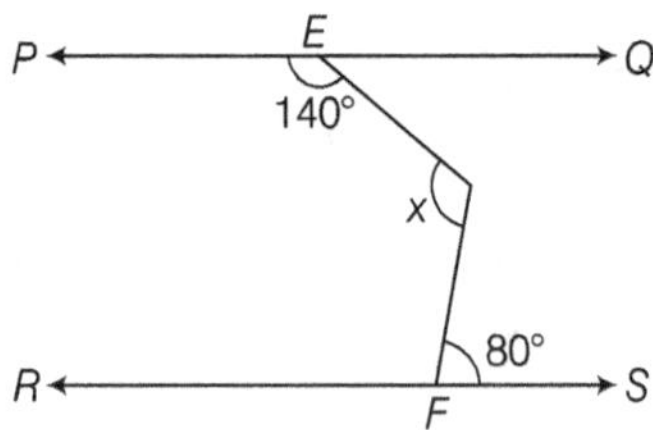

   (a) $\angle x = 40°$, $\angle y = 75°$
   (b) $\angle x = 20°$, $\angle y = 35°$
   (c) $\angle x = 40°$, $\angle y = 35°$
   (d) None of the above

7. In the given figure, AOB is a line. If $\angle a = 40°$, then measure of $\angle FOE$ is

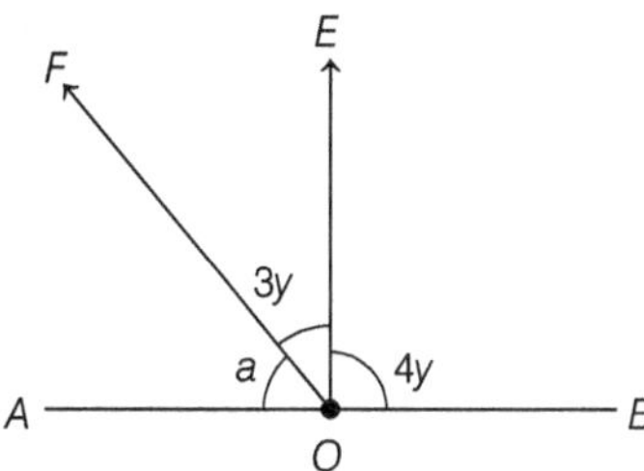

(a) 60° (b) 80°
(c) 120° (d) 160°

8.

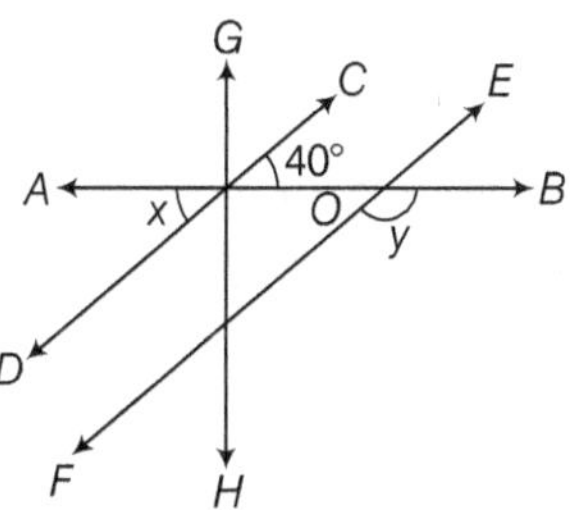

Which of the following options gives the correct values of x and y?
(a) $\angle x = 120°, \angle y = 140°$
(b) $\angle x = 140°, \angle y = 40°$
(c) $\angle x = 40°, \angle y = 140°$
(d) $\angle x = 140°, \angle y = 120°$

9. In the given figure, if $RS \parallel UT$. CD is a straight line, then find the value of $\angle RTC$.

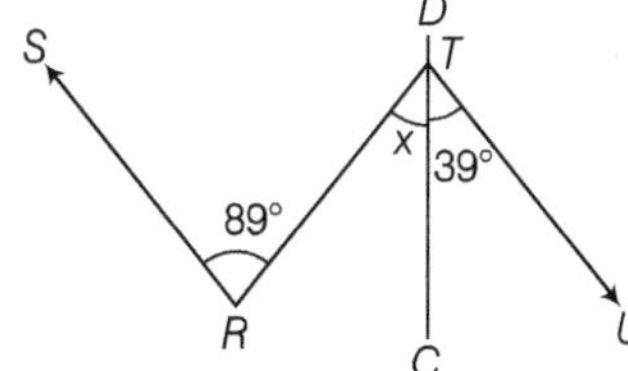

(a) 89°
(b) 39°
(c) 50°
(d) 49°

10. On the basis of given figure, which of the following is true?

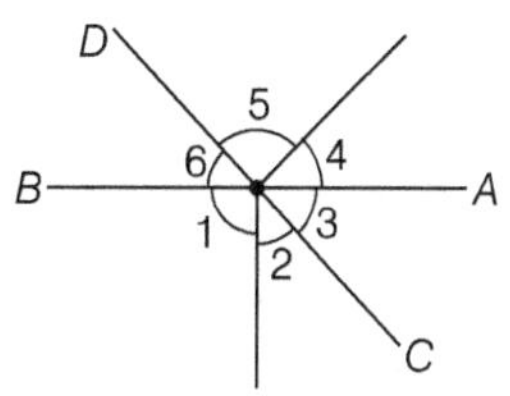

(a) $\angle 4 = \angle 5$
(b) $\angle 6 + \angle 5 = \angle 1 + \angle 2$
(c) $\angle 5 + \angle 4 = \angle 1 + \angle 2$
(d) $\angle 5 = \angle 2$

11. Match the following.

	Column A		Column B
I.	P————————Q	(i)	$\overrightarrow{PQ}$
II.	P————————→Q	(ii)	$\overleftrightarrow{PQ}$
III.	P←————————→Q	(iii)	$\overline{PQ}$

Codes

	I	II	III			I	II	III
(a)	iii	i	ii		(b)	i	ii	iii
(c)	ii	iii	i		(d)	i	iii	ii

12. Match the following.

	Column A	Column B $x =$
I.	90° ⊥ x	(i) 55°
II.	90° x 60°	(ii) 90°
III.	x 35°	(iii) 30°

Codes

	I	II	III			I	II	III
(a)	i	ii	iii		(b)	ii	iii	i
(c)	iii	i	ii		(d)	i	iii	ii

2 Marks Questions

13. In the figure given below, $EC \parallel AB$, $\angle ECD = 70°$ and $\angle BDO = 20°$. What is the value of $\angle OBD$?

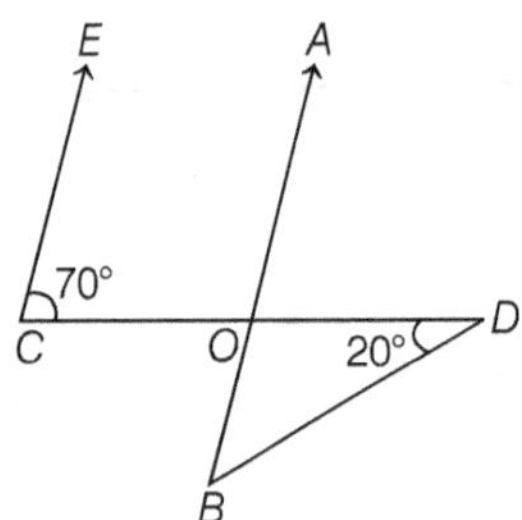

(a) 20° (b) 30°
(c) 40° (d) 50°

14. In the given figure, lines XY and WZ intersect at O. If $\angle XOV = 90°$ and $c : b = 7 : 3$, then the measure of $\angle a$ is

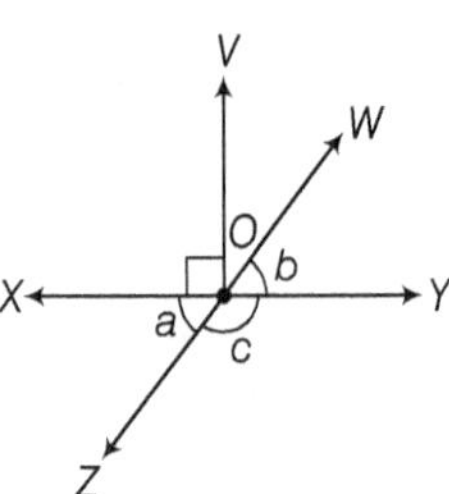

(a) 46°
(b) 54°
(c) 64°
(d) 66°

15. In the given figure, if $AC \parallel OD$ and $AO \parallel EF$. Then, measure of $\angle x$ and $\angle y$ is

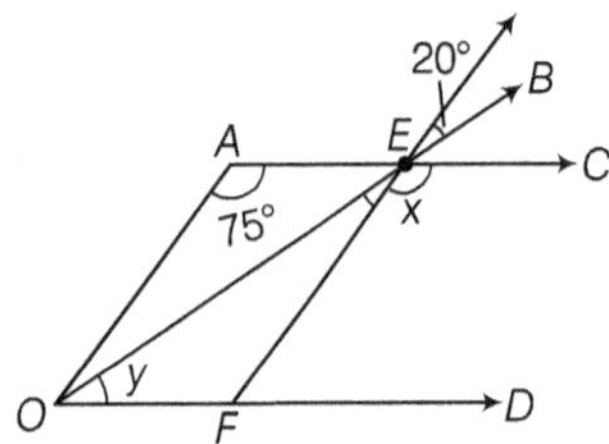

(a) $\angle x = 75°, \angle y = 95°$
(b) $\angle x = 95°, \angle y = 85°$
(c) $\angle x = 75°, \angle y = 85°$
(d) $\angle x = 95°, \angle y = 75°$

16. In the figure given below, $PQ \parallel RS$ and $PR \parallel QS$. If $\angle LPR = 35°$ and $\angle UST = 70°$, then what is $\angle MPQ$ equal to?

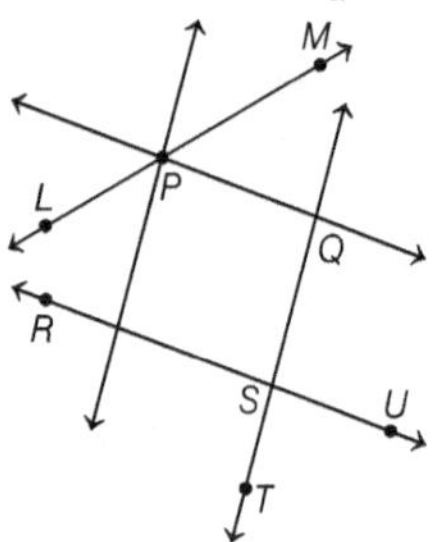

(a) 55° (b) 70° (c) 75° (d) 80°

17. In the given figure, $AB \parallel CD$ and they cut PQ and QR at E, F and G, H, respectively. If $\angle PQR = x$, then find the value of x (in degrees).

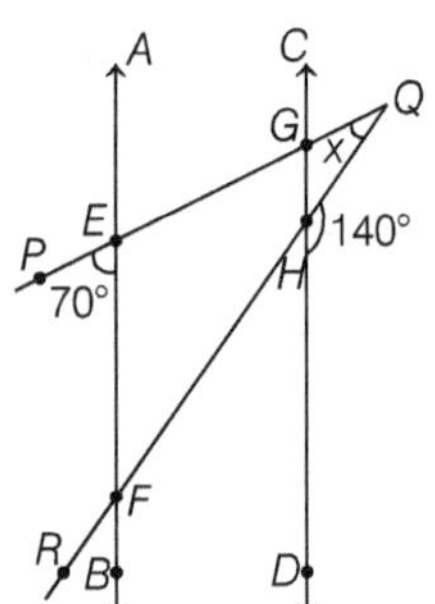

(a) 20° (b) 30° (c) 24° (d) 32°

18. In the given figure, if $AB \parallel CD \parallel XY$ and $OC \parallel EB$, $\angle ABE = 46°$ and $\angle EDC = 33°$, then $\angle e$ and $\angle OCD$ are equal to

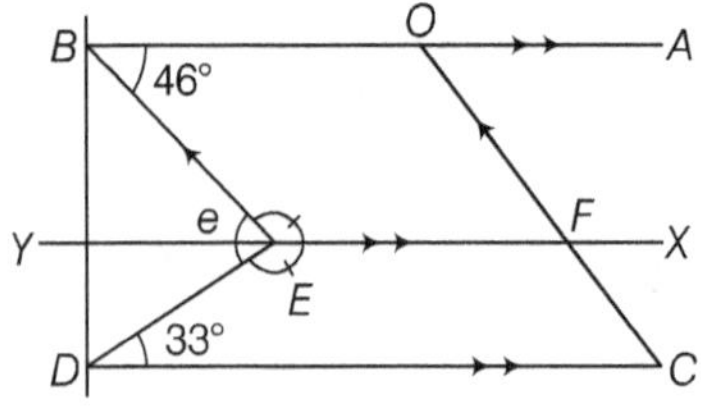

(a) $\angle e = 79°, \angle OCD = 46°$
(b) $\angle e = 101°, \angle OCD = 33°$
(c) $\angle e = 89°, \angle OCD = 46°$
(d) $\angle e = 99°, \angle OCD = 33°$

Triangle and its Properties

1 Mark Questions

1. The three angles of a triangle are in the ratio 1:2:1. What is the measure of the greatest angle?
   (a) 45°   (b) 60°
   (c) 90°   (d) 120°

2. If the angles of a triangle are in the ratio 2 : 3 : 5, then the triangle is
   (a) acute angled
   (b) obtuse angled
   (c) right angled
   (d) right angled isosceles

3. If ΔABC is an isosceles triangle with $AB = AC$, DAB and EAC are straight lines, then what is the value of x?

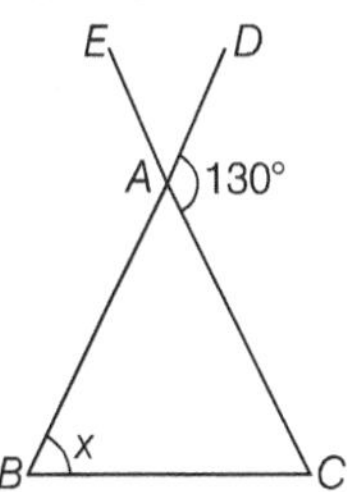

   (a) 130°
   (b) 70°
   (c) 65°
   (d) Can't be determined

4. In an isosceles triangle PQR, if $PQ = PR$ and $\angle P = 3\angle Q$, then $\angle R$ is equal to
   (a) 36°   (b) 32°
   (c) 28°   (d) 40°

5. In the given figure, not drawn to scale, $PQ = PR$ and $\angle PRS = 136°$. What is the value of x?

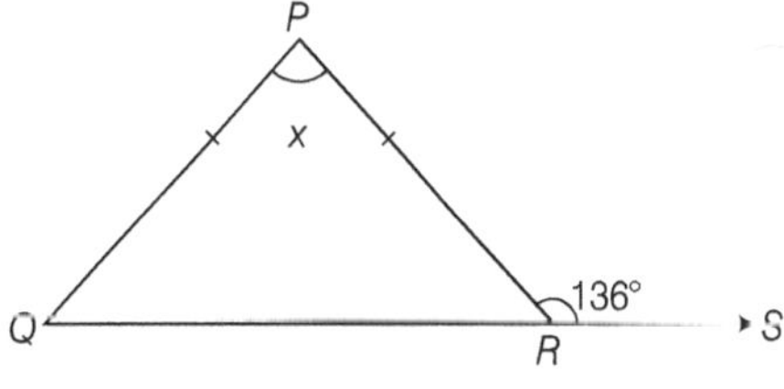

   (a) 136°   (b) 44°
   (c) 72°   (d) 92°

6. In the given figure, find the value of $\angle ABC$.

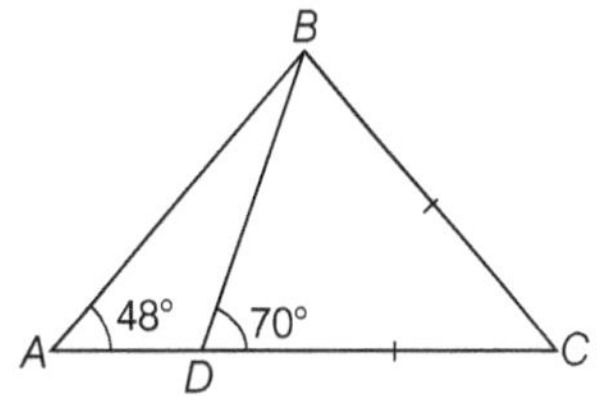

   (a) 92°   (b) 70°
   (c) 118°   (d) 42°

7. From the given figure, find the values of $\angle a, \angle b$ and $\angle c$.

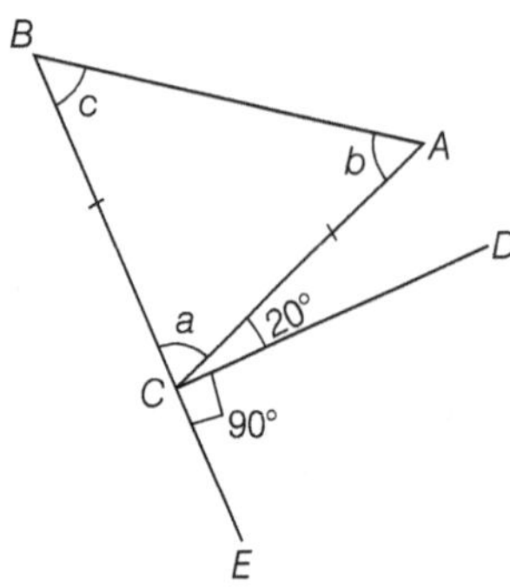

(a) $a = 55°, b = 70°, c = 70°$
(b) $a = 55°, b = 70°, c = 55°$
(c) $a = 70°, b = 55°, c = 55°$
(d) $a = 70°, b = 55°, c = 70°$

8. From the given figure, find the value of $\angle i$.

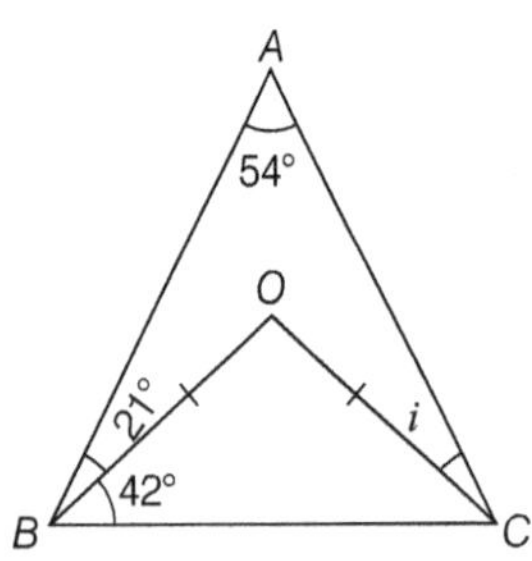

(a) $27°$ (b) $23°$
(c) $42°$ (d) $21°$

9. In the given figure,
$\angle a + \angle b + \angle c + \angle d + \angle e = \square$ right angles, then what is $\square$ in box?

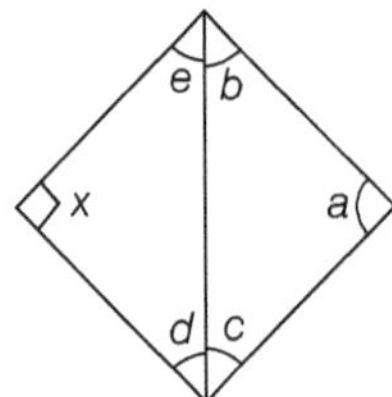

(a) 2
(b) 3
(c) 4
(d) None of these

10. In ΔABC, $\angle A = 40°$ and $\angle C = 70°$, bisectors of $\angle B$ and $\angle C$ meet at O. What is the value of $\angle BOC$?
(a) $70°$ (b) $110°$ (c) $90°$ (d) $120°$

11. In ΔPQR, if $PQ = PR$ and $PS \perp QR$, then by which of the following properties does $\Delta PQS \cong \Delta PRS$?
(a) SSS congruence rule
(b) RHS congruence rule
(c) SAS congruence rule
(d) ASA congruence rule

12. In ΔPQR and ΔXYZ, $PQ = XY$ and $QR = YZ$, where as $PR \neq XZ$. Which of the following conditions can make the two triangles congruent?
(a) $\angle P = \angle X$ (b) $\angle Q = \angle Y$
(c) $\angle R = \angle Z$ (d) None of these

13. In the given figure, $RQ = RS$ and $\angle PRQ = \angle PRS$, then which of the following is true?

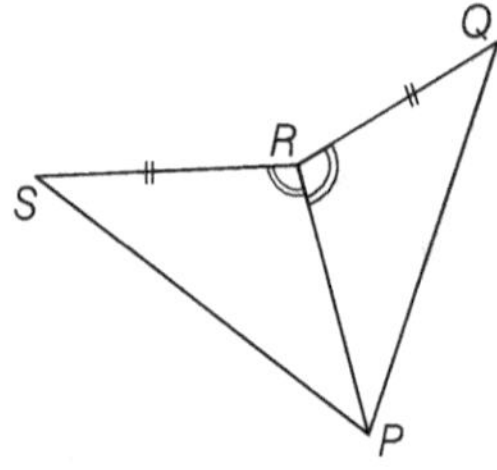

(a) $PQ = PS$ (b) $\Delta PRQ \cong \Delta PRS$
(c) $\angle PSR = \angle PQR$ (d) All of these

14. State 'T' for true and 'F' for false.
    I. By SSS property two triangles can be proved congruent.
    II. If the areas of two triangles are same, they are congruent always.
    III. The congruent figures coincide with each other.

Codes

	I	II	III		I	II	III
(a)	T	F	T	(b)	T	T	F
(c)	F	T	F	(d)	F	F	T

2 Marks Questions

15. Find the value of $\angle a$ in the given figure.

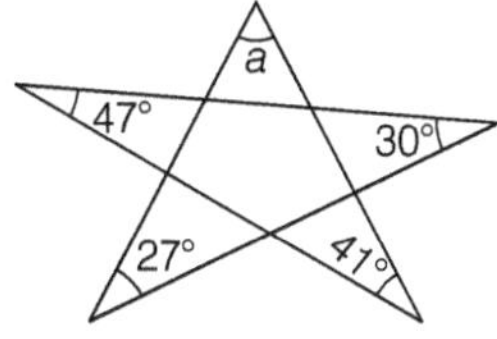

(a) 32°   (b) 41°   (c) 47°   (d) 35°

16. In thc givcn figure, $AY = CY = BY$ and $XA = XB$. What are the values of $\angle CYA$ and $\angle CBX$?

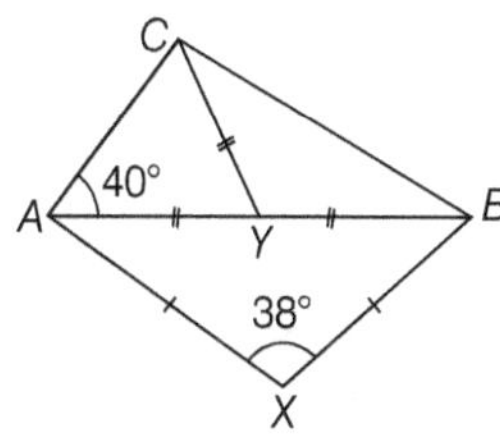

(a) 109° and 100°   (b) 120° and 139°
(c) 100° and 121°   (d) None of these

17. The skycrapers show below are connected by a sky walk with support beams. Find the length of each support beam.

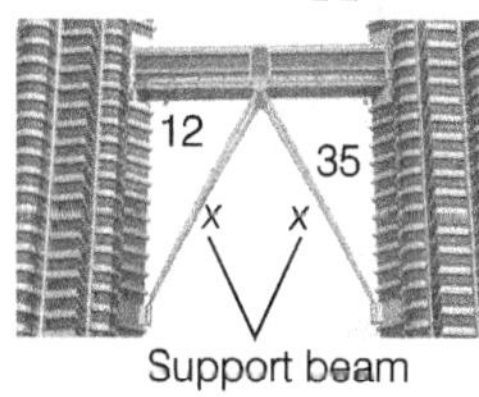

(a) 40   (b) 39   (c) 37   (d) 32

18. A beam of red light shines from point E reflects at point A and reaches point Y. $EA \perp ZY$. Find the value of x.

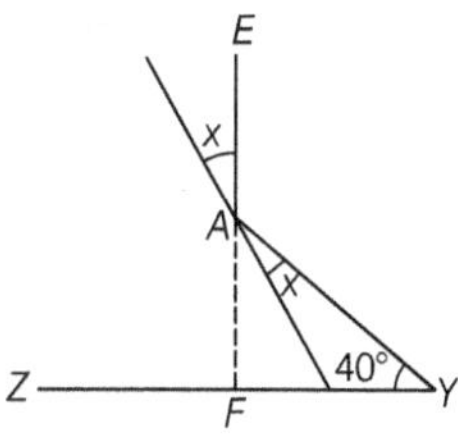

(a) 50°   (b) 30°
(c) 25°   (d) 15°

19. In the given figure, $ABCD$ is a parallelogram, AC and BD are diagonals. What is the measure of $\angle OCD$?

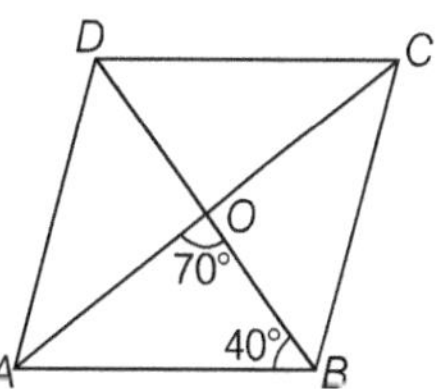

(a) 40°   (b) 70°
(c) 110°   (d) 50°

20. Amanat is designing the window shown in the photo. She wants to make ΔDRA congruent to ΔDRG. She designs the window so that $DR \perp AG$. Which of the following conditions will make the two triangles congruent?

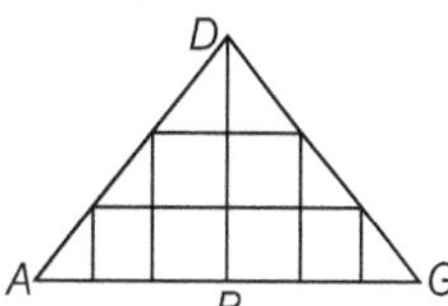

(a) $RA = RG$ (b) $DA = DG$
(c) Both (a) and (b) (d) None of these

21. Meera wants to know the width of the river given below. While doing so she stands on the edge of the river and look straight across to a point on the other edge without changing the inclination of the neck and head. She turns side ways until the vision is in line with a point on the side of the stream.

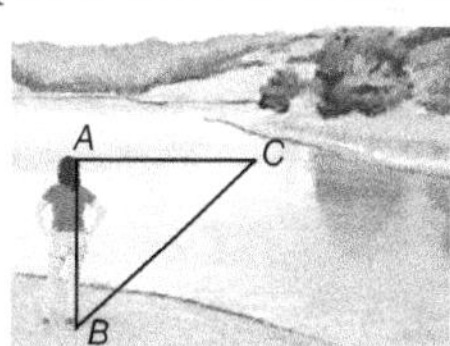
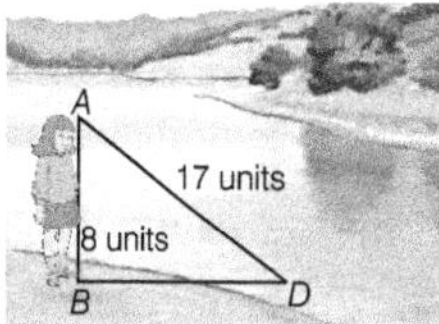

From the above description, find the value of BC.

(a) 25 units   (b) 12 units
(c) 15 units   (d) Can't be determined

Chapter
13

Symmetry

1 Mark Questions

1. Which of the following alphabets has a horizontal line of symmetry?
   (a) A (b) P
   (c) N (d) H

2. In the word 'MATH', which letter has vertical symmetry?
   (a) M, A (b) T, H
   (c) Only H (d) All of the letters

3. Which of the following letters of English Alphabet have more than one lines of symmetry?
   (a) Q (b) F
   (c) C (d) O

4. Which of the following has more than one line of symmetry?
   (a) Isosceles triangle
   (b) Scalene triangle
   (c) Rectangle
   (d) Semi-Circle

5. A square has ....
   (a) one line of symmetry
   (b) two lines of symmetry
   (c) three lines of symmetry
   (d) four lines of symmetry

6. Match the following.

	Shape		Order of symmetry
I.		(i)	2
II.	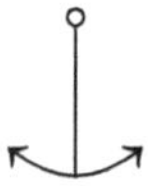	(ii)	6
III.		(iii)	No order of symmetry

	I	II	III
(a)	i	ii	iii
(b)	i	iii	ii
(c)	ii	iii	i
(d)	iii	ii	i

7. How many lines of symmetry does the given figure have?

   (a) 0 (b) 2
   (c) 3 (d) 4

8. Find the number of lines of symmetry of the given figure.

(a) No line of symmetry
(b) 2
(c) 3
(d) 4

9. How many lines of symmetry does the given figure have?

(a) 0
(b) 1
(c) 2
(d) 3

10. What are the number of lines of symmetry?

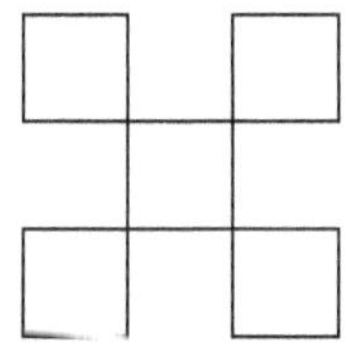

(a) 2
(b) 4
(c) 6
(d) 8

11. Which figure has only one line of symmetry?

(a) 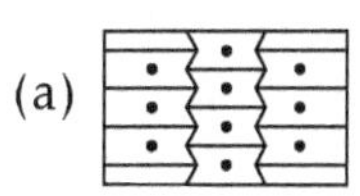
(b) 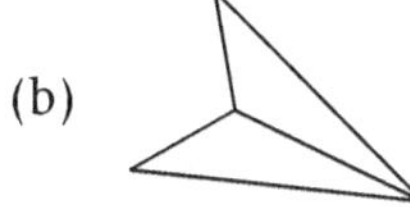
(c)
(d) None of these

12. What is the minimum number of squares that must be shaded so that the given figure will be symmetric?

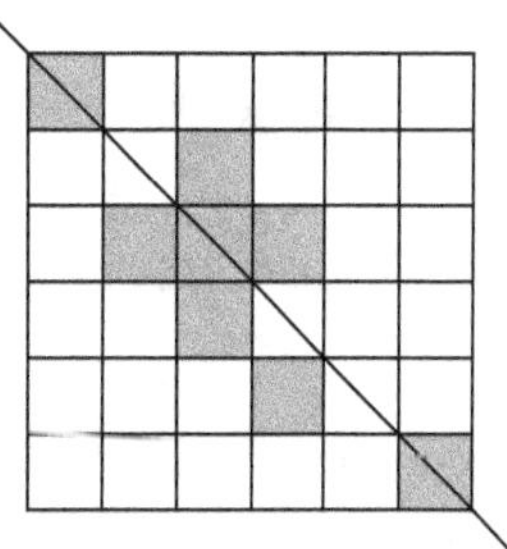

(a) 1
(b) 2
(c) 0
(d) 5

13. Match the following

	Figure	Line of symmetry	
I.		(i)	Four
II.		(ii)	One
III.		(iii)	Zero

Codes

	I	II	III
(a)	i	ii	iii
(b)	ii	iii	i
(c)	iii	i	ii
(d)	i	iii	ii

14. What is the order of rotational symmetry of a circle.

(a) 1
(b) 4
(c) 0
(d) Infinite

15. The order of rotational symmetry for the given figure is

(a) 4   (b) 1   (c) 2   (d) 3

16. What is the order of rotational symmetry of the given figure?

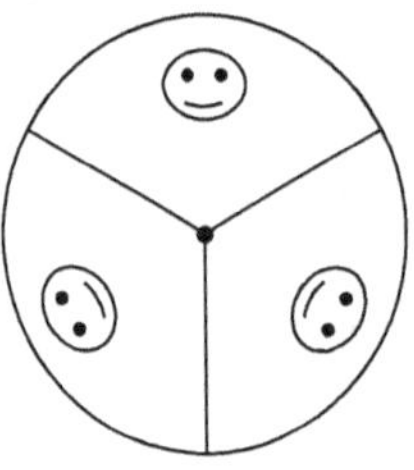

(a) 3   (b) 2   (c) 1   (d) 4

17. How many corners does this shape below have?

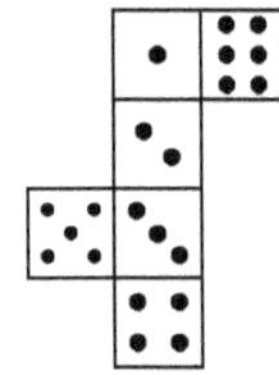

(a) 6   (b) 10   (c) 12   (d) 13

18. How many faces does this solid have?

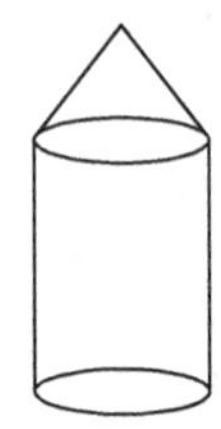

(a) 1   (b) 2
(c) 3   (d) 4

19. How many faces does the given figure have?

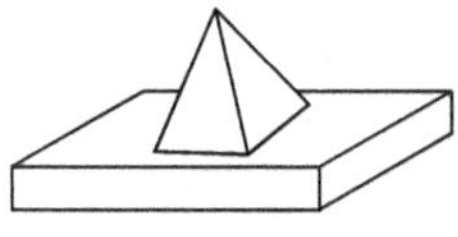

(a) 6   (b) 8
(c) 9   (d) 10

20. The net shown below forms a ....

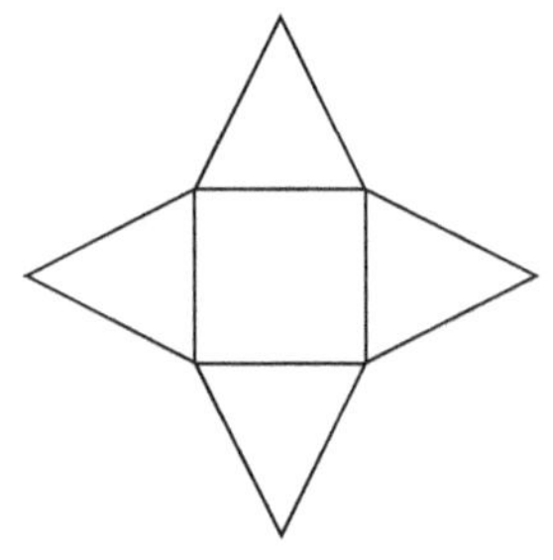

(a) Prism   (b) Cube
(c) Sphere   (d) Pyramid

2 Marks Questions

21. Which of the following solids can be obtained by folding the net below?

(a) 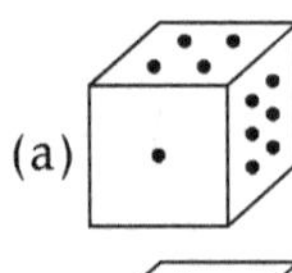   (b) 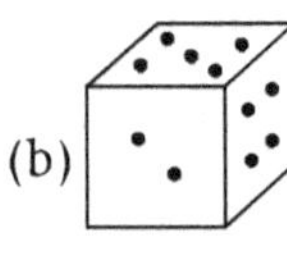

(c) 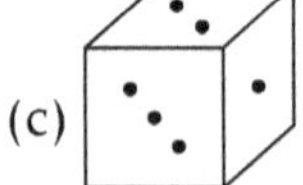   (d) 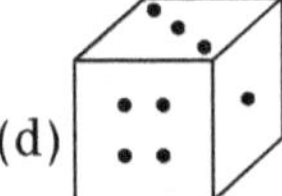

22. What will be the top view of the following figure.

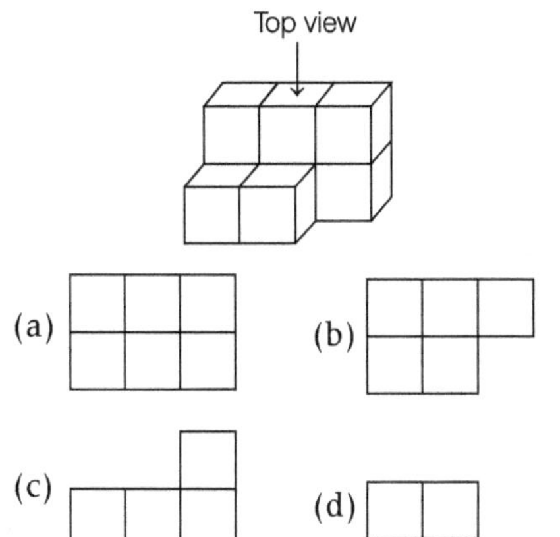

(a)   (b)

(c)   (d)

23. Match the following

	Figure		Order of rotational symmetry
I.		(i)	6
II.		(ii)	3
III.		(iii)	2
IV.		(iv)	4

	I	II	III	IV		I	II	III	IV
(a)	(i)	(iii)	(iv)	(ii)	(b)	(i)	(ii)	(iv)	(iii)
(c)	(iv)	(iii)	(ii)	(i)	(d)	(iv)	(i)	(iii)	(ii)

24. How many cubes are needed to make the solid below?

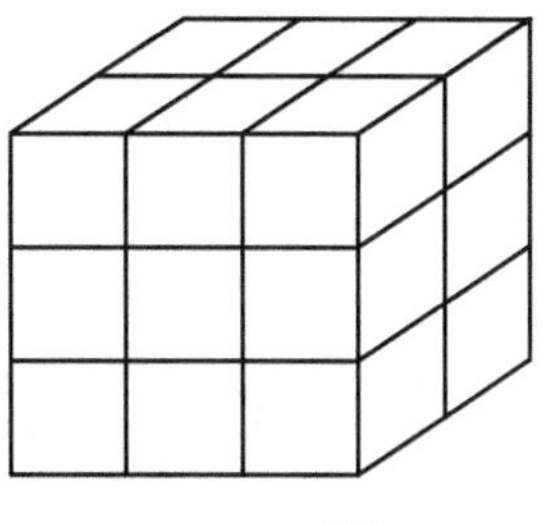

(a) 9   (b) 12
(c) 18   (d) 21

25. Which of the following figures are formed from the given net?

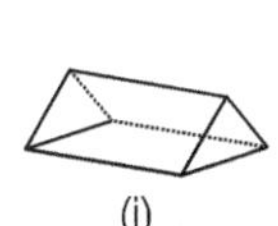 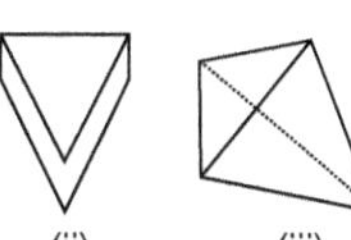 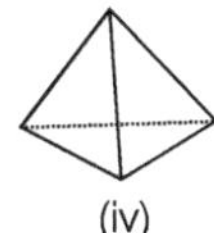
(i)   (ii)   (iii)   (iv)

(a) i, ii
(b) ii, iii
(c) iii, iv
(d) All of the above

26. Which solid figure will be formed from below given net?

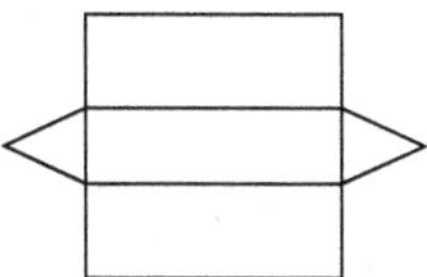

(a) Pyramid
(b) Prism
(c) Cone
(d) Frustum

Area and Perimeter

1 Mark Questions

1. The length of rectangle is increased by 25%. By what percent should its breadth be decreased so as to maintain the same area?
   (a) 20%   (b) 25%   (c) 12.5% (d) 50%

2. The length of a rectangular hall is 5 m more than its breadth. The area of the hall is 750 m^2. The length of the hall is
   (a) 15 m   (b) 22.5 m
   (c) 25 m   (d) 30 m

3. A lawn is in the form of a rectangle having breadth and length in the ratio 3 : 4. The area of the lawn is $\dfrac{1}{12}$ hectare
   The breadth of the lawn is
   (a) 25 m   (b) 50 m
   (c) 75 m   (d) 100 m

4. A marble tile measures 40 cm × 60 cm. How many tiles will be required to cover a wall of size 16 m × 18 m.
   (a) 1000   (b) 1200
   (c) 180   (d) 1600

5. The perimeter of a rectangle having area equal to 144 cm^2 and sides in the ratio 4 : 9 is
   (a) 52 cm   (b) 56 cm
   (c) 60 cm   (d) 64 cm

6. In a square field, the diagonal is 20 cm. What is the area of the square field?
   (a) 190 m^2 (b) 450 m^2
   (c) 200 m^2 (d) 100 m^2

7. One side of a rectangular field is 9 m and one of its diagonal is 20 m. Find the area of the field.
   (a) $9\sqrt{319}$ sq m
   (b) $7\sqrt{314}$ sq m
   (c) $2\sqrt{319}$ sq m
   (d) $5\sqrt{319}$ sq m

8. The maximum length of a pen that can be kept in a rectangular box of dimensions 10 cm, 8 cm, 6 cm is
   (a) 20 cm   (b) 10 cm
   (c) $10\sqrt{2}$ cm   (d) 14 cm

9. The length of diagonal of a square is $15\sqrt{2}$ cm. Its area is
   (a) 112.5 cm^2 (b) 450 cm^2
   (c) $\dfrac{225\sqrt{2}}{2}$ cm^2 (d) 225 cm^2

10. The area of the parallelogram whose length is 30 cm, width is 20 cm and one diagonal is 40 cm is
    (a) $200\sqrt{15}$ cm^2 (b) $100\sqrt{15}$ cm^2
    (c) $300\sqrt{15}$ cm^2 (d) $150\sqrt{15}$ cm^2

11. Find the area of the shaded part of the given figure if *E* and *F* are the mid-points of *DC* and *AB* respectively.

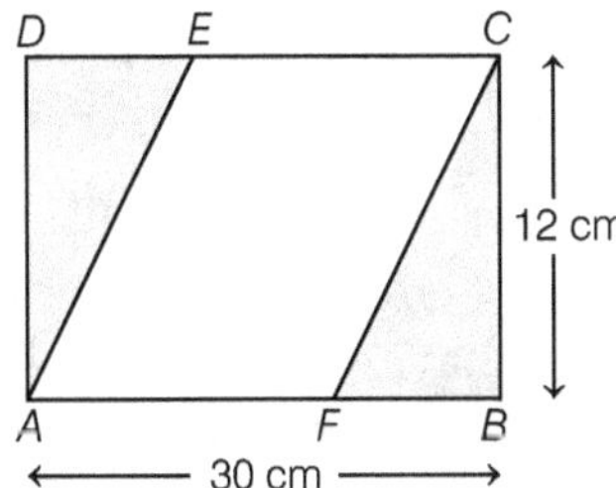

   (a) 180 cm^2 (b) 360 cm^2
   (c) 300 cm^2 (d) 160 cm^2

12. A rectangular grass plot 80 m × 60 m has 1 roads, each 10 m wide, running in the middle of it, one parallel to length and the other parallel to breadth. Find the area of roads.
   (a) 4800 sq m   (b) 3400 sq m
   (c) 1500 sq m   (d) 1300 sq m

13. The area of an equilateral triangle is $4\sqrt{3}$ sq cm. Its perimeter is
   (a) 12 cm   (b) 6 cm
   (c) 8 cm   (d) $3\sqrt{3}$ cm

14. The base of a triangle is 15 cm and height is 12 cm. The height of another triangle of double the area having the base 20 cm is
   (a) 9 cm   (b) 18 cm
   (c) 8 cm   (d) 12.5 cm

15. The hypotenuse of a isosceles right angle triangle is 5 cm. Its area will be
   (a) 5 sq cm
   (b) 6.25 sq cm
   (c) 6.50 sq cm
   (d) 12.5 sq cm

16. A circle and a square have the same perimeter. Which one of the following is correct?
   (a) Their areas are equal
   (b) The area of the circle is larger
   (c) The area of the square is $\dfrac{\pi}{2}$ times are a of circle
   (d) The area of the square is π times area of circle

17. A circular road runs around a circular ground. If the difference between the circumference of the outer circle and the inner circle is 132 m. Find the width of the road.
   (a) 7 m   (b) 20 m
   (c) 21 m   (d) 14 m

18. The area of a circular field is 61600 m^2. Find the cost of fencing it at the rate of ₹ 10.6 per metre.
   (a) ₹ 4800   (b) ₹ 9328
   (c) ₹ 1020   (d) ₹ 9450

19. A filament is in the form of a circle.
   The radius of the circle is 28 cm.
   The filament is then moulded to form a square.
   Find the side of the square formed?
   (a) 18 cm   (b) 20 cm
   (c) 44 cm   (d) 14 cm

20. The radius of a circular field is equal to the side of a square field. If the difference between the perimeter of the circular field and that of the square field is 32 m, what is the perimeter of the square field?
   (a) 38 m   (b) 42 m
   (c) 56 m   (d) 14 m

2 Marks Questions

21. State 'T' for True and 'F' for false
   1. If circumference of a circle is 22 cm, then area is 38.5 cm^2.
   2. If the ratio of areas of 2 squares is 256 : 324, then the ratio of their perimeters is 16 : 18.
   3. If the perimeter of a square is doubled, then the ratio of the original area to new area is 1 : 4.

   Codes

	1	2	3
(a)	T	T	F
(b)	F	T	T
(c)	T	T	T
(d)	T	F	F

22. A square park has each side 50 m. At each corner of the park, there is a flower bed in the form of a quadrant of radius 7 m, as shown in the figure. Find the area of remaining part of the park.

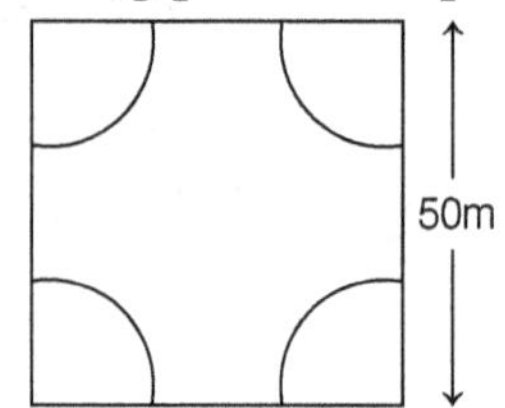

   (a) 2346 sq m   (b) 2340 sq m
   (c) 2250 sq m   (d) 2155 sq m

23. The perimeters of 2 squares are 68 cm and 60 cm. Find the perimeter of the 3rd square whose area is equal to the difference of the areas of these 2 squares.
   (a) 64 cm   (b) 60 cm
   (c) 32 cm   (d) 8 cm

24. The area of an isosceles ΔABC with $AB = AC$ and altitude $AD = 3$ cm is 12 sq cm. What is its perimeter?
   (a) 18 cm   (b) 16 cm
   (c) 14 cm   (d) 12 cm

25. The area of circle is equal to the area of a rectangle having perimeter of 50 cm and the length is more than its breadth by 3 cm. What is the diameter of the circle?
   (a) 7 cm   (b) 21 cm
   (c) 28 cm   (d) 14 cm

26. $ABCD$ is a square, E and F are the mid-points of BC and CD. What is the ratio of area of ΔAEF to that of the square $ABCD$.
   (a) 3 : 8   (b) 5 : 8   (c) 3 : 2   (d) 7 : 4

27. The diameters of 2 circles are the side of a square and the diagonal of the square. The ratio of the areas of the smaller circle and the larger circle is
   (a) 1 : 4   (b) $\sqrt{2} : \sqrt{3}$
   (c) $1 : \sqrt{2}$ (d) 1 : 2

28. In the given figure, side of each square is 1 cm. The area (in sq cm) of the shaded part is

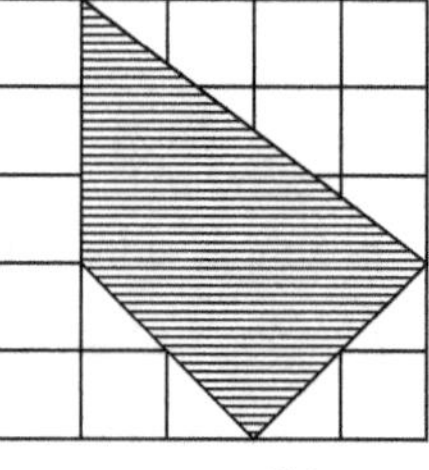

   (a) 8   (b) 9
   (c) 10   (d) 11

Chapter 15

Data Handling

1 Mark Questions

1. Employees at a retail store are paid the hourly wages listed below. What is the range of these hourly wages?

   ₹ 750, ₹ 925, ₹ 875, ₹ 950, ₹ 725 and ₹ 850
   - (a) ₹ 225
   - (b) ₹ 250
   - (c) ₹ 300
   - (d) ₹ 325

2. Find the value of x, if the mean of the following data is 36.

   8, 11, 19, 14, 13, 18, 26, x, 2x, 5
   - (a) 100
   - (b) 27
   - (c) 82
   - (d) 14

3. What is mean of Ist 10 whole numbers.
   - (a) 4.5
   - (b) 5
   - (c) 3.2
   - (d) 4

4. The average cost of 5 mangoes is ₹ 10 and the average cost of 3 of them is ₹ 9, what is the average cost of remaining 2?
   - (a) ₹ 10.1
   - (b) ₹ 9.0
   - (c) ₹ 11.5
   - (d) ₹ 21.0

5. The average temperature on Wednesday, Thursday and Friday was 25°. The average temperature on Thursday, Friday and Saturday was 24°. If the temperature was 28° on Saturday, what was the temperature on Wednesday?
   - (a) 30°
   - (b) 31°
   - (c) 26°
   - (d) 25°

6. The scores in Mathematics Examination (out of 100) of 15 students is as follows:

   12, 38, 48, 78, 36, 27, 68, 42, 19, 17, 61, 65, 47, 84, 39

   What is the median of this data?
   - (a) 47
   - (b) 42
   - (c) 36
   - (d) 60

7. The median of observations 10, 12, 14, 15, 16, $(x+2)$, 22, 24, 25, 29 and 30 arranged in ascending order is 26. Find the value of x.
   - (a) 16
   - (b) 19
   - (c) 20
   - (d) 24

8. Find the mode of the following data.

Variables	20	25	30	35	40
Frequency	3	4	6	2	5

   - (a) 30
   - (b) 32
   - (c) 6
   - (d) 40

9. Find the value of x, if the mode of the following data is 40

40, 28, 30, 40, 28, 25, 14, 25, 25, 26, 30, 40, 30, x, 28

(a) 36   (b) 40
(c) 35   (d) 25

10. Study the double bar graph shown below and answer the question that follow.

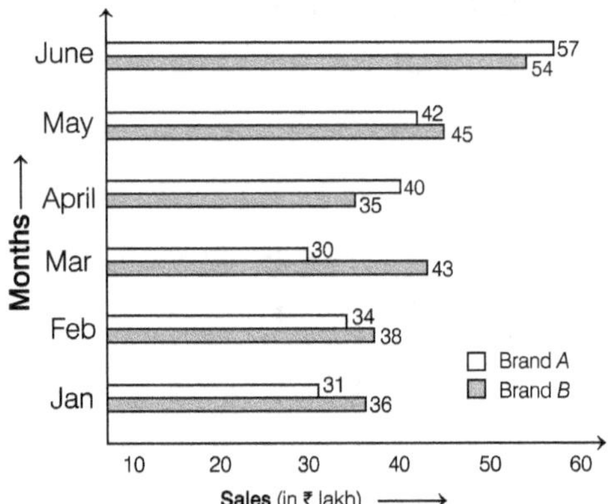

Find the average sales of brand B for the 6 months.

(a) ₹ 50.63 lakh   (b) ₹ 2 lakh
(c) ₹ 36.43 lakh   (d) ₹ 41.83 lakh

11. Study the double bar graph given below and answer the question that follow:

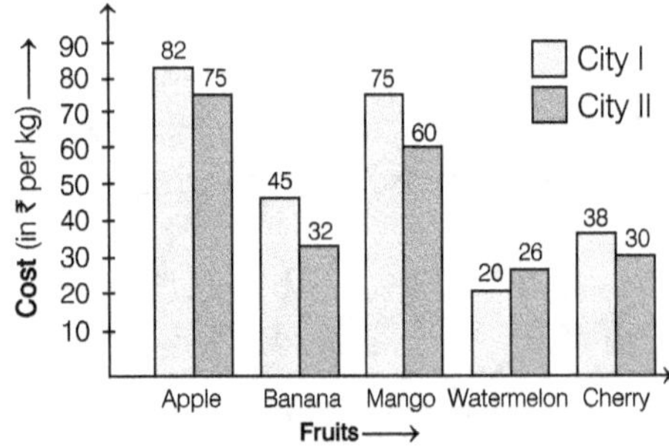

What is the average cost of fruits in city I.

(a) 50   (b) 28
(c) 30   (d) 52

12. A coin is tossed 100 times and head is obtained 59 times on tossing a coin at random. Find the probability of getting a head.

(a) $\dfrac{41}{100}$ (b) $\dfrac{59}{100}$ (c) $\dfrac{53}{100}$ (d) $\dfrac{1}{2}$

13. A die is thrown 300 times and the outcomes are noted as shown below:

Outcomes	1	2	3	4	5	6
Frequency	35	45	38	46	65	71

What is the probability of getting an even number?

(a) $\dfrac{23}{50}$ (b) $\dfrac{47}{100}$

(c) $\dfrac{27}{50}$ (d) $\dfrac{28}{71}$

14. From a bag of white and green balls, the probability of picking a white ball is $\dfrac{x}{2}$. Find the value of x if the probability of picking a green ball is $\dfrac{2}{3}$.

(a) $\dfrac{2}{3}$ (b) $\dfrac{4}{3}$ (c) $\dfrac{1}{2}$ (d) $\dfrac{1}{3}$

15. Aakash and Rishabh play a game where each is asked to select a number from 1 to 25. If the 2 numbers match, both of them win a prize. Find the probability that they will not win a prize in a single trial.

(a) $\dfrac{24}{25}$ (b) $\dfrac{1}{2}$ (c) $\dfrac{2}{25}$ (d) $\dfrac{3}{24}$

16. If 3 unbiased coins are tossed simultaneously, then the probability of exactly 2 heads is

(a) $\dfrac{1}{8}$ (b) $\dfrac{2}{8}$ (c) $\dfrac{3}{8}$ (d) $\dfrac{4}{8}$

2 Marks Questions

17. The mean age of a class of 10 students is 18 yr. If 2 students join the class, the means age increases by 2 yr.

What is the mean age of the new students?

(a) 30   (b) 20
(c) 40   (d) 60

18. The arithmetic mean of 5 consecutive integers starting with x is 'a'. What is the arithmetic mean of 9 consecutive integers that starts with $x + 2$?

(a) $2 + x + a$
(b) $20 + a$
(c) $14 + x + a$
(d) $4 + a$

19. The mean marks obtained by 300 students in a subject are 60. The mean of top 100 students was found to be 80 and the mean of last 100 students was found to be 50. The mean marks of the remaining 100 students are

(a) 70   (b) 65
(c) 60   (d) 50

20. The mean and median of 5 observations are 9 and 8 respectively. If 1 is subtracted from each observation, then the new mean and the new median will be respectively

(a) 8 and 7
(b) 9 and 7
(c) 8 and 9
(d) Cannot be determined due to insufficient data

Directions (Q. Nos. 21 and 22) Study the following bar chart and answer the given questions. Data regarding number of boys and girls studying in Stand. X of 5 different schools

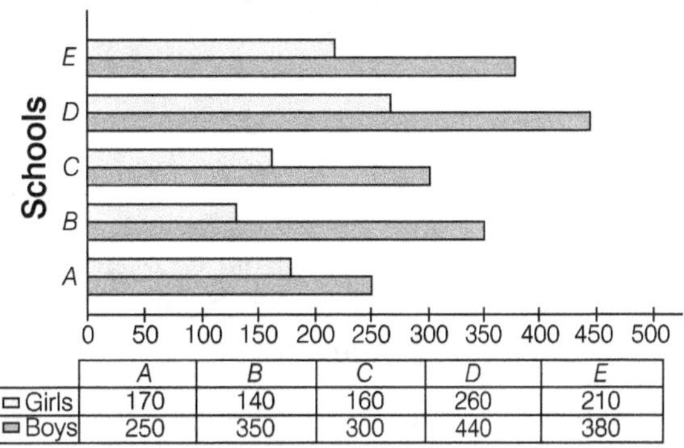

	A	B	C	D	E
□ Girls	170	140	160	260	210
▣ Boys	250	350	300	440	380

21. What is the difference between total number of boys studying in schools B and C together and the total number of girls in the same schools together?

(a) 350   (b) 200
(c) 400   (d) 309

22. Number of students (boys and girls together) Studying in class IX of school E is 20% less than those Studying in class X of the same school. How many students Studying in class IX in the same school?

(a) 506   (b) 472
(c) 420   (d) 464

23. The given line graph show the number of toys sold by a shopkeeper over 5 days.

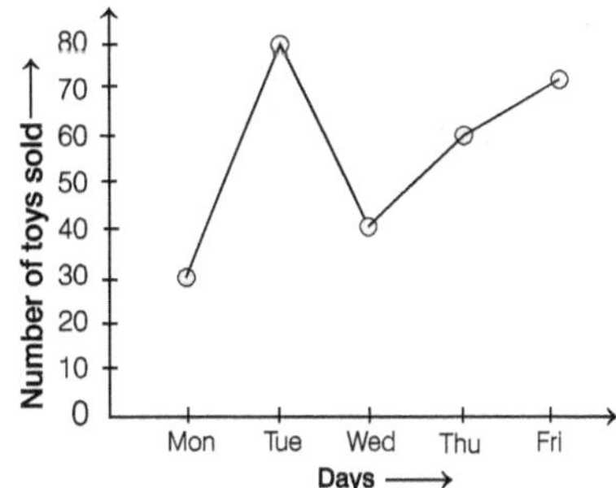

If the cost of 1 toy is ₹ 40, then how much did he earn in 5 days?

(a) ₹ 9200   (b) ₹ 10200
(c) ₹ 11200   (d) ₹ 12200

PRACTICE SET 

1 Mark Questions

1. 3 times an angle is equal to 2 times its complement. What is the value of angle?
(a) $180°$ (b) $120°$ (c) $36°$ (d) $30°$

2. Simplify and choose the correct option.
$$-[10 \times (-2) + (-25)] \div (-5)$$
(a) -9 (b) -5 (c) -2 (d) 1

3. What is the solution of $7y - 9 = -4$.
(a) $\dfrac{1}{7}$ (b) $\dfrac{1}{3}$ (c) $\dfrac{6}{7}$ (d) $\dfrac{5}{7}$

4. The following are steps involved in finding each of interior angle of 10-sided regular polygon. Arrange them in sequential order.

I. Each exterior angle $= 36°$

II. Each interior angle $= 180° - 36° = 144°$

III. Each exterior angle $= \dfrac{360°}{n} = \dfrac{360°}{10°}$
$$[\because n = 10]$$

(a) III, I, II   (b) II, I, III
(c) III, II, I   (d) II, III, I

5. The value of $\left[(\sqrt[m]{y^2})^{\frac{m}{2}} \right]^2$

(a) y^2 (b) $1/y$ (c) $\sqrt{y}$ (d) $y/2$

6. What is the order of rotational symmetry of the given figure.

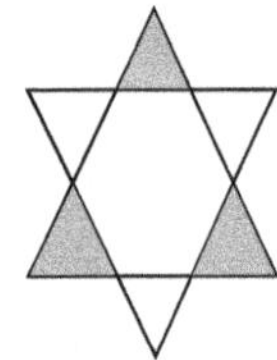

(a) 1   (b) 2   (c) 3   (d) 4

7. What would be the simple interest obtained in 7 yr on a principal of ₹ 3200 at the rate of 9% per annum?
(a) ₹ 6400   (b) ₹ 17320
(c) ₹ 6600   (d) ₹ 2016

8. Kriti bought 4 sweaters that each cost the same amount and 1 skirt that cost ₹ 20. The items she bought cost a total of ₹ 160 before tax was added.

If x represents the cost of 1 sweater, write the correct expression to show the given problem.
(a) $4x = 160 + 20$ (b) $4x + 20 = 160$
(c) $4x - 20 = 160$ (d) None of these

9. Which of the following letter have only vertical symmetry?
A, B, F, G, C
(a) A   (b) B
(c) G   (d) C

10. In the given figure, ABC is a straight line. If $EF \parallel AD$, $\angle BEG = 104°$ and $\angle BGF = 152°$, then find the values of x and y.

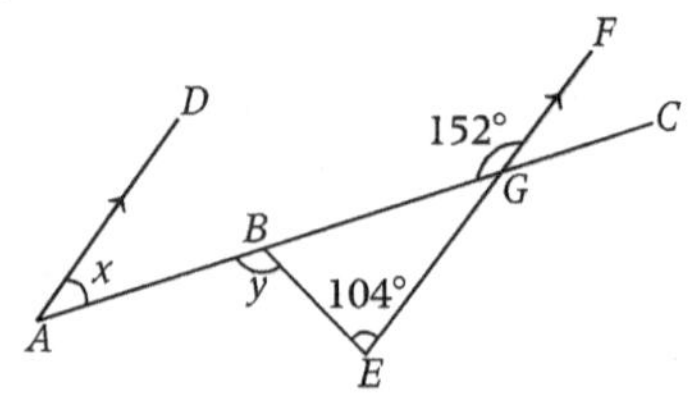

(a) $x = 132°, y = 46°$
(b) $x = 28°, y = 132°$
(c) $x = 46°, y = 114°$
(d) None of the above

11. Tom scored 553 marks out of 700 and Abrahim scored 486 marks out of 600 in English. Whose performance is better?
(a) Tom   (b) Abrahim
(c) Equal   (d) None

12. Andrew deposited ₹ 5500 and Anamika deposited ₹ 4800 in a bank. If the bank pays a simple interest of 2% per annum, then how much more interest would Andrew get than Anamika after a year?
(a) ₹ 14   (b) ₹ 96   (c) ₹ 110   (d) ₹ 206

13. The perimeter of a rectangular field is 91 m. Its length is $(2a-1)$ m and breadth is $(a+9)$ m, then what will be its length?
(a) 21.5 m (b) 24 m   (c) 16 m   (d) 18 m

14. Evaluate and choose the correct option.
$$\left(1+\frac{1}{3}+\frac{1}{5}\right)\times\left(\frac{1}{3}+\frac{1}{5}+\frac{1}{7}\right)$$
$$-\left(1+\frac{1}{3}+\frac{1}{5}+\frac{1}{7}\right)\times\left(\frac{1}{3}+\frac{1}{5}\right)$$
(a) $\dfrac{1}{5}$ (b) $\dfrac{1}{3}$ (c) $\dfrac{1}{7}$ (d) $\dfrac{1}{9}$

15. If $\triangle ABC \cong \triangle XYZ$ then, the value of $\angle A$ will be?

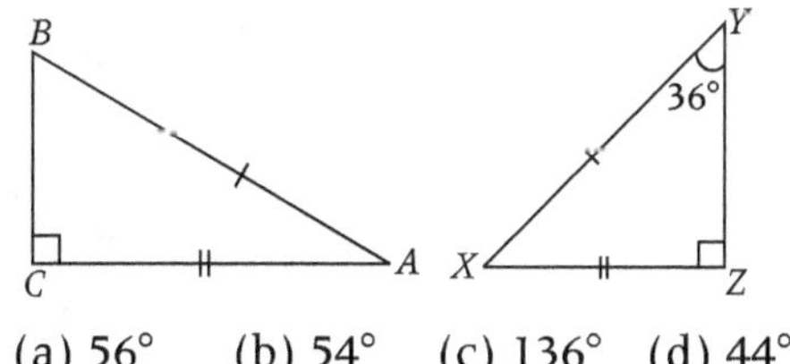

(a) 56°   (b) 54°   (c) 136°   (d) 44°

16. How many lines of symmetry does the given figure have?

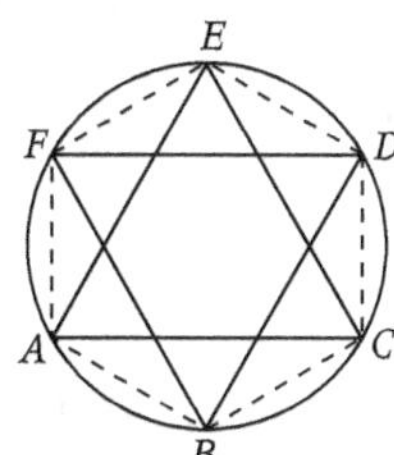

(a) 4   (b) 6   (c) 8   (d) 0

17. Which of the following means $5n+7=17$?
(a) 7 more than 5 times a number is 17
(b) 5 more than 7 times a number is 17
(c) 7 less than 5 times a number is 17
(d) 12 times a number is 17

18. The dimension of a rectangular floor of a room is 20 m × 10 m. The owner want to pave the floor by equal number of 2 different color square marbles of length 1 m. If he uses blue and white color marbles then the number of blue color marbles is
(a) 100   (b) 30
(c) 50   (d) 65

19. If $xyz=0$ then the value of $(p^x)^{zy}+(p^y)^{zx}+(p^z)^{xy}$ is
(a) p^2 (b) 1
(c) 0   (d) 3

20. Anamika and Rashmi purchased some items in their shopping. One of them bought 18 more than the other and the number of items she bought was 75% of the sum of the number of their items. Then the total number of items purchased by them is
(a) 36   (b) 28   (c) 45   (d) 54

21. If $A:B:C=5:6:7$, then $\left(\dfrac{A}{B}\right):\left(\dfrac{B}{C}\right):\left(\dfrac{C}{A}\right)$ is equal to
(a) 175 : 180 : 294   (b) 25 : 36 : 49
(c) 10 : 180 : 79   (d) 35 : 30 : 45

22. Marya earns ₹ 30000 every month. She spends 20% of her salary on rent, 80% of the remaining amount on other expenses and saves the rest. What percentage of the salary does Marya save?
(a) ₹ 4800   (b) ₹ 3600
(c) ₹ 4200   (d) ₹ 2700

23. Evaluate and choose the correct option.

$$\dfrac{17\dfrac{2}{3} + 21\dfrac{1}{2} - 9\dfrac{1}{3}}{79\dfrac{1}{2} - 49\dfrac{2}{3}}$$

(a) $4\dfrac{2}{3}$ (b) $17\dfrac{2}{6}$

(c) 1 (d) $2\dfrac{3}{5}$

24. A product is marked at 20% above cost price. It is then sold at 90% of selling price. The profit is 120. Then, cost price is equal to

(a) ₹ 1500   (b) ₹ 2000
(c) ₹ 1200   (d) ₹ 2500

25. What is the value of $\dfrac{3x - 7 + 11x + 21}{2}$, when $x = 4$?

(a) 35   (b) 42
(c) 32   (d) 70

26. A laptop costs ₹ 27900 after a 10% discount. How much would the laptop cost after a further price reduction of 5% off its original undiscounted price?

(a) ₹ 26700   (b) ₹ 26350
(c) ₹ 24630   (d) ₹ 26375

27. Mr. Puri deposits ₹ 30000 in a bank that pays an interest of 12%. If he earns an interest of ₹ 10800, then what is the timep eriod for which he kept the money?

(a) 2 yr   (b) 3 yr
(c) 4 yr   (d) 5 yr

28. The cost price of 2 skirts and 3 kurtis is ₹ 2200 and the cost price of 2 kurtis and 4 skirts is ₹ 2400. Find the ratio between the cost price of the kurti and the skirt.

(a) 10 : 7   (b) 3 : 7
(c) 6 : 13   (d) 2 : 3

29. Simplify and choose the correct option.

$$\dfrac{(2x^3z^2)^6}{8x^3y^4z^2 \cdot x^{-4}z^3}$$

(a) $\dfrac{8x^{10}z^4}{y}$ (b) $\dfrac{6xz^4}{y^{10}}$

(c) $\dfrac{8x^{10}z}{y^4}$ (d) None of these

30. Kiran had 10 paise, 25 paise and 50 paise coins in the ratio of $10 : 8 : 9$ respectively. After giving ₹ 20 to her mother she has ₹ 40.
How many 25 paise coins did she have?

(a) 59   (b) 64
(c) 72   (d) 86

31. Which of the following options is simplified value of
$(1 + 0.35 + 0.58) \times (0.35 + 0.58 + 0.78)$
$- (1 + 0.35 + 0.58 + 0.78) \times (0.35 + 0.58)$?

(a) 0.35   (b) 0.58
(c) 0.78   (d) 1

32. There are 3 blue, 4 red and 5 black coloured balls in a bag. If a ball is picked at random, what is the probability of having a blue ball?

(a) $\dfrac{4}{5}$ (b) $\dfrac{2}{3}$ (c) $\dfrac{1}{4}$ (d) $\dfrac{1}{2}$

33. Chitra deposits ₹ 7500 in saving bank and gets ₹ 10000 after 5 yr. What was the rate of interest?

(a) $8\dfrac{1}{3}\%$ (b) $6\dfrac{2}{3}\%$ (c) $5\dfrac{1}{6}\%$ (d) $1\dfrac{1}{2}\%$

34. What is the coefficient of x^2 in $-\dfrac{49}{87}Px^2 + z^2yx$

(a) $-\dfrac{49}{87}P$ (b) $-P$

(c) $\left(\dfrac{49}{87}\right)^2$ (d) 1

35. Match the following.

Figure		Lines of symmetry
I.	(i)	4
II.	(ii)	1
III.	(iii)	0

Codes

	I	II	III
(a)	ii	i	iii
(b)	i	iii	ii
(c)	iii	i	ii
(d)	i	ii	iii

36. Which of the following is a pythagoras triplet?

(a) 7, 8, 9   (b) 8, 7, 12
(c) 13, 14, 8   (d) 8, 15, 17

37. Read the following statements carefully and mark the correct option.

Statement I When a figure fits onto itself more than once during a full turn is known as rotational symmetry.

Statement II The number of times a figure fits onto itself in one full turn is called order of rotational symmetry.

(a) Both Statements I and II are correct
(b) Only Statement I is correct
(c) Only Statement II is correct
(d) None are correct

38. Match the data given in column A with their corresponding mode given in column B.

Column A	Column B
A. 1, 2, 4, 1, 2, 4, 5, 1	1. 9
B. 19, 18, 20, 21, 19, 23, 19, 18, 20	2. 11
C. 14, 11, 15, 19, 11, 15, 11, 7	3. 19
D. 7, 9, 10, 11, 9, 12	4. 1

	A	B	C	D		A	B	C	D
(a)	4	3	2	1	(b)	4	2	3	1
(c)	1	3	4	2	(d)	2	1	3	4

39. Fill in the blanks

P. Area of square pond whose perimeter is 320 m is ....

Q. If the perimeter of a square is doubled, then the ratio of original area to the new area is ....

R. If the base of the right angled triangle is 4 m and the hypotenuse is 5m long. Then its area is ....

	P	Q	R
(a)	6400 m^2	(1 : 4)	6 m^2
(b)	3200 m^2	(1 : 2)	7 m^2
(c)	6400 m^2	(2 : 3)	6 m^2
(d)	8200 m^2	(1 : 3)	6 m^2

40. State 'T' for true and 'F' for false

I.   Sum of two rational numbers is not a rational number.

II. Additive inverse of $\dfrac{1}{3}$ is $\dfrac{-1}{3}$.

III. On a number line $-\dfrac{3}{4}$ is to the left of the zero (0).

IV. $-\left(-\dfrac{3}{7}\right)$ is a negative rational number.

	I	II	III	IV		I	II	III	IV
(a)	T	F	F	T	(b)	F	T	T	F
(c)	T	T	F	F	(d)	F	F	T	T

2 Marks Questions

41. A cuboid was made using cardboard. Karishma made some changes to the size of the original cuboid. She increased the length by 10% and the breadth is $\frac{4}{5}$ of the original breadth.

The ratio of the new height to the original height is 11 : 10. If the volume of cuboid is equal to length × breadth × height, then what is the new volume of cuboid as a percentage of its original volume?

(a) 98.6%

(b) 96.8%

(c) 94.2%

(d) 92.4%

42. Choose the correct option.

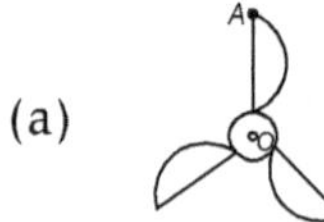
(a) It has angle of rotation equal to 120°

(b) It has angle of rotation equal to 72°

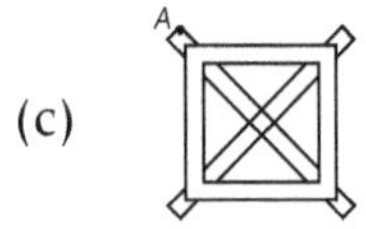
(c) It has angle of rotation equal to 90°

(d) All are correct

43. The profit gained from the sale of a TV set is ₹ 1000. If it is sold at its selling price. If it is sold at 80% of its selling price, a loss of ₹ 600 will be incurred. What is the cost price of the TV set?

(a) ₹ 7000   (b) ₹ 8000

(c) ₹ 9000   (d) ₹ 10000

44. An insurance policy pays 90% of the 1st bill on ₹ 20000 of a certain patient's medical expenses, 80% of the next ₹ 40000 and 40% of the ₹ 40000 after that. If the patient's total bill is ₹ 92000, then how much will the policy pay?

(a) ₹ 90000

(b) ₹ 84000

(c) ₹ 70000

(d) ₹ 62800

45. Simplify and choose the correct option.
$$\frac{(2\,hj^2k^{-2} \cdot h^4\,j^{-1}k^4)^0}{2h^{-3}\,j^{-4}\,k^{-2}}$$

(a) $h^8j^5k^4$

(b) $2h^6j^4k^4$

(c) $\dfrac{h^3j^4k^2}{2}$

(d) $2h^3j^4k^2$

46. In the given figure if BC is parallel to EF and $DC = DB = DA = DE = DF$. Then, what is the value sum of $\angle CDB$ and $\angle FDE$?

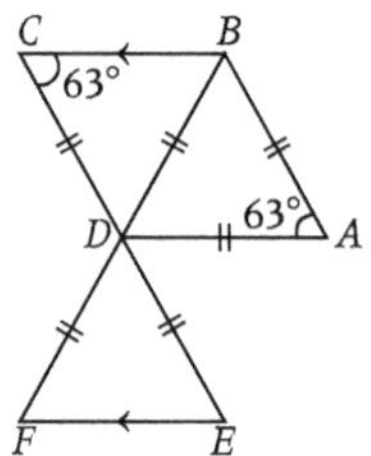

(a) 112°

(b) 108°

(c) 136°

(d) 110°

47. Study the following statements and select the correct option.

P: Only those angles which are the multiples of 15° can only be constructed using ruler and compass.

Q: We can construct an isosceles triangle in which length of its equal sides is 8.4 cm and angle between then is 90°.

(a) Both P and Q are true

(b) Both P and Q are false

(c) P is true but Q is false

(d) P is false but Q is true

48. John paid 15% less than Marie. Joseph paid 25% more than John. If the total sum of their payments is ₹ 17475, then how much did Marie paid?

(a) ₹ 7000

(b) ₹ 5190

(c) ₹ 6000

(d) ₹ 6500

Directions (Q. Nos. 49 and 50) Study the following bar graph carefully and answer the questions that follow.

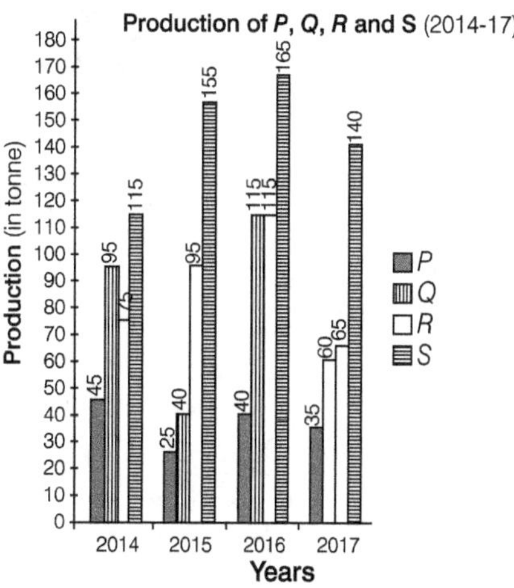

49. In which year the annual growth rate of total production (of all products) is highest?

(a) 2015   (b) 2016

(c) 2017   (d) 2019

50. Individual revenue of P, Q, R and S for the entire period (2014-17) is calculated based on the price of ₹ 9, ₹ 4, ₹ 13 and ₹ 3, respectively. Which product fetches the lowest revenue?

(a) Product P (b) Product Q

(c) Product R (d) Product S

PRACTICE SET 02

1 Mark Questions

1. Which of the following numbers is equal to 36?

(a) $\dfrac{(-2)\times(-3)\times3\times4}{-2}$

(b) $\dfrac{(-2)\times6\times(-3)\times(-2)}{-3}$

(c) $\dfrac{(-2)\times9\times(-3)\times(-2)}{3}$

(d) $\dfrac{(-2)\times3\times(-3)\times(-2)}{-1}$

2. X, Y and Z are the 3 numbers such that Y is 50% more than Z and X is 20% more than Z then $X:Y$ is

(a) $2:3$ (b) $4:5$ (c) $5:6$ (d) $7:3$

3. Chavi get marks in the ratio $1:2:3$ in three subjects. If she gets a total of 120 marks in all, what she get marks in three subjects?

(a) 20, 30, 70 (b) 30, 40, 50
(c) 10, 50, 60 (d) 20, 40, 60

4. 6000 acres of farmland have to be partitioned in the ratio $3:4:5$. What is the size of greatest part?

(a) 2500 acres (b) 1500 acres
(c) 750 acres (d) 480 acres

5. The below figure is made up of a right angled triangle and an equilateral triangle. Then, value of $\angle ABC$ is

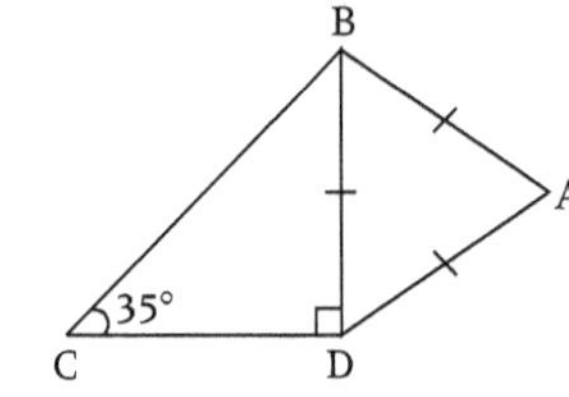

(a) $55°$ (b) $120°$ (c) $115°$ (d) $145°$

6. Albert bought a refrigerator for ₹ 52000 and spent ₹ 4000 on its repairs. If he sells at ₹ 47000 then what will be his loss percentage?

(a) 13% (b) $15\dfrac{2}{9}\%$

(c) 18% (d) $16\dfrac{1}{14}\%$

7. Poonam's salary was decreased by 50% and subsequently increased by 50%. How much percent does she loss?

(a) 25% (b) 67% (c) 12% (d) 35%

8. Cost price of 32 books is same as the selling price of 24 books. Then profit percent is

(a) $\dfrac{40}{7}\%$ (b) 60%

(c) $\dfrac{100}{3}\%$ (d) 40%

9. Find the value of P in $P\%$ of $1864 + 60 = 618.2$

(a) 49.09 (b) 72.44
(c) 29.94 (d) 83.02

10. The difference of negative 12 and 4 is multiplied by the square of 3 will be equal to

(a) -144 (b) -200
(c) -176 (d) -184

11. Observe the numbers on below given dice and find the number on the face opposite to the number 4.

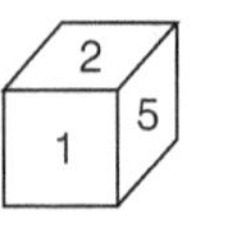

(a) 1 (b) 2 (c) 3 (d) 6

12. In the given figure, AOB is a straight line and the ray OC stand on it. If $\angle AOC = (2x-10)^\circ$ and $\angle BOC = (3x+20)^\circ$, then the value of $(5x+40)^\circ$ is equal to

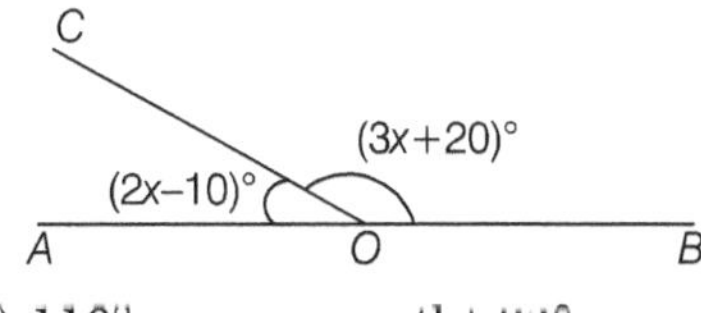

(a) 110° (b) 93°

(c) 210° (d) 195°

13. The formula for the sum of n terms is given by $S_n = (n/2)\{2a + (n-1)d\}$. If $n = 10, a = 6$ and $d = 4$, then S_n is equal to

(a) 200   (b) 240   (c) 280   (d) 300

14. In 2010, 3500000000000 prescription drug orders were filled in India. If the average price of each prescription was roughly ₹65, then how much did India pay for prescription drugs?

(a) 2.275×10^{14}

(b) 2.275×10^{10}

(c) 2.275×10^{12}

(d) None of the above

15. If $x = -2, y = 3$ and $z = -4$, then what is the value of $-4x + 5y + 2z$?

(a) 8   (b) -8 (c) 15   (d) 10

16. Sammy drew a rectangle that was w inches wide. The expression $2(2w) + 2(w)$ represents the perimeter of the rectangle that Sammy drew. Which statement relates the perimeter to the width of the rectangle?

(a) The perimeter is 6 inch more than the width

(b) The perimeter is 6 times the width.

(c) The perimeter is 2 inch more than the width

(d) The perimeter is 2 times the width

17. A travelling agent gets a commission of 4.5% on the sale of tickets. If on a certain day, he gets ₹ 31.5 as commission, then the cost of tickets sold on that day is worth

(a) ₹ 700

(b) ₹ 400

(c) ₹ 1000

(d) ₹ 3150

18. If $C = \dfrac{AX}{X+15}$ is the formula for a child's dose of medicine, where A is the adult dose in grams and Y is the child's age in year, then find the dose for a child who is 10 yr old, if the adult dose is 50 gm.

(a) 10 gm

(b) 20 gm

(c) 25 gm

(d) 40 gm

19. Which of the solid shapes shown could be made from the pattern?

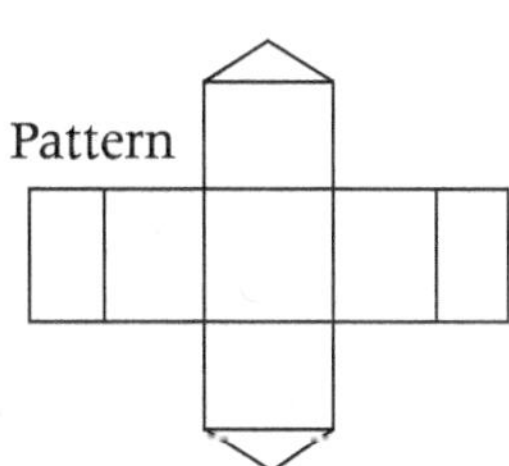

(a) 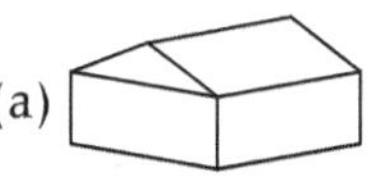   (b) 

(c)    (d) 

20. Simplify and choose the correct option.

$$63 - (-3)\{-3 - \overline{8-3}\} \div 3\{5 + (-3)(-1)\}$$

(a) 62   (b) 52

(c) 46   (d) 72

21. If $\angle 1 = 32°$ and $\angle 2$ and $\angle 3$ are complementary, then the measure of $\angle 4$ is

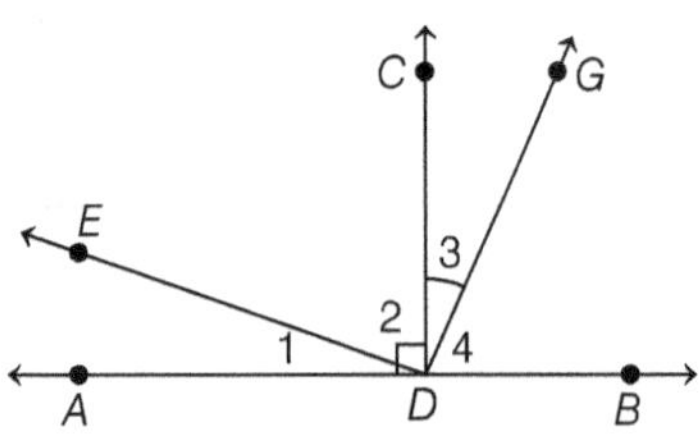

(a) 54°   (b) 32°

(c) 36°   (d) 58°

22. What is the range of the following times?

1.7 h, 6.3 h, 2.5 h, 5.1 h, 3.9 h

(a) 2.5   (b) 2.07

(c) 4.6   (d) 3.9

23. Arvind went shopping with ₹ 1500. After spending 0.75 of it on 3 identical shirts, he spent the rest of the money on 2 pairs of shoes. How much did Arvind pay for a shirt and 2 pairs of shoes?

(a) ₹ 750   (b) ₹ 800

(c) ₹ 450   (d) None of these

24. Simplify and choose the correct option.

$$\frac{2x^2y^4 \cdot 4x^2y^4 \cdot 3x}{3x^{-3}y^2}$$

(a) $10x^8y^6$ (b) $8x^8y^6$

(c) $\dfrac{8}{3}x^4y^2$ (d) $\dfrac{10}{3}x^4y^2$

25. $\dfrac{2}{5}$th of the fruits at a fruit seller were oranges and the rest were bananas. When the fruit seller bought another 148 fruits, the number of oranges added to the fruit stall was $\dfrac{1}{4}$th to total number of bananas. If the number of bananas added to the fruit stall was 80,

then the number of fruits at the fruit stall was

(a) 280   (b) 320

(c) 360   (d) 400

26. What is the value of x in the expression,

$$\frac{(16)^{2x+1}\,(64)^5}{(256)^2 \times 4} = (16)^{6x}$$

(a) 7   (b) 0

(c) 2   (d) 1

27. What is the difference between the mean and median of set $S = \{2, 4, 6, 7, 7, 13, 18, 92\}$?

(a) 10.125   (b) 11.125

(c) 11.625   (d) 14

28. If 100 square marbles of equal size were required to pave a floor of dimension 3m × 12m then length of each marble is

(a) 120 cm   (b) 144 cm

(c) 60 cm   (d) 100 cm

29. Which congruence criterion can be used to state that $\triangle AOB \cong \triangle DOC$?

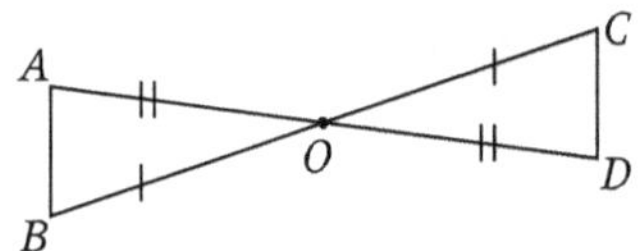

(a) ASA   (b) SAS

(c) SSS   (d) RHS

30. What is the value of $\dfrac{25P - 12}{3}$, when $P = 6$?

(a) 16   (b) 28

(c) 36   (d) 46

31. Johanson is 5 yr old. Joseph is n yr older than Johanson. What is their total age in 3 yr time?

(a) $20 + n$ (b) $9 + n$

(c) $11 + n$ (d) $16 + n$

32. ₹ 3200 is divided among A, B and C in the ratio of $3:5:8$, respectively. What is the difference between the share of B and C?

(a) ₹ 600   (b) ₹ 800

(c) ₹ 100   (d) ₹ 550

33. A certain sum of money triples itself in 5 yr at simple interest. In how many year it will be 5 times?

(a) 10 yr

(b) 8 yr

(c) 6 yr

(d) 4 yr

34. The sum of a fraction and 7 times its reciprocal is $\dfrac{11}{2}$. What is the fraction?

(a) $\dfrac{2}{3}$ (b) $\dfrac{3}{4}$

(c) $\dfrac{2}{7}$ (d) $\dfrac{7}{2}$

35. If P is the area, Q is the circumference and R is the diameter of circle, then $\dfrac{P}{QR}$ is

(a) $1:4$ (b) $2:3$

(c) $3:5$ (d) $6:7$

36. In $\triangle ABC$ if the median $AD = \dfrac{1}{2} BC$, then $\angle BAC$ is .....

(a) $60°$ (b) $45°$

(c) $90°$ (d) $120°$

37. Assertion 5 is a rational number.

Reason The square roots of all positive integers are rational.

(a) Both Assertion and Reason are correct and Reason is the correct explanation for Assertion.

(b) Both Assertion and Reason are correct but Reason is not the correct explanation for Assertion

(c) Assertion is correct but Reason is incorrect

(d) Assertion is incorrect but Reason is correct

38. Match the following.

	Column A		Column B
I.	The supplement of 80° is	(i)	$10°$
II.	The complement of 80° is	(ii)	Hypotenuse
III.	The long side of a right triangle is called	(iii)	Rectangle
IV.	A parallelogram in which an angle is 90° is called a	(iv)	Altitude
		(v)	$100°$
		(vi)	Square

     I   II III IV

(a) v   i   iv iii

(b) i   v   ii vi

(c) i   v iv vi

(d) v   i   ii iii

39. Fill in the blanks.

P. A die is rolled, the probability that even number is obtained is .....

Q. There are 4 restaurants in a town. If 3 men goes into the restaurant in a day then the probability that each goes into a different restaurant is ....

R. The simple interest on ₹ 200 for 6 yr at 5% per annum is ......

S. When an article is sold at a price lower than its cost price, then .... is incurred.

	P	Q	R	S
(a)	$\dfrac{1}{2}$	$\dfrac{3}{8}$	₹ 160	Profit
(b)	$\dfrac{2}{3}$	$\dfrac{1}{2}$	₹ 100	Loss
(c)	$\dfrac{1}{6}$	$\dfrac{2}{3}$	₹ 250	Profit
(d)	$\dfrac{1}{2}$	$\dfrac{3}{8}$	₹ 60	Loss

40. Write 'T' for true and 'F' for false

P. If the perimeter of an equilateral triangle is 45 cm, then its area is 225 cm^2

Q. The area of square inscribed in a circle of radius 5 cm is 50 cm^2

R. If the difference between circumference and radius of the circle is 37 m. Then the circumference is 7 m

S. If $\triangle ABC \cong \triangle XYZ$ and $\angle ABC = 75°$, then $\angle XYZ = 45°$

	P	Q	R	S
(a)	T	F	F	T
(b)	F	T	F	F
(c)	F	F	T	T
(d)	T	T	F	F

2 Marks Questions

41. 2 different brands of air conditioner were sold at the same price of ₹ 30400 each. The sale of the 1st set made a profit of 20% while that of the 2nd made a loss of 25%. Find the net gain/loss on the sale of the air conditioners.

(a) Gain ₹ 1520   (b) Loss ₹ 2000

(c) Loss ₹ 5067   (d) Gain ₹ 2000

42. In the given figure, $ABCD$ is a parallelogram such that $AB \parallel CD$ and $AD \parallel BC$ with opposite angles equal. If $DA = DX$, then find the values of $\angle m$ and $\angle n$.

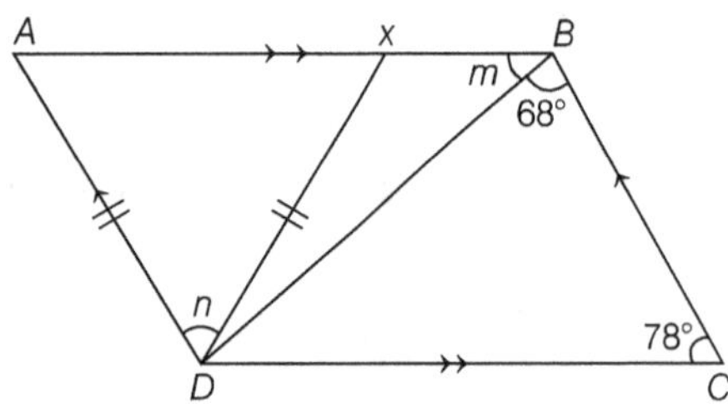

(a) $m = 24°$, $n = 34°$

(b) $m = 24°$, $n = 24°$

(c) $m = 34°$, $n = 24°$

(d) $m = 34°$, $n = 34°$

43. There were fewer than 42 students in a class. $\dfrac{1}{2}$ of the students scored A^+ in a Mathematics test. $\dfrac{1}{3}$ of them scored A in the same test and another $\dfrac{1}{7}$ of them scored B^+. The rest of the students scored B. How many students scored B in the test?

(a) 1   (b) 3   (c) 4   (d) 5

44. Simplify and choose the correct option.
$$\frac{(2m^{-1}pq^0)^{-4} \cdot 2m^{-1}p^3}{2pq^2}$$

(a) $\dfrac{m^3}{16p^2q^2}$ (b) $16p^2q^2m^3$

(c) $\dfrac{16\,m^3}{p^2q^2}$ (d) $\dfrac{1}{16m^3p^2q^2}$

45. The salary of 2 friends Mukesh and Aparna are in the ratio $4:5$. If the salary of each one increases by ₹ 6000, then the new ratio becomes $48:55$. What is Mukesh's salary?

(a) ₹ 10400   (b) ₹ 8400

(c) ₹ 10200   (d) ₹ 4800

46. A person invests ₹ 12000 as fixed deposit at a bank at the rate of 10% per annum simple interest. But due to some pressing needs, he has to withdraw the entire money after 3 yr, for which the bank allowed him a lower rate of interest. If he gets ₹ 3320 less than, what he would have got at the end of 5 yr, the rate of interest allowed by bank is

(a) $7\dfrac{8}{9}\%$ (b) $8\dfrac{7}{9}\%$

(c) $7\dfrac{5}{9}\%$ (d) $7\dfrac{4}{9}\%$

47. A circle of 3 m radius is divided into three areas by semi-circles of radii 1 m and 2 m as shown in the adjoining figure. The ratio of the three areas A, B and C will be

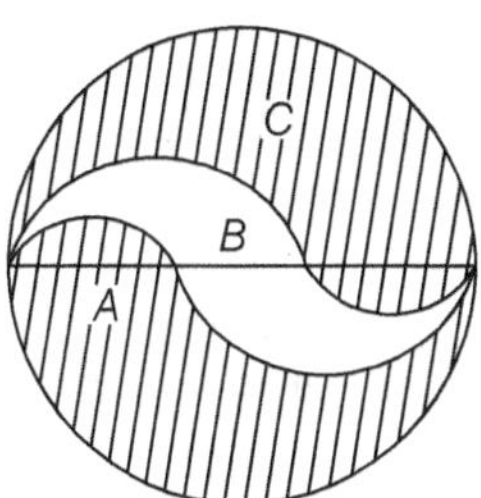

(a) $2:3:2$ (b) $1:1:1$

(c) $4:3:4$ (d) $1:2:1$

48. Manisha has 25% more seeds than Sangeeta. If Sangeeta gives 50 seeds to Manisha, she will have $\dfrac{1}{2}$ of what Manisha has. How many seeds does Sangeeta have at 1st?

(a) 75   (b) 150

(c) 200   (d) None of these

Directions (Q. Nos. 49 and 50) The following bar chart shows the production of cement (in lakh tonne) of four factories A, B, C and D over the year.

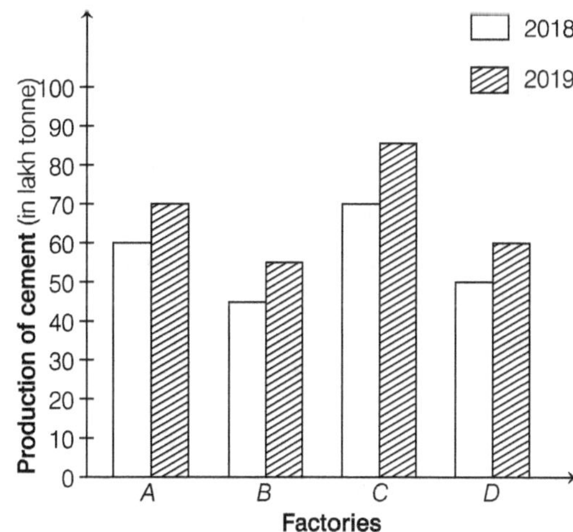

49. The percentage increase in production of cement by factory B from 2018 to 2019 is about

(a) 15.6   (b) 18.9   (c) 12.8   (d) 22.2

50. Which of the 4 factories has recorded the maximum percentage growth in production of cement from 2018 to 2019?

(a) B (b) A (c) D (d) C

Hints & Solutions

Chapter 1 : Integers

1. *(c)* Option (a), $\quad -(+100) = -100$,
Option (b), $\quad -(-2) = 2$
Option (c), $\quad (-48) = 48$
Option (d), $\quad +(-101) = -101$

2. *(b)* Going above sea level $= +20$ km
$\therefore$ Its opposite is going below sea level $= -20$ km

3. *(c)* By property, we know that integers are closed under both addition and subtraction.

4. *(b)* If $a = 2, b = 3$, then
$a - b = 2 - 3 = -1, b - a = 3 - 2 = 1$
Hence, $a - b \neq b - a$ (if $a \neq b$).

5. *(d)* Except option (d), all other options have the sum equal to -11.

6. *(a)* Consider
$-28 + 12 + 42 - 63 = 12 + 42 - 28 - 63$
$= 54 - 91$
$= -37 = 37$

7. *(b)* Consider, $-6 + (-24) - 48 = -6 - 24 - 48$
$= -78$

8. *(c)* The correct forecast from lowest to highest is
$-79°C, -70°C, -58°C, -53°C, -52°C, -48°C$

9. *(d)* Here, $\qquad D = 7$ and $A = -5$
So, $\qquad D - A = 7 - (-5) = 12$

10. *(b)* Here, $C = 2$ and $B = -2$
$\therefore \quad C + B = 0$ and $D + A = 7 - 5 = +2$
$\therefore \quad C + B < D + A$

11. *(a)* $(-1) \times (-1) \times (-1) \times (-1) \times \ldots$ 20 times $= (-1)^{20}$
$\therefore \qquad\qquad = 1 \quad [\because (-1)^n = 1,$ where n is even$]$

12. *(b)* The given statement is not correct as we know that, Product of a negative and positive integers is always negative.

13. *(b)* Given, $3 \times (-7) \times (-8) \times 9 \times 0 \times 4 \times 2 = 0$
$\because$ Any number multiplied to '0' is equal to zero.

14. *(c)* By distributive property
$2 \times (5 + 6) = (2 \times 5) \boxed{+} (2 \times 6)$
$2 \times 11 = 10 \boxed{+} 12$
$22 = 22 \qquad (\therefore \text{LHS} = \text{RHS})$
Hence, the required sign is '+'

15. *(a)* $? = (-2) \div 3 \times (-4) \div 1$
$= (-2) \times 3 \times (-4) \times 1 \qquad$ (Replaced $\div$ by $\times$)
$= (-6) \times (-4) = 24$

16. *(d)* Given, $7 \times (8 + 9) = 7 \times 8 + 7 \times 9$
Here, distributive property of multiplication over addition is used.

17. *(a)* P. 1 $\qquad$ Q. odd $\qquad$ R. less $\qquad$ S. 0

18. *(d)* Considering option (d),
$$\frac{2 \times 2 + 2 \div (-1)}{-1} = \frac{2 \times 2 - 2}{-1} = \frac{4 - 2}{-1} = -2$$

19. *(d)* I. $(-31) + 30 + (-31) + 30 + \ldots$ 30 terms
$= (-31 + 30) + (-31 + 30) + \ldots$ 15 pairs
$= -1 + -1 + -1 + \ldots 15$ times $= -15$
II. $(-7) \times 5 + 1 \times 0 = -35 + 0 = -35$
III. $42 \times (91 - 91) = 42 \times 0 = 0$
IV. $21 \div (5 - 8) = 21 \div (-3) = -7$

20. *(c)* Given,
$(-3) \;\square\; (-8) \;\square\; (-4) \;\square\; 2 \;\square\; (-2) = 3$
Considering the signs given in option (c)
$+, \div, -, \times$, we get
$(-3) + (-8) \div (-4) - 2 \times (-2)$
$= (-3) + 2 - 2 \times (-2) = (-3) + 2 + 4 = -3 + 6 = 3$

21. *(b)* Given, $\quad 100 \times \nabla = \nabla + \nabla + 98 \times 7$
$\Rightarrow \qquad 100 \times \nabla = 2\nabla + 686$
$\Rightarrow \qquad 100\nabla = 2\nabla + 686$
$\Rightarrow \qquad 98\nabla = 686 \Rightarrow \nabla = 7$
and $\qquad 153 \div \diamondsuit = 923 - 230 \times 4$
$\Rightarrow \qquad 153 \div \diamondsuit = 923 - 920$
$\Rightarrow \qquad 153 \div \diamondsuit = 3 \Rightarrow \diamondsuit = 51$
Hence, option (b) is correct.

22. *(c)* **Assertion** (A) Given,
$17 - \{(2 + \overline{7 - 3}) - 8\} = 17 - \{(2 + 4) - 8\}$
$= 17 - \{6 - 8\} = 17 - (-2) = 17 + 2 = 19$
$\therefore$ A is true and R is false.

23. *(c)* Number of tablets taken in a day $= 2A + B$
Number of tablets taken in two days
$= 2A + B + 2A + B + C = 7$ tablets
So, number of tablets taken in 30 days $= \dfrac{30}{2} \times 7$
$= 105$

24. (a) Given, $65 - (-3)\{-2 - \overline{8 - 3}\} \div 3\{5 + (-2)(-1)\}$

$= 65 - (-3)\{-2 - 5\} \div 3\{5 + 2\}$

$= 65 - (-3)\{-7\} \div 3\{7\}$

$= 65 - 21 \div 21 = 65 - 1 = 64$

25. (c)

(i) $(-10) \times (5 - 2) = -10 \times (3) = -30$

and $(-10) \times (-3) = 30$

so, $(-10) \times (5 - 2) \neq (-10) \times (-3)$

(ii) $0 \times (-51) = 0$ and $1 \times (-51) = (-51)$

so, the success or of $0 \times (-51)$ is not $1 \times (-51)$

(iii) $(-3) + (-10) = -13$ and $(-10) - (-3) = -10 + 3 = -7$

so, $(-3) + (-10)$ is less than $(-10) - (-3)$.

(iv) Integers are not always closed under division. If a and b are integers, then $a \div b$ is not necessarily an integer.

Hence, only (iii) is correct.

26. (b) We know that withdrawals are represented by '−' sign and deposits are represented by '+' sign.

∴ Final amount $= 11700 + 1925 + 3380$

$+ 4000 - 2500 - 5850 - 1000$

$= 21005 - 9350 = ₹11655$

27. (a) Original position of Mohan = 24th floor

Final position of Mohan = − 3rd floor [3rd basement]

∴ Number of floors to be covered

$= 24 - (-3) = 27$ floors

Now, speed of elevator = 1 floor/sec

So, time taken $= \dfrac{27}{1} = 27$ sec

Chapter 2 : Rational Number

1. (a) Consider, $\dfrac{2}{5} + \left(-\dfrac{5}{6}\right) + \left(-\dfrac{7}{9}\right)$

$= \dfrac{2}{5} - \dfrac{5}{6} - \dfrac{7}{9} = \dfrac{36 - 75 - 70}{90} = \dfrac{36 - 145}{90} = -\dfrac{109}{90}$

2. (c) Other rational number $= \dfrac{8}{9} - \dfrac{2}{18} = \dfrac{16 - 2}{18}$

$= \dfrac{14}{18} = \dfrac{7}{9}$

3. (d) Let the number to be added be x

and nearest natural number = 1.

So, $x + \left(\dfrac{-1}{4}\right) = 1 \Rightarrow x = 1 + \dfrac{1}{4} = \dfrac{5}{4}$

4. (b) Let x be subtracted

$\left(\dfrac{2}{3} - \dfrac{3}{4}\right) - x = -\dfrac{1}{6} \Rightarrow \dfrac{8 - 9}{12} - x = -\dfrac{1}{6}$

$\Rightarrow \quad x = -\dfrac{1}{12} + \dfrac{1}{6} = \dfrac{-1 + 2}{12} = \dfrac{1}{12}$

5. (c) Here, $A = \dfrac{4}{5}$ and $B = -\dfrac{3}{5}$

So, $A - B = \dfrac{4}{5} - \left(-\dfrac{3}{5}\right) = \dfrac{4}{5} + \dfrac{3}{5} = \dfrac{7}{5}$

6. (d) Rational number are not closed, commutative, and associative under division.

So, option (d) is correct answer.

7. (c)

$$\xleftarrow{\quad} \overset{-4/5}{\underset{}{\bullet}} \quad\quad \overset{0}{\bullet} \quad\quad\quad \overset{\frac{4}{5}}{\bullet} \xrightarrow{\quad}$$

We know that $\dfrac{-4}{-5} = \dfrac{4}{5}$

8. (d) All rational numbers satisfy the property of associativity under addition.

9. (b) The correct simplification $= \dfrac{-49}{-63} = \dfrac{7}{9}$

10. (d) Consider, $\dfrac{1}{3}, \dfrac{2}{5}, \dfrac{3}{7} = \dfrac{35}{105}, \dfrac{42}{105}, \dfrac{45}{105}$

∴ The correct sequence of numbers in ascending order is $\dfrac{1}{3} < \dfrac{2}{5} < \dfrac{3}{7}$.

11. (a) Given, $p = -\dfrac{2}{3} + \dfrac{4}{5} + 1 = \dfrac{-10 + 12 + 15}{15} = \dfrac{17}{15}$

and $q = \dfrac{2}{3} - \dfrac{4}{5} + \dfrac{7}{15} = \dfrac{10 - 12 + 7}{15} = \dfrac{5}{15}$

∴ $p > q$

12. (c) Exept option (c),

All others options lies between $\dfrac{2}{101}$ and $\dfrac{3}{71}$.

13. (c) I. $\left(\dfrac{-6}{25}\right) \times \dfrac{50}{36} = \dfrac{-1 \times 2}{6} = \dfrac{-1}{3}$

II. $\dfrac{3}{11} \times \left(\dfrac{-33}{21}\right) = \dfrac{-3}{7} = \dfrac{3}{-7}$

III. $\dfrac{5}{21} \times \left(\dfrac{42}{-9}\right) = \dfrac{10}{-9} = \dfrac{-10}{9}$

IV. $\left(\dfrac{-7}{11}\right) \times \dfrac{77}{49} = -1$

14. (c) As $\dfrac{7}{9}\left(\dfrac{-7}{11} + \dfrac{2}{11}\right) = \dfrac{7}{9} \times \dfrac{-7}{11} + \dfrac{7}{9} \times \dfrac{2}{11}$

Among all the given option (c) is the wrong statement.

15. (d) Considering option (d),

$\left(\dfrac{3}{2} \times \dfrac{1}{3}\right) + \left(\dfrac{1}{3} \times 9\right) = \left(\dfrac{1}{2}\right) + \left(\dfrac{3}{1}\right) = \dfrac{1 + 6}{2} = \dfrac{7}{2}$

∴ Reciprocal of $\dfrac{7}{2} = \dfrac{2}{7}$

16. *(b)* I. True

II. True   As, $\left(\dfrac{-16}{21} \div \dfrac{-4}{3}\right) = \dfrac{-16}{21} \times \dfrac{3}{-4} = \dfrac{4}{7}$

III. False

As, $\dfrac{9}{72}\left(=\dfrac{3}{24}\right)$ and $\dfrac{-3}{21}$ are not equivalent numbers.

IV. False

As, $\dfrac{48}{-96}$ is not in standard form.

17. *(d)* P. $\dfrac{120}{-114} = \dfrac{40}{-38} = \dfrac{20}{-19} = \dfrac{-20}{19}$

Q. Opposite

R. $-\dfrac{5}{8}$ is less than $\dfrac{-7}{-12}$ $\left(\because \dfrac{-7}{-12} = \dfrac{7}{12}\right)$

S. $\dfrac{-4}{-9} = \dfrac{4}{9} \times \dfrac{4}{4} = \dfrac{16}{36}$ and $\dfrac{1}{4} = \dfrac{1}{4} \times \dfrac{9}{9} = \dfrac{9}{36}$

$\therefore \dfrac{-4}{-9}$ is greater than $\dfrac{1}{4}$.

18. *(d)* Salary of Shehnaz = ₹ 25000

Amount spent on food $= \dfrac{1}{5} \times 25000 = ₹\,5000$

Money left $= 25000 - 5000 = ₹\,20000$

Amount spent on house rent $= \dfrac{3}{10} \times 20000$

$= ₹\,6000$

Money left $= ₹(20000-6000) = ₹\,14000$

Amount spent on education of children

$= 14000 \times \dfrac{9}{28} = ₹\,4500$

Money left $= ₹(14000 - 4500) = ₹\,9500$

19. *(c)* I. Commutative property

II. Associative property

III. Distributive property

20. *(d)* Consider, $\dfrac{5}{6}, \dfrac{7}{12}, \dfrac{13}{18}, \dfrac{23}{24}$

Convert to equivalent fractions, $\dfrac{60}{72}, \dfrac{42}{72}, \dfrac{52}{72}, \dfrac{69}{72}$

$\therefore$ Greatest number $= \dfrac{69}{72} = \dfrac{23}{24}$

Smallest number $= \dfrac{42}{72} = \dfrac{7}{12}$

$\because$ Required percentage $= \dfrac{\frac{7}{12}}{\frac{23}{24}} \times 100 = \dfrac{7}{12} \times \dfrac{24}{23} \times 100$

$= \dfrac{1400}{23} = 60\dfrac{20}{23}$

21. *(a)* Speed of train $= \dfrac{2024}{15}$ km/h, Time taken $= \dfrac{25}{4}$ h

Distance $= \dfrac{2024}{15} \times \dfrac{25}{4}$

$= \dfrac{506}{15} \times 25 = \dfrac{506 \times 5}{3} = \dfrac{2530}{3}$ km

22. *(b)* Share got by eldest son $= \dfrac{1}{3}$

Remaining land $= 1 - \dfrac{1}{3} = \dfrac{2}{3}$

Share got by the daughter $= \dfrac{2}{5} \times \dfrac{2}{3} = \dfrac{4}{15}$

So, remaining land $= \dfrac{2}{3} - \dfrac{4}{15} = \dfrac{10-4}{15} = \dfrac{6}{15} = \dfrac{2}{5}$

Hence, share of land got by youngest child

$= 25000 \times \dfrac{2}{5} = 10000$ sq m

23. *(b)* $\left(1 - \dfrac{1}{2}\right)\left(1 - \dfrac{1}{3}\right)\left(1 - \dfrac{1}{4}\right)\left(1 - \dfrac{1}{5}\right)\ldots\left(1 - \dfrac{1}{100}\right)$

$= \left(\dfrac{1}{2}\right)\left(\dfrac{2}{3}\right)\left(\dfrac{3}{4}\right)\left(\dfrac{4}{5}\right)\ldots\left(\dfrac{99}{100}\right) = \dfrac{1}{100}$

Chapter 3 : Fractions and Decimals

1. *(b)* Number of parts = 26

Number of shaded parts = 10

$\therefore$ Required fraction $= \dfrac{10}{26} = \dfrac{5}{13}$

2. *(b)* We know that, $\dfrac{3}{4}$ of $8 = \dfrac{3}{4} \times 8 = 6$

So, option (b) has 6 parts shaded out of 8.

3. *(d)* By definition, Improper fractions have numerator greater than denominator.

4. *(d)* $\dfrac{6}{13}, \dfrac{3}{5}, \dfrac{5}{6}, \dfrac{1}{4}$

Converting them into equal denominator, we get

$\dfrac{720}{1560}, \dfrac{936}{1560}, \dfrac{1300}{1560}, \dfrac{390}{1560}$

$\therefore$ $\dfrac{1}{4} < \dfrac{6}{13} < \dfrac{3}{5} < \dfrac{5}{6}$

So, $\dfrac{1}{4}$ is closest to '0'.

5. *(b)* Consider, $\dfrac{1}{9}$ and $\dfrac{1}{11}$

Converting them into equivalent fractions, we have

$\dfrac{11}{99}$ and $\dfrac{9}{99}$

To have 19 as numerator multiply both the fractions by $\dfrac{2}{2}$,

So we get $\dfrac{22}{198}, \dfrac{18}{198}$ i.e. $\dfrac{22}{198} > \dfrac{19}{198} > \dfrac{18}{198}$

Hence, 198 is the correct whole number to fill the box.

6. *(a)* Required fraction $= 10\dfrac{9}{44} - 2\dfrac{37}{44} = \dfrac{449}{44} - \dfrac{125}{44}$

$$= \dfrac{324}{44} = \dfrac{81}{11} = 7\dfrac{4}{11}$$

7. *(c)* Given, $x = \dfrac{6}{25}, y = \dfrac{3}{5}$

$\therefore \quad \dfrac{x}{y} = \dfrac{\frac{6}{25}}{\frac{3}{5}} = \dfrac{6}{25} \times \dfrac{5}{3} = \dfrac{2}{5}$

8. *(c)* Given, $a * b = \dfrac{a \times b}{a + b}$

$\therefore \quad 21 * 3 = \dfrac{21 \times 3}{21 + 3} = \dfrac{21 \times 3}{7} = \dfrac{9}{1}$

9. *(b)* Total quantity of both ingredients for 1 pack

$$= 3\dfrac{1}{2} + 2\dfrac{1}{3} = \dfrac{7}{2} + \dfrac{7}{3} = \dfrac{21 + 14}{6} = \dfrac{35}{6}$$

Now, cups required for 10 such packets

$$= 10 \times \dfrac{35}{6} = 5 \times \dfrac{35}{3} = \dfrac{175}{3} = 58\dfrac{1}{3}$$

So, it is between 50 and 60 cups.

10. *(a)* Total number of games $= 12 + 4 = 16$

Number of games lost by team $= 4$

So, fraction of games lost by team $= \dfrac{4}{16}$

11. *(a)* I. True

II. False

As, product of proper and improper fraction is less than the improper fraction.

III. False

As, $2\dfrac{2}{5} + 2\dfrac{1}{5} = \dfrac{12}{5} + \dfrac{11}{5} = \dfrac{23}{5} \neq 2$

IV. False As, reciprocal of $\dfrac{7}{8}$ is $\dfrac{8}{7}$

V. False

A mixed fraction can converted to a improper fraction.

12. *(c)* $0.321 = \dfrac{321}{1000}$

13. *(b)* Option (b) shows correct ascending order.

14. *(d)* We have, $14.63 - \dfrac{1}{6} \times 0.6 = 14.63 - 0.1 = 14.53$

15. *(b)* To multiply a decimal by 100, we move the decimal point in the number to the right by two places.

16. *(c)* We know that,

$73.47 \times 100 = 92 \times 73.47 + 8 \times \boxed{73.47}$

17. *(a)* Price per litre on Tuesday $= \dfrac{616.8}{12} = ₹\,51.4$

Price per litre on Friday $= \dfrac{817.5}{15} = ₹\,54.5$

On Tuesday, Marshall gets better price.

18. *(a)* Let the decimal be x.

Clue 1. It is between $\dfrac{2}{5}$ and $\dfrac{3}{5}$ or it is between 0.4 and 0.6.

Clue 2. It is greater than $\dfrac{1}{2}$ i.e. greater than 0.5.

$\therefore$ x lies between 0.5 and 0.6.

Clue 3. Multiple of 11

$\therefore$ It can be 0.55. Aman gave the correct answer.

19. *(b)* Number of parts $= 36$

Number of shaded parts $= 12$

To have fraction $\dfrac{4}{9}$, we shall convert it into an equivalent fraction having denominator equal to 36.

So, we have $\dfrac{4 \times 4}{9 \times 4} = \dfrac{16}{36}$

$\therefore$ Required number of triangles to be shaded

$$= 16 - 12 = 4$$

20. *(c)* Given,

$$\left(1 - \dfrac{2}{3}\right) \times \left(1 - \dfrac{2}{5}\right) \times \left(1 - \dfrac{2}{7}\right) \times \left(1 - \dfrac{2}{9}\right) \times \ldots \times \left(1 - \dfrac{2}{99}\right)$$

$$= \dfrac{1}{3} \times \dfrac{3}{5} \times \dfrac{5}{7} \times \dfrac{7}{9} \times \ldots \times \dfrac{97}{99} = \dfrac{1}{99}$$

21. *(b)* Given, $\dfrac{1}{1 + \dfrac{1}{2 + \dfrac{1}{3 + \dfrac{1}{2}}}} = ?$

$$= \dfrac{1}{1 + \dfrac{1}{2 + \dfrac{2}{7}}} = \dfrac{1}{1 + \dfrac{7}{16}} = \dfrac{16}{23}$$

22. *(c)* Consider, $\dfrac{\dfrac{5}{3} + 1\dfrac{1}{2} \text{ of } \dfrac{7}{3}}{2 + 2\dfrac{2}{3}} = \dfrac{\dfrac{5}{3} + \dfrac{3}{2} \times \dfrac{7}{3}}{2 + \dfrac{8}{3}}$

$$= \dfrac{\dfrac{5}{3} + \dfrac{7}{2}}{\dfrac{2}{1} + \dfrac{8}{3}} = \dfrac{\dfrac{10 + 21}{6}}{\dfrac{6 + 8}{3}} = \dfrac{31}{6} \times \dfrac{3}{14}$$

$$= \dfrac{31}{28} = \dfrac{31}{4} \times \dfrac{1}{7}$$

62

But Mihir answered $= \dfrac{1}{7}$

$\therefore$ His answer is $\dfrac{31}{4}$ times wrong.

23. (c) I. 100   II. Dividing
III. 16.92   IV. 0.07

24. (c) I. False
As, to multiply a number by 1000, we move the decimal point to the right by three place.
  II. False As, $4.7 \div 10 = 0.47 \neq 47$
  III. True As, $4.06 \times 100 = 406$
  IV. False According to the question,
Cost of 5 apples $= ₹ \, 2.15$

Cost of 1 apple $= ₹ \, \dfrac{2.15}{5}$

$\therefore$ Cost of 40 apples $= ₹ \, \dfrac{2.15}{5} \times 40 = ₹ \, 17.2$

So, given statement is false.

25. (a) **Store A** Cost of 1 pair of jeans and 2 shirts
      $= ₹ \, 399.7 + ₹ \, 444.8 = ₹ \, 844.5$
Store B Cost of 1 pair of jeans and 2 shirts
      $= ₹ 449.9 + ₹ \, 224.8 + ₹ \, 224.8 = ₹ \, 899.5$
Store C Cost of 1 pair of jeans and 2 shirts
      $= ₹ 499.5 + ₹ 204.6 + ₹ \, 204.6 = ₹ 908.7$
$\therefore$ Store A is most economical.

26. (c) We have, jeans C : $₹ \, 499.5$

Shirt A : $₹ \, 444.8 \div 2 = ₹ \, 222.4$
1 shirt B : $₹ \, 224.8$
Total amount to be spend
      $= ₹ 499.5 + ₹ 2224 + ₹ 224.8 = ₹ \, 946.7$
Money left $= ₹ (1000 - 946.7) = ₹ 53.3$

27. (b) Cheapest jeans are from store A:
$\therefore$ Cost of 2 jeans from store A $= ₹ \, 399.7 \times 2 = ₹ \, 799.4$
and cheapest shirt is from store C, costing $₹ \, 204.6$.
So, total money required $= ₹ \, (799.4 + 204.6) = ₹ 1004$
$\therefore$ Extra money required $= ₹ \, (1004 - 1000) = ₹ 4$

Chapter 4. Exponents and Powers

1. (a) $-2187 = (-3) \times (-3) \times (-3) \times (-3) \times (-3) \times (-3) \times (-3)$
      $= (-3)^7$

2. (d) $\dfrac{2^0 + 3^0 + 4^0}{2^0 \times (3^0 + 4^0)} = \dfrac{1+1+1}{1 \times (1+1)} = \dfrac{3}{2}$

3. (a) $x^y + y^x = 1^2 + 2^1 = 1 + 2 = 3$

4. (a) Given, $\left(\dfrac{4}{5}\right)^3 \times \left(\dfrac{4}{5}\right)^{b+8} = \left(\dfrac{5}{4}\right)^{-11}$

$\Rightarrow \left(\dfrac{4}{5}\right)^{b+8+3} = \left(\dfrac{4}{5}\right)^{11}$ $[\because a^m \times a^n = a^{m+n}]$

$\Rightarrow \left(\dfrac{4}{5}\right)^{b+11} = \left(\dfrac{4}{5}\right)^{11}$ $\Rightarrow b + 11 = 11$

$\Rightarrow \quad\quad b = 0$

5. (b) Given, $2^x = 4^y = 8^z = 64$

$\because \quad\quad 2^x = 64 \Rightarrow 2^x = 2^6 \Rightarrow x = 6$
Now, $\quad 4^y = 64 \Rightarrow 4^y = 4^3$
$\Rightarrow \quad\quad y = 3$ and $8^z = 64 \Rightarrow 8^z = 8^2$
$\Rightarrow \quad\quad z = 2$
$\therefore \quad x + y + z = 6 + 3 + 2 = 11$

6. (c) Given, $5^x = 999$,

Consider, $5^{x-3} = \dfrac{5^x}{5^3}$ $\left[\because \dfrac{a^m}{a^n} = a^{m-n}\right]$

$= \dfrac{999}{125}$

7. (b) Consider, $\dfrac{(a^2 b^3 c)^2}{a^4 b^6 c^2} = \dfrac{a^4 b^6 c^2}{a^4 b^6 c^2} = 1$

8. (c) Consider, $\left(\dfrac{169}{225}\right)^{\frac{1}{2}} \times \left(\dfrac{125}{27}\right)^{\frac{2}{3}} \times \left(\dfrac{81}{4}\right)^{\frac{1}{2}}$

$= \dfrac{(13^2)^{\frac{1}{2}}}{(15^2)^{\frac{1}{2}}} \times \dfrac{(5^3)^{\frac{2}{3}}}{(3^3)^{\frac{2}{3}}} \times \dfrac{(9^2)^{\frac{1}{2}}}{(2^2)^{\frac{1}{2}}}$

$= \dfrac{13}{15} \times \dfrac{5^2}{3^2} \times \dfrac{9}{2}$ $[\because (a^m)^n = (a)^{m \times n}]$

$= \dfrac{13}{15} \times \dfrac{25}{9} \times \dfrac{9}{2} = \dfrac{65}{6}$

9. (c) Consider, $\dfrac{\left(\dfrac{-1}{3}\right)^6}{\left(\dfrac{-1}{3}\right)^5} \div \dfrac{\left(\dfrac{-1}{27}\right)}{\left(\dfrac{-1}{9}\right)} = \left(\dfrac{-1}{3}\right)^{6-5} \div \dfrac{9}{27}$

      $[\because a^m \div a^n = a^{m-n}]$

$= \dfrac{-1}{3} \div \dfrac{1}{3} = -1$

10. (d) Consider, $\dfrac{2x^2 y}{3x} \cdot \dfrac{9xy^2}{y^4} = 6x^{2+1-1} \cdot y^{1+2-4}$

$= 6x^2 y^{-1} = \dfrac{6x^2}{y}$

11. (a) Consider, $\left(\dfrac{m^3 p^5}{n^7}\right)^6 \times \left(\dfrac{m^2 n^0 p^3}{m^4 n^2}\right)^3$

$= \dfrac{m^{18} p^{30}}{n^{42}} \times \dfrac{m^6 p^9}{m^{12} n^6}$

$= m^{18+6-12} p^{30+9} n^{-42-6}$

$= m^{12} p^{39} n^{-48} = \dfrac{m^{12} p^{39}}{n^{48}}$

12. *(d)* Given, $(5x^7y^3z^{-1})^2 \times (2xy^{-5})^3 \times (2y^{-3}z^2)^3$

$$= 5^2 x^{14} y^6 z^{-2} \times 2^3 x^3 y^{-15} \times 2^3 y^{-9} z^6$$

$$= 25 \times 8 \times 8 \times x^{14+3} \times y^{6-15-9} \times z^{-2+6}$$

$$= 1600 \times x^{17} \times y^{-18} \times z^4 = \frac{1600x^{17}z^4}{y^{18}}$$

13. *(b)* $9.9 \times 10^{-6} = \dfrac{9.9}{10^6} = \dfrac{9.9}{1000000} = \dfrac{99}{1000000} \times \dfrac{1}{10}$

$$= 0.0000099$$

14. *(c)* We have, $0.000000748 = \dfrac{748}{1000000000}$

$$= \frac{748}{10^9} = 748 \times 10^{-9} = 7.48 \times 10^{-7}$$

15. *(b)* I. $(2^2)^3 = 2^6$ and $2^{2^3} = 2^8 \Rightarrow (2^2)^3 < 2^{2^3}$

II. $(4^4)^{\frac{1}{2}} = 4^{\frac{4}{2}} = 4^2 = 16 \Rightarrow (2^4) = 4 \times 4 = 16$

$\therefore (4^4)^{\frac{1}{2}} = 2^4$

III. $\left(3^{\frac{1}{3}}\right)^9 = 3^{\frac{9}{3}} = 3^3 = 27$

$\left(81^{\frac{1}{4}}\right)^2 = \left(3^{4 \times \frac{1}{4}}\right)^2 = 3^2 = 9 \Rightarrow (3^{\frac{1}{3}})^9 > \left(81^{\frac{1}{4}}\right)^2$

16. *(d)* Consider, $\left(\dfrac{24a^3b^{-8}}{6a^{-5}b^2}\right)^{\frac{-1}{2}} = (4a^{3+5}b^{-8-2})^{\frac{-1}{2}}$

$$[\because a^m \div a^n = a^{m-n}, a^m \times a^n = a^{m+n}]$$

$$= (4a^8b^{-10})^{\frac{-1}{2}} = 4^{\frac{-1}{2}} a^{\frac{-8}{2}} b^{\frac{-10 \times (-1)}{2}} = \frac{1}{2}a^{-4} b^5 = \frac{b^5}{2a^4}$$

17. *(c)* Total area of land $= 2^{17}$ sq miles

Area of pieces to be cut-out $= 16^2 = (2^4)^2$

$$[\because (a^m)^n = a^{m \times n}]$$

$$= 2^8$$

Number of pieces of land $= \dfrac{2^{17}}{2^8} = 2^{17-8} = 2^9$

$$[\because a^m \div a^n = a^{m-n}]$$

18. *(d)* Amount spent by each household $= ₹ \, 40000$

Number of such households $= 1 \times 10^8$

$\therefore$ Total amount spent $= ₹ \, 40000 \times 1 \times 10^8$

$$= ₹(4 \times 10^4 \times 10^8) \, [\because 10^4 = 10000]$$

$$= ₹ \, (4 \times 10^{12}) \, [\because a^m \times a^n = a^{m+n}]$$

19. *(a)* $(-1)^{101} + (-1)^{102} + (-1)^{103} + ... + (-1)^{200}$

$$= \{(-1)^{101} + (-1)^{103} + ... + (-1)^{199}\}$$

$$+ \{(-1)^{102} + (-1)^{104} + ... + (-1)^{200}\}$$

$$= \{(-1) + (-1) + ...50 \text{ times}\} + \{(1) + (1) + ... 50 \text{ times}\}$$

$$= -50 + 50 = 0$$

20. *(a)* Consider, $7^4 \left[\left(\dfrac{6}{7}\right)^2 + \left(\dfrac{6}{7}\right) - \left(\dfrac{6}{7}\right)^3\right] + (-7)^3$

$$\left[\left(\dfrac{6}{7}\right) + 1 - \left(\dfrac{6}{7}\right)^2\right] \times 6$$

$$= 7^4 \times \frac{6}{7}\left[\frac{6}{7} + 1 - \left(\frac{6}{7}\right)^2\right] + (-7)^3 \times 6\left[\frac{6}{7} + 1 - \left(\frac{6}{7}\right)^2\right]$$

$$= 7^3 \times 6\left[\frac{6}{7} + 1 - \left(\frac{6}{7}\right)^2\right] - 7^3 \times 6\left[\frac{6}{7} + 1 - \left(\frac{6}{7}\right)^2\right] = 0$$

21. *(c)* I. $\dfrac{6^3 \times 9^2 \times 25^2}{3^2 \times 4^2 \times 15^4} = \dfrac{2^3 \times 3^3 \times 3^4 \times 5^4}{3^2 \times 2^4 \times 3^4 \times 5^4}$

$$= 2^{-1} \times 3^1 = \frac{3}{2}$$

II. $\dfrac{3^8 \times 16^2 \times 7^5}{81^2 \times 2^5 \times 49^2} = \dfrac{3^8 \times 2^8 \times 7^5}{3^8 \times 2^5 \times 7^4} \, [\because (a^m)^n = (a)^{m \times n}]$

$$= 3^{8-8} \times 2^{8-5} \times 7^{5-4}$$

$$= 1 \times 2^3 \times 7 = 8 \times 7 = 56$$

III. $\dfrac{15^4 \times 21^3}{3^3 \times 5^2 \times 7^3} = \dfrac{5^4 \times 3^4 \times 3^3 \times 7^3}{3^3 \times 5^2 \times 7^3}$

$$= 5^2 \times 3^4 \times 1 = 5^2 \times 3^4$$

22. *(c)* Consider, $\left(\dfrac{a^{5b-3} \times a^{3-2b}}{a^{4b-6} \times a^{2b-9}}\right)^{\frac{-8}{6}}$

$$= \left(\frac{a^{5b-3+3-2b}}{a^{4b-6+2b-9}}\right)^{\frac{-8}{6}} = \left(\frac{a^{3b}}{a^{6b-15}}\right)^{\frac{-8}{6}}$$

$$[\because a^m \div a^n = a^{m-n}, a^m \times a^n = a^{m+n}]$$

$$= (a^{3b-6b+15})^{\frac{-4}{3}} = (a^{-3b+15})^{\frac{-4}{3}}$$

$$= (a^{b+5})^{-4} = a^{4b-20}$$

23. *(a)* Given, Mass of Earth $= 5.9 \times 10^{24}$ kg

Mass of Pluto $= 1.3 \times 10^{22}$ kg

Required difference $= 5.9 \times 10^{24} - 1.3 \times 10^{22}$

$$= (5.9 \times 10^2) \times 10^{22} - 1.3 \times 10^{22}$$

$$= 590 \times 10^{22} - 1.3 \times 10^{22}$$

$$= 588.7 \times 10^{22} = 5.887 \times 10^{24}$$

24. *(a)* Consider, $\left(\dfrac{p^{a^4}}{p^{b^4}}\right)^{\frac{1}{a^2+b^2}} \times \left(\dfrac{p^{b^4}}{p^{c^4}}\right)^{\frac{1}{b^2+c^2}}$

$$\times \left(\frac{p^{c^4}}{p^{a^4}}\right)^{\frac{1}{c^2+a^2}}$$

$$= (p^{a^4 - b^4})^{\frac{1}{a^2 + b^2}} \times (p^{b^4 - c^4})^{\frac{1}{b^2 + c^2}} \times (p^{c^4 - a^4})^{\frac{1}{c^2 + a^2}}$$

$$= p^{\frac{(a^2 - b^2)(a^2 + b^2)}{a^2 + b^2}} \times p^{\frac{(b^2 - c^2)(b^2 + c^2)}{b^2 + c^2}} \times p^{\frac{(c^2 - a^2)(c^2 + a^2)}{c^2 + a^2}}$$

$$= p^{a^2 - b^2} \times p^{b^2 - c^2} \times p^{c^2 - a^2}$$

$$= p^{a^2 - b^2 + b^2 - c^2 + c^2 - a^2} = p^0 = 1$$

25. *(a)* Given that, $xyz = 1$

Then, $\dfrac{1}{(1 + x + y^{-1})} + \dfrac{1}{(1 + y + z^{-1})} + \dfrac{1}{(1 + z + x^{-1})}$

$$= \frac{1}{\left(1 + x + \dfrac{1}{y}\right)} + \frac{1}{\left(1 + y + \dfrac{1}{z}\right)} + \frac{1}{\left(1 + z + \dfrac{1}{x}\right)} \left[\because a^{-1} = \frac{1}{a}\right]$$

$$= \frac{y}{y + xy + 1} + \frac{1}{1 + y + xy} + \frac{1}{1 + \dfrac{1}{xy} + \dfrac{1}{x}}$$

$$= \frac{y}{y + xy + 1} + \frac{1}{1 + y + xy} + \frac{xy}{xy + 1 + y} = \frac{1 + xy + y}{1 + xy + y} = 1$$

26. *(c)* Here, $a^x = b^y = c^z$

Let $a^x = b^y = c^z = K$, then $a = K^{1/x}$, $b = K^{1/y}$

and $c = K^{1/z}$

$\therefore abc = 1 \Rightarrow K^{\left(\frac{1}{x} + \frac{1}{y} + \frac{1}{z}\right)} = 1 \Rightarrow K^{\left(\frac{1}{x} + \frac{1}{y} + \frac{1}{z}\right)} = K^0$

On comparing, we get

$$\frac{1}{x} + \frac{1}{y} + \frac{1}{z} = 0 \Rightarrow \frac{xy + yz + zx}{xyz}$$

or $\quad xy + yz + zx = 0$

Chapter 5. Ratio and Proportion

1. *(c)* Let consequent be x

Then, according to the question,

$$\frac{75}{x} = \frac{3}{4} \Rightarrow x = \frac{75 \times 4}{3} = 100$$

2. *(d)* Let $p = 5k$, $q = 7k$

Then, $\dfrac{5p + 3q}{2p - q} = \dfrac{5(5k) + 3(7k)}{2(5k) - 7k} = \dfrac{25k + 21k}{10k - 7k} = \dfrac{46k}{3k}$

$$= \frac{46}{3} = 46 : 3.$$

3. *(a)* According to the question,

$$\frac{p}{5} = \frac{12}{20} \Rightarrow p = \frac{12}{20} \times 5 = 3$$

4. *(a)* According to the question,

$$\left(\frac{p}{q}\right) \times \left(\frac{q}{r}\right) = \frac{3}{4} \times \frac{2}{3} = \frac{1}{2}$$

$$\therefore \qquad\qquad p : r = 1 : 2$$

5. *(c)* Let the fourth proportion is x.

Then, $72 : 168 :: 150 : x$

$$\frac{72}{168} = \frac{150}{x} \Rightarrow x = \frac{168 \times 150}{72} = 350$$

6. *(b)* Equivalent ratio of $105 : 135$ is $7 : 9$.

$\therefore$ Correct option is (b)

7. *(a)* Let 1 rupee coin $= 3x$, 2 rupee coin $= 4x$

5 rupee coin $= 5x$

According to the question,

So, $\qquad 3x + 2(4x) + 5(5x) = 360 \Rightarrow 36x = 360$

$\therefore \qquad\qquad\qquad\qquad\qquad x = 10$

$\therefore$ 1 rupee coins $= 3 \times 10 = 30$

2 rupee coins $= 4 \times 10 = 40$

5 rupee coins $= 5 \times 10 = 50$

8. *(b)* Share of Anil $= \dfrac{5}{8} \times 10000 = 5 \times 1250 = ₹\, 6250$

Share of Ajay $= \dfrac{3}{8} \times 10000 = 3 \times 1250 = ₹\, 3750$

9. *(b)* Let the income be x.

According to the question,

$$\frac{8}{3} = \frac{x}{1332} \Rightarrow x = \frac{10656}{3} = ₹\, 3552$$

We know that,

Expenditure = Income − Saving

$\therefore$ Expenditure $= ₹\, 3552 - ₹\, 1332 = ₹\, 2220$

10. *(a)* Let the present age of Aman and her mother be $3x$ and $11x$.

According to the question,

$$11x - 3x = 24 \Rightarrow 8x = 24 \Rightarrow x = 3$$

So, Aman's present age $= 3x = 3 \times 3 = 9$ yr

Aman's mother present age $= 11 \times 3 = 33$ yr

Ratio of their ages after 3 yr $= \dfrac{9 + 3}{33 + 3} = \dfrac{12}{36} = \dfrac{1}{3}$

$$= 1 : 3$$

11. *(c)* B's share $= \dfrac{9}{7 + 9} \times$ total amount

$$\Rightarrow \quad 7200 = \frac{9}{16} \times \text{total amount}$$

Total amount $= \dfrac{7200 \times 16}{9} = 800 \times 16 = ₹\, 12800$

12. *(d)* $6A = 4B$ and $4B = 9C$

$$\frac{A}{B} = \frac{4}{6} = \frac{2}{3} = \frac{6}{9} \Rightarrow \frac{B}{C} = \frac{9}{4}$$

$\therefore \quad A : B : C = 6 : 9 : 4$

13. *(a)* $\because x : y = 3 : 1 \Rightarrow \dfrac{x}{y} = \dfrac{3}{1}$

$$\frac{x^3 - y^3}{x^3 + y^3} = \frac{\left(\frac{x}{y}\right)^3 - 1}{\left(\frac{x}{y}\right)^3 + 1} = \frac{(3)^3 - 1}{(3)^3 + 1} = \frac{26}{28} = 13:14$$

14. *(d)* Let number are $3x$ and $4x$.

$\therefore$ Their HCF $= x$

We know that,

$$\text{LCM} \times \text{HCF} = \text{Product of numbers}$$

$$\Rightarrow \quad 180 \times x = 3x \times 4x \Rightarrow x = \frac{180}{12} = 15$$

$\therefore$ First number $= 3 \times 15 = 45$

15. *(a)* Let marks obtained in Science $= x$

Let marks obtained in English $= 2x$

Then, marks obtained in Maths $= 3x$

$\therefore \quad x + 2x + 3x = 180$

$$\Rightarrow \quad 6x = 180 \Rightarrow x = \frac{180}{6} = 30$$

Hence, marks obtained in Science $= 30$

16. *(b)* Let the two positive integers be $9x$ and $7x$.

$\therefore \qquad 9x \times 7x = 1575$

$$\Rightarrow \qquad x^2 = \frac{1575}{63} = 25 \Rightarrow x = 5$$

$\therefore$ Smaller integer $= 7 \times 5 = 35$

17. *(c)* Let two numbers be $3x$ and $4x$.

According to the question,

$$\frac{3x + 6}{4x + 6} = \frac{4}{5} \Rightarrow 16x + 24 = 15x + 30$$

$$\Rightarrow \qquad x = 6$$

$\therefore$ Difference between the numbers $= 4x - 3x$

$$x = 6$$

18. *(b)* According to the question,

$$5 : 825 :: 12 : x$$

$$\Rightarrow \qquad x = \frac{12 \times 825}{5} = ₹ 1980$$

19. *(a)* Let the quantity of milk and water be $4x$ and $3x$ litres respectively. Then,

$$\frac{4x}{3x + 5} = \frac{4}{5} \Rightarrow 20x = 12x + 20$$

$$8x = 20 \Rightarrow x = 2.5$$

$\therefore$ Quantity of milk $= 4 \times 2.5 = 10$ litres

20. *(d)* Let A and B be $4x$ and $5x$, respectively.

$\therefore \qquad B^2 - A^2 = (5x)^2 - (4x)^2$

$$= 25x^2 - 16x^2 = 9x^2$$

$\because \qquad 9x^2 = 81 \Rightarrow x^2 = 9 \Rightarrow x = 3$

$\therefore$ Value of $A = 4x = 4 \times 3 = 12$

21. *(b)* $A : B : C = \dfrac{1}{2} : \dfrac{1}{3} : \dfrac{1}{4} = \dfrac{1}{2} \times 12 : \dfrac{1}{3} \times 12 : \dfrac{1}{4} \times 12$

$$[\because \text{LCM of 2, 3 and 4} = 12]$$

$$= 6 : 4 : 3$$

A's share $= \dfrac{6}{13} \times 2600 = ₹ 1200$

B's share $= \dfrac{4}{13} \times 2600 = ₹ 800$

C's Share $= \dfrac{3}{13} \times 2600 = ₹ 600$

22. *(b)* Let x be added to the numbers so that they becomes continued fraction.

$$\Rightarrow \qquad \frac{94 + x}{24 + x} = \frac{100 + x}{26 + x}$$

$$\Rightarrow (94 + x)(26 + x) = (100 + x)(24 + x)$$

$$\Rightarrow 2444 + x^2 + 120x = 2400 + x^2 + 124x$$

$$\Rightarrow \qquad 4x = 44 \Rightarrow x = 11$$

23. *(c)* Let x must be subtracted.

$$\frac{6 - x}{7 - x} = \frac{16}{21}$$

$$\Rightarrow \qquad 126 - 21x = 112 - 16x$$

$$\Rightarrow \qquad 21x - 16x = 126 - 112 \Rightarrow 5x = 14$$

Hence, it is clear that if 3 is subtracted from each term of $6 : 7$, then ratio will be less than $= 16 : 21$

24. *(b)* Let the age of father $= 5x$ yr

and the age of son $= 2x$ yr

According to the question,

$$5x \times 2x = 1000 \Rightarrow 10x^2 = 1000$$

$$\Rightarrow \qquad x^2 = 100 \Rightarrow x = \sqrt{100} = 10$$

$\therefore$ Father's age after 10 yr $= (5x + 10)$

$$= 5 \times 10 + 10 = 60 \text{ yr}$$

25. *(b)* If three parts be x, y and z, then

$$\frac{x}{2} = \frac{y}{3} = \frac{z}{5} \Rightarrow x : y : z = 2 : 3 : 5$$

$\therefore \qquad x = \dfrac{2}{10} \times 990 = 198$

$$y = \frac{3}{10} \times 990 = 297 \text{ and } z = \frac{5}{10} \times 990 = 495$$

26. *(c)* Let the incomes of two persons be $7x$ and $3x$ respectively.

Expenditure of first person $= 7x - 300$

Expenditure of second person $= 3x - 300$

According to the question,

$$\frac{7x - 300}{3x - 300} = \frac{5}{2} \Rightarrow 14x - 600 = 15x - 1500$$

$$\Rightarrow \qquad x = 900$$

$\therefore$ Income of first person $= 7x = 7 \times 900 = ₹ 6300$

Chapter 6 : Percentage

1. *(d)* Required per cent = 40% of $70 = \dfrac{40}{100} \times 70 = 28$

and $70\% \; 40 = \dfrac{70}{100} \times 40 = 28$

$\therefore \qquad$ Sum $= 28 + 28 = 56$

2. *(b)* Required per cent $= \dfrac{4500}{7500} \times 100 = 60\%$

3. *(d)* 45% of x + 30% of 90 = 30% of 210

$\Rightarrow \qquad \dfrac{45}{100} x + \dfrac{30 \times 90}{100} = \dfrac{30}{100} \times 210$

$\Rightarrow \qquad \dfrac{45}{100} x + 27 = 63$

$\Rightarrow \qquad \dfrac{45}{100} x = 63 - 27 = 36 \Rightarrow x = \dfrac{36 \times 100}{45} = 80$

4. *(b)* Let the number be x.

According to the question,

$\dfrac{25}{100} x + 30 = x \;\; \Rightarrow \;\; \dfrac{1}{4} x + 30 = x$

$\Rightarrow \qquad 30 = x - \dfrac{1}{4} x \Rightarrow 30 = \dfrac{3}{4} x \Rightarrow x = 40$

5. *(c)* Number of pupils who were late $= \dfrac{5}{100} \times 1600$

$= 80$

So, the number of pupils who were punctual

$= 1600 - 80 = 1520$

6. *(d)* Number of goats = 30, Per cent increase = 20%

$\therefore$ Number of goats increased = 30 of 20%

$= 30 \times \dfrac{20}{100} = 6$

7. *(a)* Ratio of grey tiles to white tiles = 3 : 5

Number of white tiles used = 45

$\therefore$ Number of grey tiles used $= \dfrac{45}{5} \times 3 = 27$

$\therefore$ Total number of tiles used = 27 + 45 = 72

Percentage of grey tiles used $= \dfrac{27}{72} \times 100 = \dfrac{3}{8} \times 100$

$= \dfrac{300}{8} = \dfrac{75}{2} = 37.5\%$

8. *(c)* Percentage increased in number of students = 3%

Let the students earlier be x.

We have, 3% of x = 42

$\Rightarrow \qquad \dfrac{3}{100} \times x = 42 \;\; \Rightarrow \;\; x = 1400$

9. *(c)* Total number of students = 600

Number of students who go for the picnic = 126

$\therefore$ Number of students who did not go for the picnic

$= 600 - 126 = 474$

$\therefore$ In percentage,

$= \dfrac{\text{Students who do not go for picnic}}{\text{Total students}} \times 100$

$= \dfrac{474}{600} \times 100 = 79\%$

10. *(a)* Let the total number of people be 100.

$\therefore$ Number of men = 40% of 100 = 40

and number of women = 100 − 40 = 60

Number of members who married

$= \dfrac{20}{100} \times 40 + \dfrac{30}{100} \times 60 = 8 + 18 = 26$

$\therefore$ Percentage of married members $= \dfrac{26}{100} \times 100 = 26\%$

11. *(c)* Earlier price of gasoline drops = ₹ 2.00

New price of gasoline drops = ₹ 1.90

Decrease in price = ₹ 2.00 − ₹ 1.90 = ₹ 0.10

Per cent decrease in price $= \dfrac{0.10}{2.00} \times 100 = 5\%$

12. *(a)* Percentage of commission = 5%

Amount of sales = ₹ 15000

$\therefore$ Amount of commission earned $= 15000 \times \dfrac{5}{100}$

$= ₹ 750$

13. *(c)* Marks scored in mathematics = 97

Marks scored in English = 94

Marks scored in Hindi = 46

Total marks = 237

For overall percentage to be 80%.

Total marks required to be score = 80% of 400 = 320

So, marks to be scored in Science = 320 − 237 = 83

14. *(b)* Let the marks obtained by Deepak be x.

Then the marks obtained by Rohit = $(x + 9)$

Then, according to the question,

$(x + 9) = \dfrac{56}{100} (x + 9 + x)$

$\Rightarrow \qquad 25(x + 9) = 14(2x + 9) \Rightarrow 3x = 99$

$\therefore \qquad\qquad x = 33$

So, their marks are 42 and 33.

15. *(b)* Length of rectangle = 40 cm

Breadth of rectangle = 30 cm

Decrease in length = 20%

$\therefore$ New length $= (100 - 20)\%$ of $40 = \dfrac{80}{100} \times 40 = 32$

New area = 32 × 30 = 960 sq cm

16. *(c)* Number of apples $= 180$

Percentage of number of red apples $= 40\%$

So, number of green apples $= \dfrac{60}{100} \times 180 = 108$

Percentage of green apples which are bad in quality $= 25\%$

So, number of green apples which are not bad

$$= \dfrac{75}{100} \times 108 = 81$$

17. *(c)* Let total budget be ₹ x

$\therefore$ 15% of $x = 3000000$

$\Rightarrow$ $\dfrac{15x}{100} = 3000000$

$\Rightarrow$ $x = \dfrac{3000000 \times 100}{15}$

$\therefore$ Total budget $= $ ₹ 20000000

18. *(c)* Children who are below $10 y = 20\%$

Number of boys $= \dfrac{2}{3}$ [below 10 yr]

$\therefore$ Number of girls $= \dfrac{1}{3}$ [below 10 yr]

Also given number of girls $= 22$ [below 10 yr]

$\therefore$ Number of children below

10 yr $= 22 \times 3 = 66$

Total number of children who participated $= \dfrac{66 \times 100}{20}$

$= 330$

19. *(c)* Let the maximum marks be x.

Now, according to the question,

30% of $x = 30 + 30 \Rightarrow \dfrac{30x}{100} = 30 + 30$

$\dfrac{30x}{100} = 60$ $\Rightarrow$ $x = 200$

20. *(d)* Let the total number of staffs be 100.

$\therefore$ Female staff $= 40$

$\therefore$ Votes cast by females $= \dfrac{40}{100} \times 40 = 16$.

and votes cast by males $= \dfrac{60}{100} \times 60 = 36$.

Votes cast by both (males + females) $= 16 + 36 = 52$

$\therefore$ Percentage votes obtained $= 52\%$

21. *(c)* **Statement 1**

New price $= 92\%$ of $15000 = \dfrac{92}{100} \times 15000$

$= $ ₹ 13800 (True)

Statement 2

Let the actual price of rice be ₹ y per kg.

Amount of rice bought in ₹ $100 = \dfrac{100}{y}$

Price of rice after 10% decrease $= 90\%$ of $y = \dfrac{9}{10} y$

Now, amount of rice bought in ₹ $100 = \dfrac{1000}{9y}$

According to the question, $\dfrac{1000}{9y} - \dfrac{100}{y} = 5$

$\Rightarrow$ $y = \dfrac{100}{9 \times 5} = $ ₹ $\dfrac{20}{9} = $ ₹ $2\dfrac{2}{9}$ (True)

22. *(d)* Let the marks of 1st students be x.

Then, marks of 2nd students be $(x + 10)$.

According to the question,

$$(x + 10) = \dfrac{75}{100} (2x + 10)$$

$\Rightarrow$ $x + 10 = \dfrac{3}{4}(2x + 10) \Rightarrow x + 10 = \dfrac{3}{2}(x + 5)$

$\Rightarrow$ $2x + 20 = 3x + 15$

$\therefore$ $x = 5$ and $x + 10 = 15$

Hence, the marks obtained by them are 15 and 5.

23. *(b)* Let the number of boys and girls be x and y respectively.

Total sum of ages of boys $= 20x$

and total sum of ages of girls $= 16y$

Given that, $\dfrac{20x + 16y}{x + y} = 18$

$\Rightarrow$ $20x + 16y = 18x + 18y$

$\Rightarrow$ $2x = 2y \Rightarrow x = y$

Hence, percentage of boys in group is 50%.

24. *(c)* I. 10% of 2 km $= \dfrac{10}{100} \times 2 = \dfrac{2}{10}$ km

$= \dfrac{2}{10} \times 1000$ m $[\because 1$ km $= 1000$ m$]$

$= 200$ m

II. 1 min $= 60$ sec

20 min $= 20 \times 60$ sec $= 1200$ sec

Required per cent $= \dfrac{144}{1200} \times 100 = 12\%$

III. $\dfrac{7}{5}$ of 200 cm $= \dfrac{7}{5} \times 200 = 280$ cm

Now, $x\%$ of 28 m $= 280$ cm

$\Rightarrow$ $\dfrac{x}{100} \times 28 \times 100 = 280$ cm $[\because 1$ m $= 100$ cm$]$

$\Rightarrow$ $x = 10$

IV. 25% of x kg $= 600$ gm

$\Rightarrow$ $\dfrac{25}{100} \times x \times 100 = 600$ gm $[\because 1$ kg $= 100$ gm$]$

$\Rightarrow$ $250\,x = 600$ gm

$\Rightarrow$ $25x = 60$ gm $\Rightarrow x = 2.4$

25. *(b)* I. $400\% = \dfrac{400}{100} = 4$ II. $\dfrac{1}{4} = 0.25 = \dfrac{25}{100} = 25\%$

III. $0.02 = \dfrac{2}{100} = 2\%$ IV. $6\dfrac{1}{4}\% = \dfrac{25}{4}\%$

V. $10\% = \dfrac{10}{100} = \dfrac{1}{10}$

Chapter 7. Profit and Loss

1. *(d)* $\therefore$ Amount of profit earned $= CP \times \dfrac{\text{Profit }\%}{100}$

$$= \dfrac{48000 \times 15}{100} = ₹\,7200$$

2. *(c)* CP of 1 battery $= ₹\,2$, SP of 4 batteries $= ₹\,10$

$\therefore$ SP of 1 battery $= \dfrac{10}{4} = ₹\,2.5$

$\therefore$ Profit $= SP - CP = ₹\,(2.5 - 2.0) = ₹\,0.5$

So, profit per cent $= \dfrac{\text{Profit }\%}{CP} \times 100 = \dfrac{0.5}{2} \times 100 = 25\%$

3. *(b)* CP of play station game pack $= ₹\,7000$
SP of play station game pack $= ₹\,6090$
Loss $= CP - SP = ₹\,(7000 - 6090) = ₹\,910$

$\therefore$ Loss per cent $= \dfrac{\text{Loss}}{CP} \times 100 = \dfrac{10}{7000} \times 100 = 13\%$

4. *(b)* CP of a scooter $= ₹\,20000$, profit $= 12\%$

$\because SP = \dfrac{100 + \text{Profit}\%}{100} \times CP$

$\therefore SP = \dfrac{100 + 12}{100} \times 20000 = \dfrac{112}{100} \times 20000$

$= 112 \times 200 = ₹\,22400$

5. *(c)* SP of the article $= ₹\,1980$ and profit $= 10\,\%$

$\because \quad CP = \dfrac{100}{100 + \text{Profit}\%} \times SP$

$\therefore \quad CP = \dfrac{100}{100 + 10} \times 1980 = \dfrac{100}{110} \times 1980 = ₹\,1800$

6. (c) Given, SP of 10 apples $= ₹\,1$ and Gain $= 40\%$

CP of 10 apples $= \left(\dfrac{100}{100 + \text{Gain}\%}\right) \times SP = \dfrac{100}{140} \times 1 = ₹\,\dfrac{5}{7}$

Since, $₹\,\dfrac{5}{7}$ yield 10 apples.

$\therefore ₹\,1$ will yield $10 \times \dfrac{7}{5} = 14$ apples.

7. *(a)* $CP = 10.80 \times 4 = 43.20$

Then, $SP = 0.80 \times 48 = 3840$

Loss $\% = \dfrac{CP - SP}{CP} \times 100 = \dfrac{43.20 - 28.80}{43.20} \times 100$

$= \dfrac{480}{43.20} \times 100 = 11.11\% = \dfrac{100}{9}\%$

8. *(a)* SP of toy $= ₹\,750$ and profit per cent $= 20\%$

$\therefore \quad CP = \dfrac{SP \times 100}{(100 + \text{Profit }\%)} = \dfrac{750 \times 100}{120} = ₹\,625$

9. *(a)* Let $CP = 5x$ and $SP = 3x$

Loss $= CP - SP = 5x - 3x = 2x$

$\therefore$ Loss $\% = \dfrac{\text{Loss}}{CP} \times 100\% = \dfrac{2x}{5x} \times 100\% = 40\%$

10. *(c)* Here, $CP = ₹\,250$ per kg

$SP = ₹\,10$ per 50 gm $= 10 \times \dfrac{1000}{50}$ per kg

$= ₹\,200$ per kg   [There will be a loss]

$\because \quad CP > SP$

$\therefore$ Loss $\% = \dfrac{CP - SP}{CP} \times 100 = \dfrac{250 - 200}{250} \times 100 = 20\%$

11. *(a)* $\because$ Total CP of typewriter $= ₹\,(1200 + 200) = ₹\,1400$
and SP of the typewriter $= ₹\,1680$

$\therefore$ Profit $= SP - CP = ₹\,(1680 - 1400) = ₹\,280$

Profit $\% = \dfrac{\text{Profit}}{CP} \times 100\% = \dfrac{280}{1400} \times 100 = 20\%$

12. *(d)* Let $SP = ₹\,x \Rightarrow CP = ₹\,\dfrac{95x}{100} = ₹\,\dfrac{19x}{20}$

Profit $= SP - CP = ₹\left(x - \dfrac{19x}{20}\right) = ₹\,\dfrac{x}{20}$

$\therefore$ Profit $\% = \dfrac{\text{Profit}}{CP} \times 100 = \dfrac{\frac{x}{20}}{\frac{19x}{20}} \times 100 = \dfrac{100}{19} = 5.26\%$

13. *(b)* Let CP and SP be $₹\,x$ and $₹\,y$ respectively.
When profit triples, then
$3(y - x) = (2y - x) \Rightarrow y = 2x$

Profit $= ₹\,(y - x) = ₹\,(2x - x) = ₹\,x$

$\therefore$ Profit $\% = \left(\dfrac{x}{x} \times 100\right) = 100\%$

14. *(c)* Let SP of 1 pencil $= ₹\,1$
$\therefore$ SP of 36 pencils $= ₹\,36$
Loss $= ₹\,4$
$\therefore$ CP of 36 pencils $= 36 + 4 = ₹\,40$

$\therefore$ Loss percent $= \dfrac{\text{Loss}}{CP} \times 100 = \dfrac{4}{40} \times 100 = 10\%$

15. *(c)* Let CP of the watch be $₹\,x$.
According to the question,
$$\dfrac{75 - x}{x} \times 100 = x$$

$$\left[\because \text{Profit }\% = \dfrac{SP - CP}{CP} \times 100\right]$$

$\Rightarrow \qquad (75 - x) \times 100 = x^2$

$$x^2 + 150x - 50x = 7500$$

$$x(x + 150) - 50(x + 150) = 0$$

$$(x + 150)(x - 50) = 0 \Rightarrow x = ₹\,50$$

16. *(c)* Let the CP be 100.s

Since profit is 25%, the SP becomes 125

Now if CP and SP are interchanged, then CP becomes 125 and SP becomes 100.

$$\therefore \text{Loss \%} = \frac{\text{CP} - \text{SP}}{\text{CP}} \times 100 = \frac{25}{125} \times 100 = 20\%$$

17. (d) Let total number of apples purchased by man is 200. i.e. 100 at ₹ 3/apple and 100 for ₹ 4/apple

Total lost price after mixing $= 100 \times 3 + 100 \times 4$

$$= ₹\,700$$

SP of 1 apple after mixing = ₹ 3/apple

Total SP $= 200 \times 3 = ₹\,600$

$$\text{Loss\%} = \frac{(\text{CP} - \text{SP})}{\text{CP}} \times 100 = \frac{700 - 600}{700} \times 100$$

$$= \frac{100}{7} = 14\frac{2}{7}\%$$

18. *(d)* CP of 1 lemon $= ₹\,\dfrac{3}{4}$, SP of 1 lemon $= ₹\,\dfrac{4}{5}$

$\because$ SP > CP

$$\therefore \text{Gain} = \text{SP} - \text{CP} = \frac{4}{5} - \frac{3}{4} = \frac{16 - 15}{20} = \frac{1}{20}$$

$$\text{Gain\%} = \left(\frac{\text{Gain}}{\text{CP}} \times 100\right)\% = \left(\frac{1}{20} \times \frac{4}{3} \times 100\right)\% = 6\frac{2}{3}\%$$

19. *(b)* **Statement 1**

Let CP of commodity $= ₹\,x$

$$\therefore \qquad 524 - x = x - 452$$

$$\Rightarrow 2x = 524 + 452 \Rightarrow x = \frac{976}{2} = ₹\,488 \text{ (false)}$$

Statement 2

Let SP of 1 m cloth be ₹ 1.

$\therefore$ SP = ₹ 25, gain = ₹ 5

CP = SP − gain = 25 − 5 = ₹ 20

$$\therefore \text{Gain \%} = \frac{\text{gain}}{\text{CP}} \times 100 = \frac{5}{20} \times 100 = 25\% \text{ (true)}$$

20. *(c)* Let SP $= ₹\,x$

$$\therefore \text{Profit} = 20\% \text{ of } ₹\,x = \frac{20 \times x}{100} = ₹\,\frac{x}{5}$$

$$\Rightarrow \text{CP} = \text{SP} - \text{Profit} = ₹\left(x - \frac{x}{5}\right) = ₹\,\frac{4x}{5}$$

Hence, Profit % $= \dfrac{\text{Profit}}{\text{CP}} \times 100\%$

$$= \frac{\dfrac{x}{5}}{\dfrac{4x}{5}} \times 100\% = \frac{100}{4}\% = 25\%$$

21. *(a)* Let quantity of green tea and lemon tea be $5x$ and $4x$.

Total CP of both varieties tea

$$= 5x \times 200 + 4x \times 300 = 2200x$$

Total SP $= (5x + 4x) \times 275 = ₹\,2475x$

$$\therefore \text{Profit\%} = \frac{\text{SP} - \text{CP}}{\text{CP}} \times 100 = \frac{2475 - 2200}{2200} \times 100$$

$$= 12.5\%$$

22. *(b)* Buying price of VCD player $= \dfrac{5500 \times 80}{100}$

$$= ₹\,4400$$

She wants profit $= 10\%$

$\therefore$ SP of VCD player = CP + 10% of CP

$$= \text{CP}\left(1 + \frac{10}{100}\right) = \text{CP}\left(\frac{110}{100}\right)$$

$$= \frac{4400 \times 110}{100} = ₹\,4840$$

Chapter 8 : Simple Interest

1. *(c)* Amount after 2 yr = ₹ 840

Amount of 4 yr = ₹ 920

$\therefore$ SI for 2 yr = ₹ 920 − ₹ 840 = ₹ 80

So, SI for 4 yr = ₹ 160

$\therefore$ Principle amount = ₹ (920 − 160) = ₹ 760

2. *(b)* $\qquad \text{SI} = \dfrac{P \times R \times T}{100} \Rightarrow 150 = \dfrac{P \times 4 \times \frac{6}{12}}{100}$

$$\Rightarrow \qquad P = \frac{150 \times 100}{4 \times \frac{1}{2}} \quad \therefore \quad P = ₹7500$$

3. *(a)* $\qquad \text{SI} = \dfrac{P \times R \times T}{100}$

$$\Rightarrow \qquad 1080 = \frac{3000 \times 12 \times T}{100} \qquad [T \rightarrow \text{Time}]$$

$$\therefore \qquad T = \frac{1080 \times 100}{3000 \times 12} = 3\text{yr}$$

4. *(c)* Let $P = ₹\,x$ and SI $= ₹\,\dfrac{2x}{5}$

$$\text{SI} = \frac{P \times R \times T}{100}$$

Now, $\dfrac{2x}{5} = \dfrac{x \times 8 \times T}{100} \Rightarrow T = \dfrac{2 \times 100}{5 \times 8} = 5\text{yr}$

5. *(d)* Let principal be ₹P. Then, SI is $₹\,\dfrac{1}{3}P$.

According to the question, $\dfrac{1}{3}P = \dfrac{P \times 8 \times 4}{100}$

$$\Rightarrow \frac{1}{3} = \frac{8 \times 4}{100} \text{ [data inadequate]}$$

6. *(c)* As the interest rate increases by 2%.

$\therefore$ SI increase $= \dfrac{5000 \times 3 \times 2}{100} = 300$

She would get $= ₹\ 7000 + ₹\ 300 = ₹\ 7300$

7. *(c)* Let the principal be P and rate of interest be $R\ \%$

$\therefore$ Required ratio $= \dfrac{\left(\dfrac{P \times R \times 12}{100}\right)}{\left(\dfrac{P \times R \times 20}{100}\right)} = \dfrac{12}{20} = \dfrac{3}{5} = 3 : 5$

8. *(b)* Let rate $= R\ \%$ and time $= R$ yr

Then according to question,

$\dfrac{1200 \times R \times R}{100} = 432 \Rightarrow 12R^2 = 432$

$\Rightarrow \qquad R^2 = 36 \quad \Rightarrow \quad R = 6\%$

9. *(c)* SI $=$ Amount $-$ Principal $= 3P - P = 2P$

Rate, $R = \dfrac{\text{SI} \times 100}{P \times T} = \dfrac{2P \times 100}{P \times 5} = 40\%$

10. *(d)* SI paid by Feroz

$\text{SI}_1 = \dfrac{P_1 \times R_1 \times T_1}{100} = \dfrac{6400 \times 15 \times 7}{100 \times 2} = ₹\ 3360$

SI paid by Rashmi

$\text{SI}_2 = \dfrac{P_2 \times R_2 \times T_2}{100} = \dfrac{6400 \times 15 \times 5}{100} = ₹\ 4800$

$\therefore$ Difference between SI's $= ₹\ (4800 - 3360) = ₹\ 1440$

11. *(c)* SI for Sara $= \dfrac{8000 \times 6 \times 5}{100} = ₹\ 2400$

SI for Alisha $= \dfrac{12000 \times 8 \times 25}{100} = ₹\ 2400$

Hence, both get equal

12. (c) $\therefore$ Simple interest $= \dfrac{(P \times T \times R)}{100}$

$\therefore$ SI paid by Rishu $= \dfrac{8000 \times \dfrac{9}{2} \times 8}{100} = ₹\ 2880$

Amount $=$ Principal amount $+$ Interest

$\qquad = ₹\ 8000 + 2880 = ₹\ 10880$

13. *(b)* Given, $P_1 = ₹\ 1550,\ T_1 = 2\,\text{yr},$

$\qquad P_2 = ₹\ 1450$ and $T_2 = 2\,\text{yr}$

According to the question,

$\dfrac{P_1 \times R \times T_1}{100} - \dfrac{P_2 \times R \times T_2}{100} = 20$

$\Rightarrow \dfrac{1550 \times 2 \times R}{100} - \dfrac{1450 \times 2 \times R}{100} = 20$

$\Rightarrow \qquad \dfrac{200R}{100} = 20$

$\Rightarrow \qquad\qquad R = 10\%$

14. *(c)* Simple Interest (SI) $=$ Amount $-$ Principal

$\qquad\qquad = 8000 - 6000 = ₹\ 2000$

$\because \qquad \text{SI} = \dfrac{P \times R \times T}{100} \Rightarrow 2000 = \dfrac{6000 \times R \times 4}{100}$

$\Rightarrow \qquad R = \dfrac{2000 \times 100}{6000 \times 4} = \dfrac{25}{3}\%$

Again, $A = ₹\ 700,\ P = ₹\ 525,\ \text{SI} = A - P$

$\Rightarrow \qquad 700 - 525 = \dfrac{525 \times \dfrac{25}{3} \times T}{100}$

$\Rightarrow \qquad T = \dfrac{175 \times 100 \times 3}{525 \times 25} = 4\,\text{yr}$

15. *(b)* Let 1st part $= P_1 = ₹\ x$

then 2nd part $= P_2 = ₹\ (60000 - x)$

According to the question,

$\Rightarrow \dfrac{x \times 4 \times 1}{100} + \dfrac{(60000 - x) \times 5 \times 1}{100} = 2560$

$\Rightarrow \qquad 4x + 300000 - 5x = 256000$

$\Rightarrow \qquad x = 300000 - 256000 = ₹\ 44000$

16. *(c)* Let the Principal $= ₹\ P$

$\therefore \quad \text{SI} = ₹\ (P - 312) \quad \therefore \quad \text{SI} = \dfrac{P \times R \times T}{100}$

$\Rightarrow \qquad P - 312 = \dfrac{P \times 6 \times 8}{100}$

$\Rightarrow \qquad 100P - 31200 = 48P$

$\Rightarrow \qquad 52P = 31200 \quad \Rightarrow P = ₹\ 600$

17. *(a)* I.

$\therefore \text{SI} = \dfrac{1000 \times 2 \times 1}{100} \qquad \left[\because \text{SI} = \dfrac{P \times R \times T}{100}\right]$

$\qquad = ₹\ 20$

II. $\therefore \quad \text{SI} = \dfrac{500 \times 3 \times 2}{100} = ₹\ 30$

III. $\therefore \quad \text{SI} = \dfrac{250 \times 4 \times 4}{100} = ₹\ 40$

18. *(b)* Let 1st part $= ₹\ x$ and 2nd part $= ₹\ (10000 - x)$

According to the question,

$\dfrac{x \times 12 \times 4}{100} = \dfrac{(10000 - x) \times 16 \times 4.5}{100}$

$\Rightarrow \qquad 48x = (10000 - x) \times 16 \times 4.5$

$\Rightarrow \qquad \dfrac{48x}{4.5 \times 16} = (10000 - x) \Rightarrow \dfrac{48x \times 10}{45 \times 16} = 10000 - x$

$\Rightarrow \qquad \dfrac{2}{3}x = 10000 - x \Rightarrow \dfrac{2}{3}x + x = 10000$

$\Rightarrow \qquad \dfrac{5x}{3} = 10000 \Rightarrow x = 10000 \times \dfrac{3}{5} = 6000$

1st part $= ₹\ 6000$

2nd part $= 10000 - x = ₹\ 10000 - ₹\ 6000 = ₹\ 4000$

19. *(c)* Let the amount received by Anish be ₹ x.
Then, amount received by Anuj is = ₹ $(20000 - x)$.
According to the question,
$$\frac{x \times 12 \times 2}{100} = \frac{(20000 - x) \times 8 \times 2}{100}$$
$\Rightarrow \qquad 12x = 160000 - 8x$
$\Rightarrow \qquad 20x = 160000 \Rightarrow x = ₹\, 8000$
$\therefore$ Anish received = ₹ 8000,
whereas Anuj received = ₹ 12000.

20. *(d)* Let time be t yr
According to the question,
$$300 + \frac{300 \times 4 \times t}{100} + 600 + \frac{600 \times 6 \times t}{100} = 1092$$
$$12t + 36t = 1092 - 900$$
$\Rightarrow \qquad 48t = 192 \quad \Rightarrow \quad t = \dfrac{192}{48} = 4\,\text{yr}$

Chapter 9. Algebraic Expression

1. *(c)* Consider the terms,
$$9a(2b - a) = 18ab - 9a^2$$
and $-6b(4a - 2b) = -24ab + 12b^2$
$\therefore 18ab$ and $-24ab$ are like terms.

2. *(b)* $? = \left(3m + \dfrac{1}{2n}\right)^2 - \left(3m - \dfrac{1}{2n}\right)^2$
$= \left(3m + \dfrac{1}{2n} + 3m - \dfrac{1}{2n}\right)\left(3m + \dfrac{1}{2n} - 3m + \dfrac{1}{2n}\right)$
$[\because a^2 - b^2 = (a + b)(a - b)]$
$= 6m \cdot \dfrac{2}{2n} = \dfrac{6m}{n}$

3. *(a)* Consider, $[(2a^3b)^3][(4a^2b^2)]$
$= [(2^3 a^9 b^3)(4a^2 b^2)] = [(8a^9 b^3)(4a^2 b^2)] = 32a^{11}b^5$

4. *(d)* Consider, $3y = 15 \Rightarrow y = 5$
and $2x = 16 \Rightarrow x = 8$
So, $3x + 2y = 3 \times 8 + 2 \times 5 = 24 + 10 = 34$

5. *(a)* Consider, $3h + 45 - 12 + (3 \times 5)h$
$= 3h + 45 - 12 + 15h$
$= 18h + 33 = 18 \times 10 + 33$
$= 180 + 33 = 213$

6. *(d)* Given, $C = \dfrac{5}{9}(F - 32)$
Substitute, $F = 32$, we get
$C = \dfrac{5}{9}(32 - 32) = 0$

7. *(c)* Number of skirts Meera has = $4q$
Number of skirts Tara has = $12q$
and Number of skirts Lara has = $2q$
Number of skirts Meera and Lara have
$= 4q + 2q = 6q$
$\therefore$ Difference of number of skirts
Tara has from the combined number of skirts of
Meera and Lara $= 12q - 6q = 6q = 6 \times 5\ [\because q = 5]$
$= 30$

8. *(c)* Required expression
$= (-2x^3 + 5x^2 - x + 8) - (5x^2 - 4x + 12)$
$= -2x^3 + 5x^2 - x + 8 - 5x^2 + 4x - 12$
$= -2x^3 + 3x - 4$

9. *(a)* Required expression
$= 3x^2 + 2x + 1 - (x + x^2 + 6)$
$= 3x^2 + 2x + 1 - x^2 - x - 6 = 2x^2 + x - 5$

10. *(c)* Consider, $\dfrac{pq + pr}{ps} = \dfrac{p(q + r)}{p \times s} = \dfrac{q + r}{s}$

11. *(b)* Consider, $12a + 14b - 3b - 11c + 8.5a$
$= 12a + 8.5a + 14b - 3b - 11c$
$= 20.5a + 11b - 11c$

12. *(a)* Consider, $\left(\dfrac{2}{5}a^4 - 2a + 7\right)$
$$-\left(-\dfrac{3}{10}a^4 + 6a^3\right) - (2a^2 - 7)$$
$= \dfrac{2}{5}a^4 - 2a + 7 + \dfrac{3}{10}a^4 - 6a^3 - 2a^2 + 7$
$= \dfrac{2}{5}a^4 + \dfrac{3}{10}a^4 - 6a^3 - 2a^2 - 2a + 7 + 7$
$= \dfrac{7}{10}a^4 - 6a^3 - 2a^2 - 2a + 14$

13. *(b)* $(2a^3 - 3)(5a^3 - 2)$
$= 2a^3 \times 5a^3 + 2a^3(-2) - 3 \times 5a^3 - 3 \times (-2)$
$= 10a^6 - 4a^3 - 15a^3 + 6 = 10a^6 - 19a^3 + 6$

14. *(c)* Given, $A = 10w^3 + 20w^2 - 55w + 60$,
$$B = -25w^2 + 15w - 10$$
and $\qquad C = 5w^2 - 10w + 20$
$\therefore A + B - C = 10w^3 + 20w^2 - 55w + 60$
$$+ (-25w^2) + 15w - 10 - (5w^2 - 10w + 20)$$
$= 10w^3 + 20w^2 - 55w + 60 - 25w^2 + 15w - 10$
$$-5w^2 + 10w - 20$$
$= 10w^3 - 10w^2 - 30w + 30$

15. *(d)* Area of rectangle = $l \times b$

Here, $l = 33y$ m and $b = 10x$ m

$\therefore$ Area = $33y \times 10x = 330xy\,\text{m}^2$

16. *(b)* Perimeter of regular pentagon = $5l$

where, l = Side = $(3x + 1)$ inch

$\therefore$ Perimeter = $5 \times (3x + 1) = (15x + 5)$ inch

17. *(a)* Given, $S_n = \dfrac{n(n + 1)}{2}$

$\therefore$ Sum of first 20 natural numbers,

$$S_{20} = \frac{20(20 + 1)}{2} = \frac{20 \times 21}{2} = 210$$

18. *(c)* I. $x^2 + y^2 + 3xy$

$$= 1^2 + (-2)^2 + 3(1) \times (-2) = 1 + 4 - 6 = -1$$

II. $x^2 + x^2y + xy^2 + y^2$

$$= (1)^2 + (1)^2 \times (-2) + 1 \times (-2)^2 + (-2)^2$$

$$= 1 - 2 + 4 + 4 = 7$$

III. $x^2 + y^2 - 3xy = (1)^2 + (-2)^2 - 3 \times 1 \times (-2)$

$$= 1 + 4 + 6 = 11$$

IV. $(x^2 - y^2) = (1)^2 - (-2)^2 = 1 - 4 = -3$

19. *(a)* I. Trinomial   II. 4

    III. $7y - 4x$ IV. Unlike terms

20. *(d)* Given, $P = 2387.74t + 155211.46$

and $M = 1164.16\,t + 7562243$

$\therefore$ Female population, $F = P - M$

$$= 2387.74\,t + 155211.46 - 1164.16\,t - 75622.43$$

$$= 1223.58\,t + 79589.03$$

21. *(a)* The cost of 1 dozen of eggs = a

Cost of 1 bread = ₹b and Cost of 1 bottle of juice = c

$\therefore$ Total money = ₹$a + 3b + 5c$

22. *(d)* Area of house = $l \times b = x \times 1.5x = 1.5x^2$

Area of land = $3x \times (x + 20) = 3x^2 + 60x$

Remaining area of land = $3x^2 + 60x - 1.5x^2$

$$= 1.5x^2 + 60x$$

where, $x = 30$, then area = $1.5\,(30)^2 + 60 \times 30$

$= 1.5 \times 900 + 1800 = 1350 + 1800 = 3150$ sq units

23. *(d)* Monthly salary of Max = ₹ $5445q$

Money saved by him = 30%

$\therefore$ Money spent by him = 70% of $5445q = \dfrac{7}{10} \times 5445q$

Money given to parents = $\dfrac{1}{2} \times \dfrac{7}{10} \times 5445q$

$$= \frac{1}{2} \times \frac{7}{10} \times 5445 \times 8 = ₹15246$$

Money used to buy guitar = $\dfrac{3}{4} \times 15246 = ₹11434.5$

Amount of money left = $15246 - 11434.5 = 3811.50$

24. *(c)* Cost of vaccum cleaner = ₹ $154.25K$

Cost of additional pipe = ₹ $15.2K$

Cost of 3 vaccum sets = $3 \times 154.25K = ₹\,462.75K$

Cost of 5 additional pipe = $5 \times 15.2K = ₹\,76K$

$\therefore$ Total cost = $(462.75 + 76)\,K = ₹\,538.75\,K$

Chapter 10. Simple Equation

1. *(b)* Let x be the number.

Then, one-third of the number = $\dfrac{x}{3}$

We have, $\dfrac{x}{3} = x - 10$

or one-third of a number is 10 less than the number itself.

2. *(d)* Let the number be x.

According to the question,

$$9 - \frac{2}{3}x = 10 \quad \Rightarrow \quad 9 - 10 = \frac{2}{3}x$$

$$\Rightarrow \qquad -1 = \frac{2}{3}x \quad \Rightarrow \quad x = -\frac{3}{2}$$

3. *(b)* $\dfrac{4}{5}x - 2 = 2 \Rightarrow \dfrac{4}{5}x = 4 \Rightarrow x = 5$

4. *(c)* Step V must be $16x - 18x = -1$

$$\Rightarrow \qquad -2x = -1 \quad \Rightarrow \quad x = \frac{1}{2}$$

5. *(c)* Option (a), $5 - x = 9$

$\Rightarrow x = 5 - 9 \quad \Rightarrow x = -4$ (correct)

Option (b), $14 + x = 10$

$\Rightarrow x = 10 - 14 = -4$ (correct)

Option (c), $\dfrac{20}{(-x)} = 4$

$$\Rightarrow \qquad x = \frac{20}{-4} = -5\,(\text{Not correct})$$

Option (d), $9x = -36 \Rightarrow x = -4$ (correct)

6. *(a)* Let one angle be x.

$\therefore$ other angle = $180° - x$

[$\because$ Sum of two supplementary angle be $180°$]

According to the question,

$$x - (180° - x) = 74°$$

$\Rightarrow \quad x - 180° + x = 74° \Rightarrow 2x = 254° \Rightarrow x = 127°$

7. *(b)* Let the two consecutive odd number be x and $x + 2$.

$\therefore \qquad x + x + 2 = 184 \Rightarrow 2x = 182$

$\Rightarrow \qquad x = 91$

$\therefore$ The greater number $= 91 + 2 = 93$

8. (d) $\dfrac{4x-5}{7} + \dfrac{x+11}{21} = \dfrac{1}{3}$

$\Rightarrow \dfrac{12x-15+x+11}{21} = \dfrac{1}{3}$

$\Rightarrow 13x - 4 = 7 \Rightarrow 13x = 11 \Rightarrow x = \dfrac{11}{13}$

9. (a) According to the question, $4x + 7 = 47$

10. (b) Option (b), $7x - \dfrac{5}{3} = \dfrac{47}{3} + \dfrac{5x}{3}$

$\Rightarrow \qquad 7x - \dfrac{5x}{3} = \dfrac{52}{3} \Rightarrow \dfrac{16x}{3} = \dfrac{52}{3}$

$\Rightarrow \qquad x = \dfrac{52}{16} = \dfrac{13}{4} = 3\dfrac{1}{4}$ (correct)

11. (b) Let the height of the pole be x.

According to the question,

$$\dfrac{x}{4} + \dfrac{2x}{5} + 21 = x \Rightarrow x - \dfrac{x}{4} - \dfrac{2x}{5} = 21$$

$\Rightarrow \qquad \dfrac{20x - 5x - 8x}{20} = 21 \Rightarrow 7x = 21 \times 20$

$\Rightarrow \qquad x = 60$

12. (c) Let Rakesh has x pens.

According to the question, $4x + 8 = 48$

$\Rightarrow \qquad 4x = 40 \Rightarrow x = 10$

13. (b) Let $\angle B$ be x.

$\therefore \qquad \angle A = 3x$ and $\angle C = x - 20°$

We know that, $\angle A + \angle B + \angle C = 180°$

$\Rightarrow \qquad 3x + x + x - 20° = 180°$

$\Rightarrow \qquad 5x - 20° = 180°$

$\Rightarrow \qquad 5x = 200° \Rightarrow x = 40°$

14. (c) Let ₹ x be the amount donated in a Relief Fund by Subramaniam.

$\therefore$ The amount donated by Naidu will be ₹ $(x + 125)$.

According to the question,

$x + (x + 125) = 975$

$\qquad 2x + 125 = 975 \Rightarrow 2x = 975 - 125$

$\qquad 2x = 850 \Rightarrow x = \dfrac{850}{2}$

$\Rightarrow \qquad x = ₹ 425$

15. (b) Let x be the number of boys in the school.

$\therefore$ The number of girls in the school will be $= x + 50$.

Then, $x + (x + 50) = 1070$

$\qquad 2x + 50 = 1070 \Rightarrow 2x = 1070 - 50$

$\qquad 2x = 1020 \Rightarrow x = 510$

So, the number of girls in the school will be

$\qquad = 510 + 50 = 560$

16. (d) Let x be the age of the girl.

$\therefore$ The age of the father will be $= (x + 28)$ yr

Then, $x + (x + 28) = 50 \Rightarrow 2x + 28 = 50$

Then, $2x = 50 - 28 \Rightarrow 2x = 22 \Rightarrow x = \dfrac{22}{2} = 11$ yr

Hence, age of the girl is 11 yr and her father's age is

$\qquad = 11 + 28 = 39$ yr.

17. (b) Let the number of ₹ 2 coins be y.

$\therefore$ The number of ₹ 1 coins $= 3y$.

According to the question,

$\qquad 2 + y + 1 \times 3y = 120 \Rightarrow 5y = 120$

$\Rightarrow \qquad y = \dfrac{120}{5} = 24$

$\therefore$ Number of ₹ 1 coins $= 3 \times 24 = 72$.

18. (d) I. $2x = 3x - 3 \Rightarrow x = 3$

II. $\dfrac{2}{3}x - 3 = 5 \Rightarrow \dfrac{2}{3}x = 8 \Rightarrow x = 12$

III. $72 - 8x = 0 \Rightarrow 72 = 8x \Rightarrow x = 9$

19. (d) I. True

As, $\qquad 5x - 6 = 8x - 4$

$\Rightarrow \qquad 8x - 5x = 4 - 6 \Rightarrow x = -\dfrac{2}{3}$

II. False

Let the number be x.

$\qquad \dfrac{1}{5} \times x = 5 + \dfrac{1}{10} \times x \Rightarrow \dfrac{x}{5} - \dfrac{x}{10} = 5$

$\qquad \dfrac{x}{10} = 5 \qquad \Rightarrow x = 50 \neq -10$

III. True

The given statement is true.

IV. True

The given statement is true.

20. (c) I. Total number of prizes $= 40$

Number of Ist prizes $= x$

$\therefore$ Number of 2nd prizes $= 40 - x$

II. Total value of prizes in terms of x

$\qquad = 3000x + 2000(40 - x)$

III. Equation formed

$\Rightarrow \qquad 3000x + 2000(40 - x) = 90000$

$\Rightarrow \quad 3000x + 80000 - 2000x = 90000$

$\Rightarrow \qquad 1000x + 80000 = 90000$

21. (a) Let the number of toys be x.

If one child gets one toy each, then one of the child is left with no toy.

So, number of children $= (x + 1)$

If one toy is given to two children to share, then one toy will be left extra.

Now, number of children $= (x-1) \times 2 = 2x - 2$

We have, $\qquad x+1 = 2x - 2 \Rightarrow x = 3$

$\therefore$ Number of toys $= 3$

and number of children $= 2 \times 3 - 2 = 4$

22. *(d)* Option (a), $2(x-3) = 5$

$\Rightarrow \qquad 2x - 6 = 5 \Rightarrow 2x = 11$

$\Rightarrow \qquad x = \dfrac{11}{2}$ (not correct)

Option (b), $5 - 3x = 10 \Rightarrow 5 - 10 = 3x$

$\Rightarrow \qquad -5 = 3x \quad \Rightarrow \quad x = \dfrac{-5}{3}$ (not correct)

Option (c) $\dfrac{1}{4}x - 2 = 7 \Rightarrow \dfrac{1}{4}x = 9$

$\Rightarrow \qquad x = 36$ (not correct)

23. *(a)* Let the depth be d.

Increase in temperature for each kilometre of depth

$$= 30^\circ C$$

Given, temperature $= 110^\circ C$

According to the question,

$110 = 20 + 30d \Rightarrow 110 - 20 = 30d \Rightarrow 90 = 30d$

$\Rightarrow \qquad d = 3$

24. *(a)* I. $\dfrac{3}{4}(7x - 1) - \left(2x - \dfrac{1-x}{2}\right) = x + \dfrac{3}{2}$

$\Rightarrow \dfrac{21}{4}x - \dfrac{3}{4} - 2x + \dfrac{1}{2} - \dfrac{x}{2} = x + \dfrac{3}{2}$

$\Rightarrow \dfrac{21}{4}x - 2x - \dfrac{x}{2} - x = \dfrac{3}{2} + \dfrac{3}{4} - \dfrac{1}{2}$

$\Rightarrow \dfrac{21x - 8x - 2x - 4x}{4} = \dfrac{6 + 3 - 2}{4}$

$\Rightarrow \qquad 7x = 7 \Rightarrow x = 1$ (correct)

II. $\left[\left(y - \dfrac{1}{2}\right) \times 4 + 25\right] \div 3 = 10$

$\Rightarrow \quad [4y - 2 + 25] \times \dfrac{1}{3} = 10$

$\Rightarrow \qquad 4y + 23 = 30 \Rightarrow 4y = 7$

$\Rightarrow \qquad y = \dfrac{7}{4}$ (Not correct)

Chapter 11. Lines and Angles

1. *(c)* Let the angle be x.

Then, its supplement $= (180^\circ - x)$

According to the question,

$x - 3(180^\circ - x) = 40^\circ$

$\Rightarrow x - 540^\circ + 3x = 40^\circ \Rightarrow 4x = 580^\circ$

$\Rightarrow \qquad x = 145^\circ$

2. *(b)* 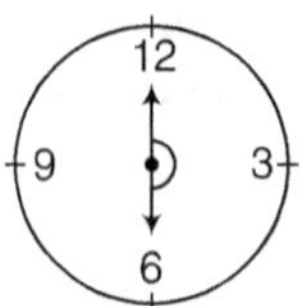

The angle formed is of measure 180° or straight angle.

3. *(c)* In the given figure,

$\qquad 2S = 100^\circ \qquad$ [vertically opposite angles]

$\therefore \qquad S = 50^\circ$

4. *(c)* From figure,

$\qquad \angle y + \angle y + 78^\circ = 180^\circ$ [linear pair]

$\therefore \qquad 2\angle y = 180^\circ - 78^\circ \Rightarrow 2\angle y = 102^\circ$

$\therefore \qquad \angle y = 51^\circ$

5. *(a)* 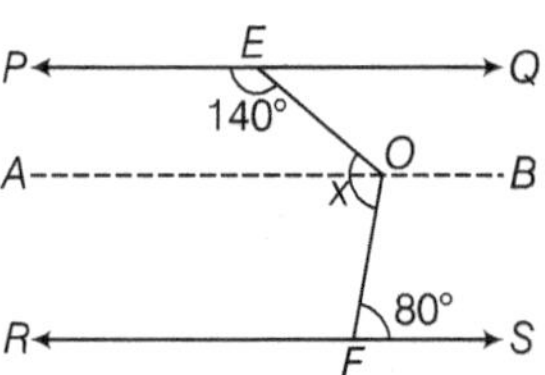

Draw $AB \parallel PQ \parallel RS$

$\therefore \qquad \angle EOA = 180^\circ - 140^\circ = 40^\circ$

[since, interior angles on the same side of transversal are supplementary]

$\because \qquad \angle AOF = \angle OFS \qquad$ [alternate angles]

$\therefore \qquad \angle AOF = 80^\circ$

Now, $\qquad \angle x = \angle EOA + \angle AOF$

$\qquad\qquad = 40^\circ + 80^\circ = 120^\circ$

6. *(c)* We have,

$\qquad 3x + 5^\circ + x + 15^\circ = 180^\circ$

$\Rightarrow \qquad 4x + 20^\circ = 180^\circ$

$\Rightarrow \qquad 4x = 160^\circ \Rightarrow x = 40^\circ$

Also, $y + 20^\circ + 4y - 15^\circ = 180^\circ$

$\Rightarrow \qquad 5y + 5^\circ = 180^\circ \Rightarrow 5y = 175^\circ$

$\Rightarrow \qquad y = 35^\circ$

$\therefore \qquad \angle x = 40^\circ$ and $\angle y = 35^\circ$

7. *(a)* Given, AOB is a line and $\angle a = 40^\circ$.

$\because \qquad \angle a + 3y + 4y = 180^\circ$ [linear pair]

$\therefore \qquad 40^\circ + 3y + 4y = 180^\circ$

$\Rightarrow \qquad 7y = 140^\circ \Rightarrow y = 20^\circ$

$\therefore \qquad \angle FOE = 3y = 60^\circ$

8. *(c)* From figure

$\qquad \angle x = 40^\circ \qquad$ [vertically opposite angles]

Now, $CD \parallel EF$

$\therefore \qquad \angle EOA = 180^\circ - 40^\circ = 140^\circ$

[interior angles on the same side of transversal]

Now, $\angle y = \angle EOA$ [vertically opposite angles]
$\therefore$ $\angle y = 140°$

9. *(c)* We have, $RS \parallel UT$

Also, TR is a transversal.

$\therefore$ $\angle SRT = \angle RTU$ [alternate angles]
$\Rightarrow$ $89° = x + \angle CTU$
$\Rightarrow$ $89° = x + 39° \Rightarrow \quad x = 50°$
$\therefore$ $\angle RTC = 50°$

10. *(c)* From figure,
    $\angle 6 = \angle 3 \dots$ (i) [vetically opposite angles]
CD is a straight line.
$\therefore \quad \angle 5 + \angle 4 + \angle 3 = \angle 1 + \angle 2 + \angle 6$
$\Rightarrow \angle 5 + \angle 4 = \angle 1 + \angle 2$ [from Eq. (i)]

11. *(a)* I. Line segment PQ or $\overline{PQ}$

    II. Ray PQ or $\overrightarrow{PQ}$

    III. Line PQ or $\overleftrightarrow{PQ}$

12. *(b)* I. $x = 90°$

    II. $x + 60° + 90° = 180°$ [linear pair]
    $\therefore$ $x = 30°$
    III. $x + 35° = 90°$ [complementary]
    $\Rightarrow \quad x = 55°$

13. *(d)* Given that, $EC \parallel AB$

$\therefore \angle ECO + \angle AOC = 180°$
$\Rightarrow$ $\angle AOC = 180° - 70° = 110°$
$\therefore$ $\angle BOD = \angle AOC = 110°$
         [vertically opposite angles]
Now, in $\triangle OBD$,
    $\angle BOD + \angle ODB + \angle OBD = 180°$
$\therefore$ $110° + 20° + \angle OBD = 180°$
$\Rightarrow$ $\angle OBD = 50°$

14. *(b)* Given, $\angle XOV = 90°$ and $c : b = 7 : 3$

Let $c = 7x$ and $b = 3x$
$\because$ $\angle c + \angle b = 180°$ [linear pair]
$\therefore$ $7x + 3x = 180°$
$\Rightarrow$ $10x = 180° \Rightarrow x = 18°$
    $b = 3 \times 18 = 54°$

Now, $\angle a = \angle b$ [vertically opposite angles]
$\therefore$ $\angle a = 54°$

15. *(c)* Given, $EF \parallel AO$

$\therefore$ $\angle A = \angle CEF$ [corresponding angles]
$\therefore$ $\angle x = \angle CEF = 75°$
Also, $\angle OEF = 20°$ [vertically opposite angles]
Now, $AC \parallel OD$ and OB is the transversal.
    $\angle OFE = x = 75°$

In $\triangle OFE$, $\angle y + \angle OFE + \angle OEF = 180°$
$\Rightarrow$ $\angle y + 75° + 20° = 180°$
$\Rightarrow$ $\angle y = 180° - 95° = 85°$

16. *(c)* We have, $\angle UST = 70°$

$\therefore \angle QSR = \angle UST = 70°$ [vertically opposite angles]
Again, $\angle SRP + \angle QSR = 180°$ [cointerior angles]
$\Rightarrow$ $\angle SRP = 180° - 70° = 110°$
Again, $\angle RPQ = 180° - \angle SRP$
         $= 180° - 110° = 70°$
Now, $\angle LPR + \angle RPQ + \angle MPQ = 180°$
         [$\because$ sum of all angles on a line is $180°$]
$\therefore 35° + 70° + \angle MPQ = 180°$
$\Rightarrow$ $\angle MPQ = 75°$

17. *(b)* Since, $AB \parallel CD$ and PQ is transversal.

    $\angle PEF = \angle EGH$ [corresponding angles]
$\Rightarrow$ $\angle EGH = 70°$ [$\because \angle PEF = 70°$]
Now, $\angle EGH + \angle HGQ = 180°$ [linear pair]
$\Rightarrow \angle HGQ = (180° - 70°) = 110°$
Also, $\angle DHQ + \angle GHQ = 180°$ [linear pair]
$\Rightarrow \angle GHQ = (180 - 140)° = 40°$
In $\triangle GQH$,
$\angle GQH + \angle GHQ + \angle HGQ = 180°$
         [$\because$ sum of the angles in a triangle is $180°$]
$\Rightarrow$ $x + 40° + 110° = 180°$
$\Rightarrow$ $x + 150° = 180° \Rightarrow x = 30°$

18. *(a)* $\because AB \parallel XY$ and BE transversal

    $\angle BEY = \angle ABE = 46°$
$\therefore$ $\angle YED = \angle EDC$ [alternate angles]
    $\angle YED = 33°$
Now, $\angle e = \angle YED + \angle BEY = 33° + 46° = 79°$
$\because OC \parallel EB$
$\therefore$ $\angle OFE = \angle BEY = 46°$ and $XY \parallel CD$
$\therefore$ $\angle OCD = \angle OFE = 46°$

Chapter 12. Triangle, Properties and Congruence

1. *(c)* The three angles of the triangle are x, $2x$ and x.

Now, by angle sum property
    $x + 2x + x = 180°$
$\Rightarrow$ $4x = 180° \Rightarrow x = 45°$
So, the greatest angle $= 2x = 90°$

2. *(c)* Let the angles be $2x$, $3x$ and $5x$.

Then, $2x + 3x + 5x = 180°$
$\Rightarrow$ $10x = 180° \Rightarrow x = 18°$
$\therefore$ The angles are $36°$, $54°$, $90°$. Hence, it is a right angled triangle.

3. *(c)* In $\triangle ABC$, $AB = AC$

$\therefore$ $\angle ABC = \angle ACB$

[angles opposite to equal sides are also equal]

Now, $\angle ABC + \angle ACB = 130°$ [exterior angle property]

$\therefore$ $x + x = 130°$

$\Rightarrow$ $2x = 130° \Rightarrow x = 65°$

4. *(a)* Given, $PQ = PR$

$\therefore$ $\angle PQR = \angle PRQ$

i.e. $\angle Q = \angle R$ ...(i)

Also, $\angle P = 3\angle Q$ ...(ii)

We have,

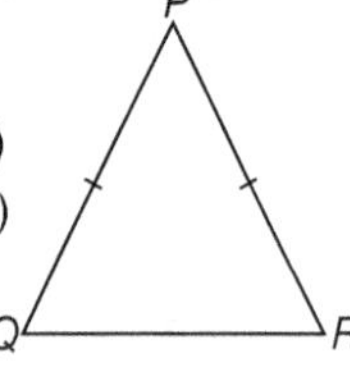

$\angle P + \angle Q + \angle R = 180°$ [angle sum property]

$\Rightarrow 3\angle Q + \angle Q + \angle Q = 180°$

[from Eqs. (i) and (ii)]

$\Rightarrow$ $5\angle Q = 180° \Rightarrow \angle Q = 36°$

$\therefore$ $\angle R = 36°$

5. *(d)* In the given figure, $\angle PRS$ is the exterior angle.

$\therefore$ $\angle PRS + \angle PRQ = 180°$ [linear pair]

$\Rightarrow$ $\angle PRQ = 180° - 136° = 44°$

Also, $\angle PRQ = \angle PQR$ [$\because$ angles opposite to equal sides are also equal]

$\therefore$ $\angle PQR = 44°$

We have, $x + \angle PQR = 136°$ [exterior angles]

$\Rightarrow$ $x + 44° = 136°$

$\therefore$ $x = 136° - 44° = 92°$

6. *(a)* Given, $BC = CD$

$\therefore$ $\angle CBD = \angle CDB = 70°$

[angles opposite to equal sides are also equal]

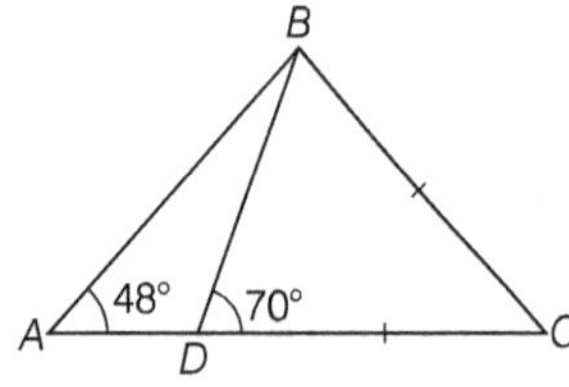

Also, $\angle BDC = \angle BAD + \angle ABD$

[exterior angle property]

$70° = 48° + \angle ABD$

$\Rightarrow$ $\angle ABD = 70° - 48° = 22°$

So, $\angle ABC = \angle ABD + \angle CBD$

$= 22° + 70° = 92°$

7. *(c)* In the given figure,

$\angle a + 20° + 90° = 180°$ [linear pair]

$\Rightarrow$ $\angle a = 180° - 110° = 70°$

Also, $\angle c = \angle b$

$\therefore$ $\angle b + \angle c = 90° + 20°$

$\Rightarrow$ $\angle b + \angle b = 90° + 20°$ [$\because \angle c = \angle b$]

$\Rightarrow$ $2\angle b = 110°$

$\Rightarrow$ $\angle b = 55°$

$\therefore \angle a = 70°$, $\angle b = 55°$ and $\angle c = 55°$

8. *(d)* In the given figure, $OB = OC$

$\therefore$ $\angle OBC = \angle OCB$

$\Rightarrow$ $\angle OCB = 42°$ [$\because \angle OBC = 42°$]

Also, in $\triangle ABC$,

$\angle A + \angle B + \angle C = 180°$

$\Rightarrow 54° + (42° + 21°) + \angle C = 180°$

$\Rightarrow$ $54° + 63° + \angle C = 180° \Rightarrow \angle C = 63°$

$\because$ $i + \angle OCB = 63°$

$\Rightarrow$ $i + 42° = 63°$

$\Rightarrow$ $i = 63° - 42° = 21°$

9. *(b)* We have,

$\angle a + \angle b + \angle c + \angle d + \angle e + \angle x = 180° + 180°$

$\Rightarrow \angle a + \angle b + \angle c + \angle d + \angle e + 90° = 360°$

[$\because \angle x = 90°$]

$\Rightarrow \angle a + \angle b + \angle c + \angle d + \angle e = 360° - 90°$

$= 270° = 3 \times 90°$

10. *(b)* In $\triangle ABC$,

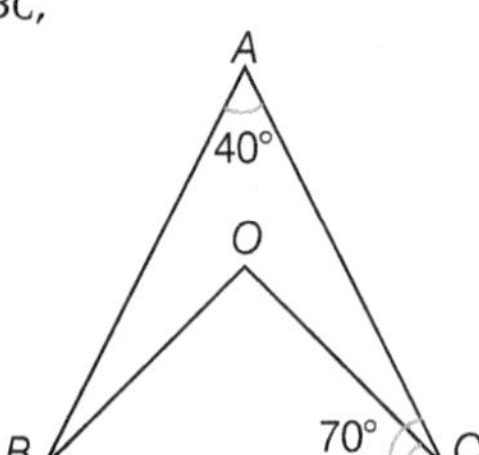

$\angle A + \angle B + \angle C = 180°$ [angle sum property]

$40° + \angle B + 70° = 180°$

$\Rightarrow$ $110° + \angle B = 180° \Rightarrow \angle B = 70°$

Now OB and OC are bisectors of $\angle B$ and $\angle C$, respectively

$\therefore$ $\angle OBC = \angle OCB = 35°$

Now, $\angle BOC = 180° - (\angle OBC + \angle OCB)$

$= 180° - (35° + 35°) = 180° - 70° = 110°$

11. *(b)* In $\triangle PSQ$ and $\triangle PSR$,

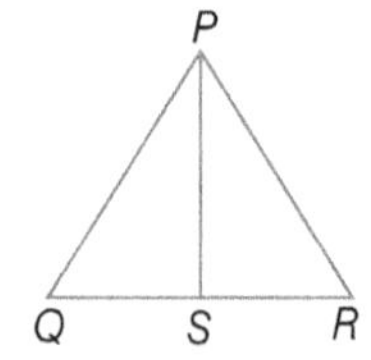

$\angle PSQ = \angle PSR$ [90°]

$PQ = PR$ [given]

$PS = PS$ [common]

$\therefore$ $\triangle PQS \cong \triangle PRS$ [by RHS rule

12. *(b)*

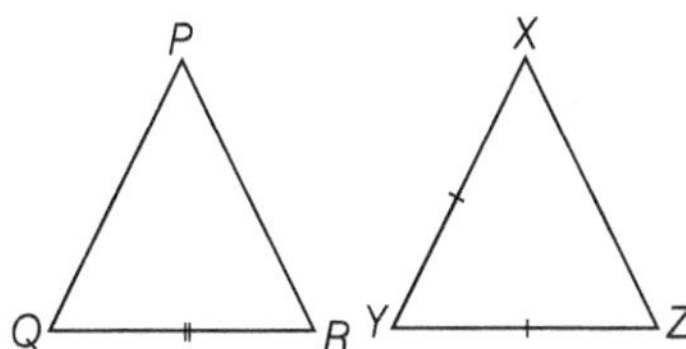

In ΔPQR and ΔXYZ
$$PQ = XY \text{ and } QR = YZ$$
when $\angle Q = \angle Y$
Then, $\Delta PQR \cong \Delta XYZ$ [by SAS property]

13. *(d)* In, ΔPRS and ΔPRQ,

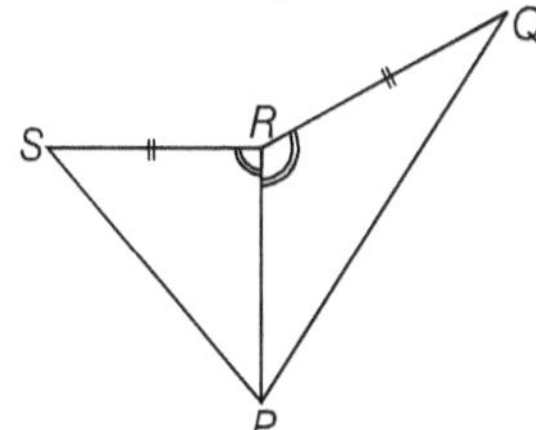

$PR = PR$	[common side]
$\angle PRQ = \angle PRS$	[given]
$RQ = RS$	[given]

So, $\Delta PRS \cong \Delta PRQ$
$\Rightarrow$ $PS = PQ$ [by CPCT]
and $\angle PSR = \angle PQR$ [by CPCT]
So, all options are true.

14. *(a)* I. True.

The SSS rule states that: If 3 sides of 1 triangle are equal to 3 sides of another triangle, then the triangles are congruent.

II. False.

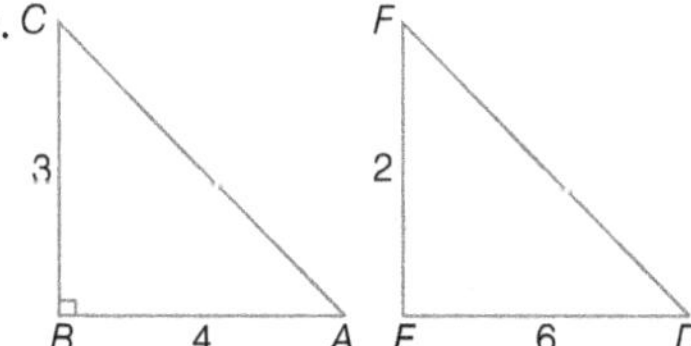

Area of ΔABC and ΔDEF are not equal but ΔABC and ΔDEF not congruent.

III. True

Congruent figures will coincide each other.

15. *(d)*

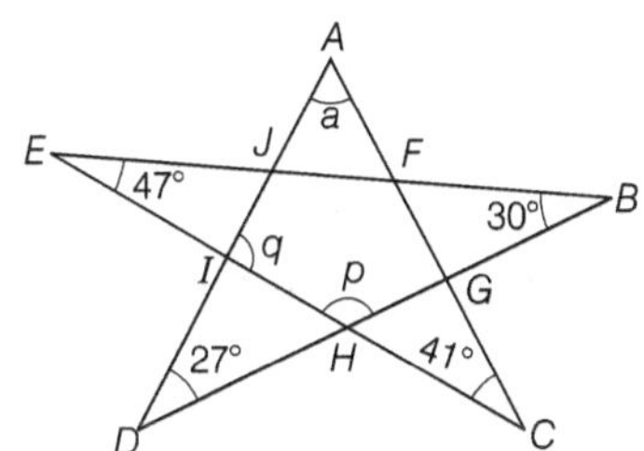

Consider ΔHEB,
$$\angle p + \angle HEB + \angle HBE = 180°$$
$\Rightarrow$ $\angle p + 47° + 30° = 180°$
$\Rightarrow$ $\angle p = 180° - 77° = 103°$
$\therefore$ $\angle DIH = 103° - 27°$ [exterior angle property]
$$= 76°$$
Now, $\angle q = 180° - 76° = 104°$ [linear pair]
In ΔIAC,
     $\angle q + \angle a + \angle ACI = 180°$ [sum of three angles]
$\Rightarrow$ $104° + \angle a + 41° = 180°$
$\Rightarrow$ $145° + \angle a = 180° \Rightarrow \angle a = 180° - 145°$
$\therefore$ $\angle a = 35°$

16. *(c)* In the given figure,

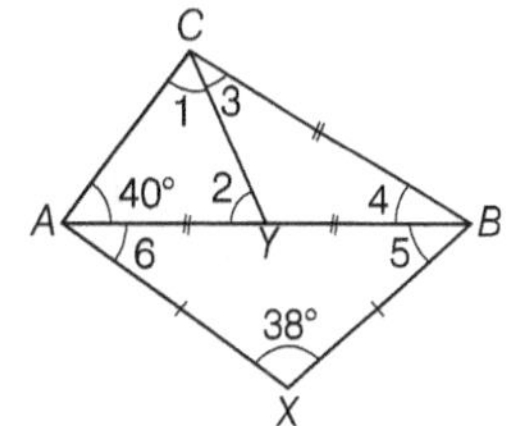

$$AY = CY \quad \Rightarrow \quad \angle 1 = 40°$$
[angle opposite to equal sides are also equal]
Also, $\angle 1 + \angle 2 + \angle CAY = 180°$
                              [angle sum property]
     $\angle 2 = 180° - (40° + 40°) = 180° - 80°$
     $\angle CYA = \angle 2 = 100°$
$\therefore$ $\angle CYB = 180° - 100° = 80°$
In ΔCYB, $80 + \angle 4 + \angle 3 = 180°$
$\Rightarrow$ $2\angle 3 = 100°$ $[\because \angle 3 = \angle 4]$
$\Rightarrow$ $\angle 4 = 50°$
In ΔAXB, $6 + 38° + \angle 5 = 180°$
$\Rightarrow$ $2\angle 5 = 142°$ $[\because \angle 5 = \angle 6]$
$\Rightarrow$ $\angle 5 = 71°$
Now, $\angle CBX = \angle 4 + \angle 5 = 50° + 71° = 121°$

17. *(c)*

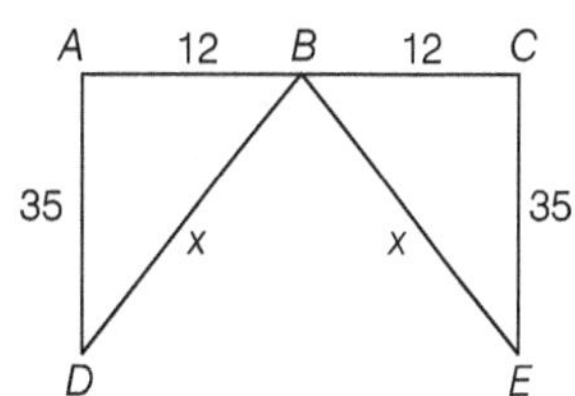

In the given figure, ΔDAB and ΔECB are right angled triangles at A and C, respectively.
Consider ΔBAD, BD is the hypotenuse.
$\therefore$ $BD^2 = AD^2 + AB^2$
$\Rightarrow$ $x^2 = 35^2 + 12^2$
$\Rightarrow$ $x^2 = 1225 + 144$

$\Rightarrow \qquad x^2 = 1369$

$\Rightarrow \qquad x = \sqrt{1369} \Rightarrow x = 37$

18. *(c)* In the given figure,

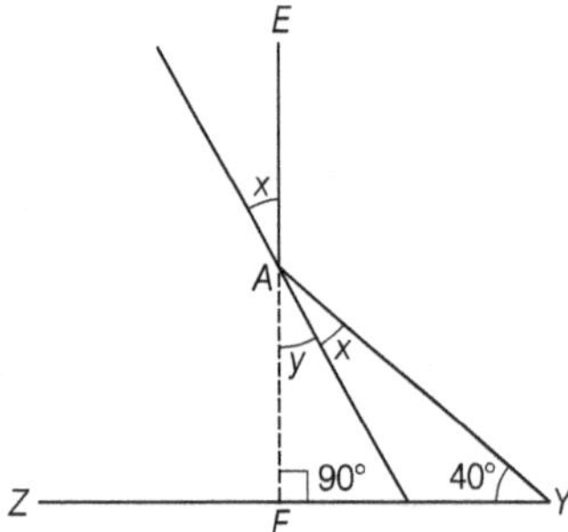

In $\triangle AFY$,

Here, $\angle AFY + \angle AYF + \angle FAY = 180°$

$\qquad\qquad\qquad\qquad$ [angle sum property]

$\Rightarrow \qquad 90° + 40° + \angle FAY = 180°$

$\Rightarrow \qquad\qquad\qquad \angle FAY = 50°$

$\Rightarrow \qquad\qquad\qquad \angle x + \angle y = 50°$

$\Rightarrow \qquad\qquad\qquad 2\angle x = 50° \quad [\because \angle x = \angle y]$

$\Rightarrow \qquad\qquad\qquad \angle x = 25°$

19. *(b)*

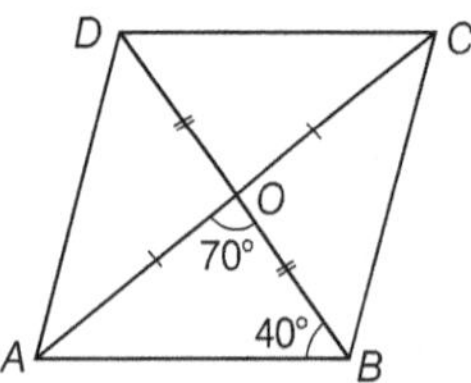

Given, $ABCD$ is a parallelogram.

then $AB \| CD$ and DB transversal

$\therefore \quad \angle ODC = 40°$

$\qquad \angle COD = \angle AOB = 70°$ (vertically opposite)

In $\triangle OCD$, $\angle ODC + \angle COD + \angle OCD = 180°$

$\Rightarrow \qquad 40° + 70° + \angle OCD = 180°$

$\Rightarrow \qquad \angle OCD = 180° - 110° = 70°$

20. *(c)* In $\triangle DRA$ and $\triangle DRG$,

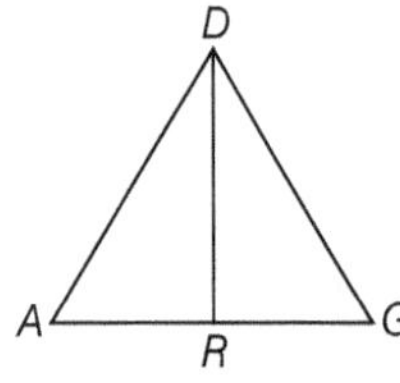

$\qquad\qquad \angle DRA = \angle DRG \qquad [DR \perp AG]$

$\qquad\qquad DR = DR \qquad\qquad$ [common]

if $\qquad\qquad RA = RG$ or $DA = DG$

Then, $\qquad\qquad \triangle DRA \cong \triangle DRG \qquad$ [by SAS rule]

21. *(c)*

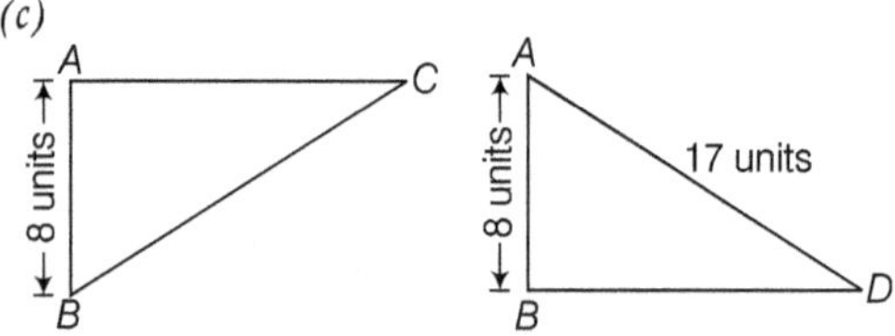

Consider, $\triangle ABD$ which is a right angled triangle.

$\therefore \qquad\qquad AD^2 = AB^2 + BD^2$

$\Rightarrow \qquad\qquad 17^2 = 8^2 + BD^2$

$\Rightarrow \qquad\qquad BD^2 = 289 - 64$

$\Rightarrow \qquad\qquad BD^2 = 225$

$\Rightarrow \qquad\qquad BD = 15$

From the given conditions,

$\qquad\qquad \triangle ABC \cong \triangle ABD$

$\Rightarrow \qquad\qquad BC = BD \qquad\qquad$ [by CPCT]

$\therefore \qquad\qquad BC = 15 \text{ units}$

Chapter 13 : Symmetry

1. *(d)*

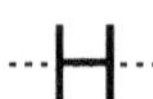

H has a horizontal line of symmetry.

2. *(d)*

All letters have vertical lines of symmetry.

3. *(d)* The letters Q and F have no line of symmetry.
The letter C has one line of symmetry.
Only letter O has more than one line of symmetry.

4. *(c)* An Isosceles triangle has only one line of symmetry.
Scalene triangle has no line of symmetry.
Semi-circle has only one line of symmetry.
Rectangle have two lines of symmetry.

5. *(d)*

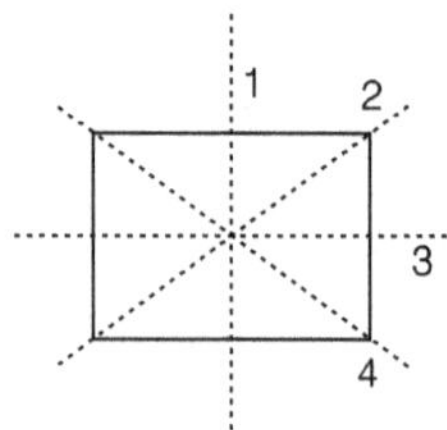

$\therefore$ A square has four lines of symmetry.

6. *(b)* I. Rectangle has order of symmetry equal to 2.
II. This figure has no order of symmetry.
III. It has 6 order of symmetry.

7. *(b)*

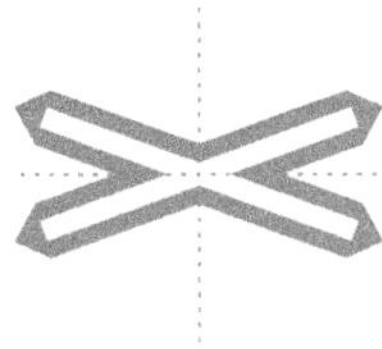

There are 2 lines of symmetry.

8. *(c)*

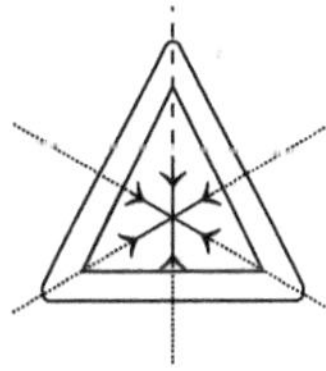

∴ For the given figure, the number of lines of symmetry = 3

9. *(d)*

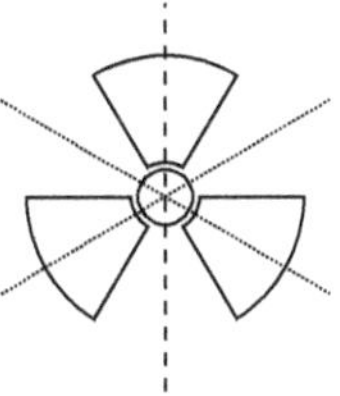

It has 3 lines of symmetry.

10. *(b)*

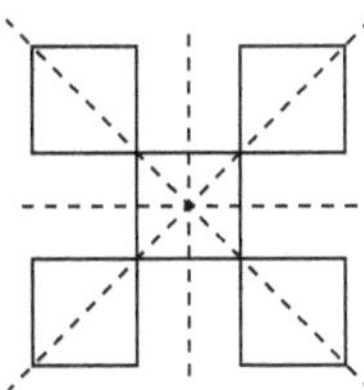

It has 4 lines of symmetry.

11. *(b)* Other figures have more than one line of symmetry except figure (b).

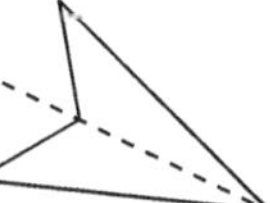

12. *(a)* The minimum number of square that must be shaded is 1.

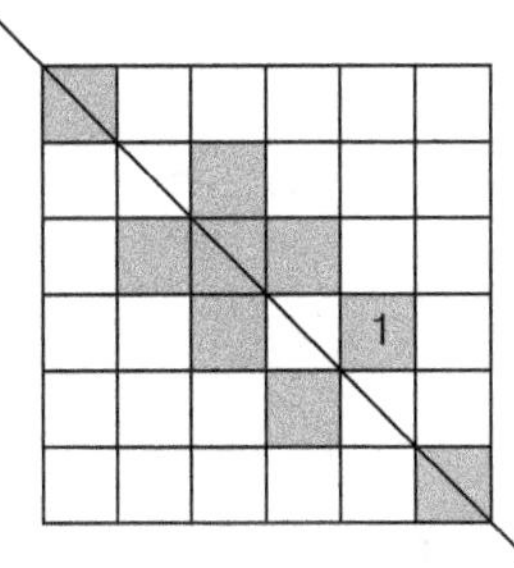

13. *(b)* I. It has one line of symmetry.
II. It has no line of symmetry.
III. It has four lines of symmetry.

14. *(d)* A circle has an infinite order of rotational symmetry.

15. *(d)*

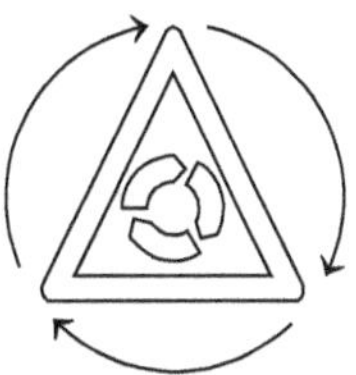

It has 3 as the order of symmetry.

16. *(a)* The given figure has 3 as the order of symmetry.

17. *(c)*

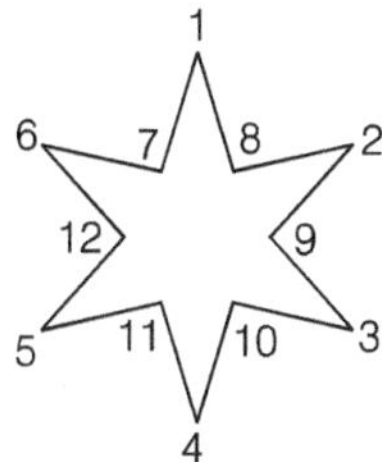

So, it has 12 corners.

18. *(c)* The solid figure has 3 faces.

19. *(d)* The given figure has 10 as the order of symmetry. So, it has 10 faces.

20. *(d)*

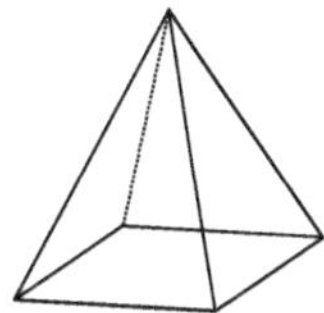

The figure formed is a pyramid.

21. *(a)* The given figure has the following conditions.
1 is opposite to 3.   2 is opposite to 4.
5 is opposite to 6.

22. *(b)* The top view of the given figure is

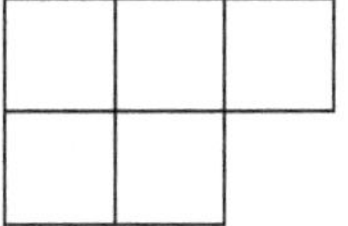

Hence, the correct option is (b).

23. *(c)* I. On rotating the given shape by 90°, the shape remains same. Thus, the order of rotational symmetry of the given shape is 4.

II. Oval fits on to itself 2 time during a full rotation of 360°.

So, oval has rotational symmetry of order 2.

III. If we rotate equilateral triangle by 120° it will always look the same.

∴ Order of rotation is 3 for equilateral triangle.

IV. Figure IV is a hexagon whose all sides are equal.

∴ The order of rotation for hexagon is 6.

24. *(c)* 18 cubes are needed to make the given figure.

25. *(c)* The given figure is a net for triangular pyramid. So, figures (iii) and (iv) are formed by given figure.

26. *(b)* Prism is formed by the given net.

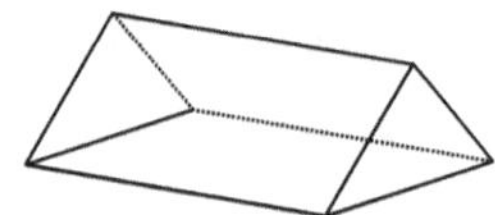

Chapter 14. Area and Perimeter

1. *(a)* Let the length and breadth of the rectangle be l and b, respectively and breadth $x\%$ decreases.

Then, new length $= \dfrac{125}{100}\, l$ and new breadth

$$= \dfrac{(100 - x)b}{100}$$

According to the question, area of the rectangle remains same.

$$\therefore \qquad lb = \dfrac{125}{100}\, l \times \dfrac{(100 - x)}{100}\, b$$

$$\Rightarrow \qquad 100 - x = 80 \quad \therefore \quad x = 20\%$$

2. *(d)* Let breadth of rectangular hall be x m.

∴ Length of rectangular hall is $(x + 5)$ m

According to the question,

$$(x + 5)x = 750$$

$$\Rightarrow \qquad x^2 + 5x - 750 = 0$$

$$\Rightarrow x^2 + 30x - 25x - 750 = 0$$

$$\Rightarrow \quad x(x + 30) - 25(x + 30) = 0$$

$$\Rightarrow \qquad (x - 25)\,(x + 30) = 0$$

$$\Rightarrow \qquad\qquad x = 25 \qquad [\because x \ne -30]$$

Hence, length of hall $= 25 + 5 = 30$ m

3. *(a)* Let $l = 4x$ and $b = 3x$ ∴ Area $= 4x \times 3x$

$$\Rightarrow \dfrac{1}{12} \times 10000 = 4x \times 3x \quad [1 \text{ hecture} = 10000\,\text{m}^2]$$

$$\Rightarrow \qquad x^2 = \dfrac{10000}{12 \times 12} \quad \Rightarrow \quad x = \dfrac{100}{12}$$

Hence, breadth of the lawn $= \dfrac{3 \times 100}{12} = 25$ m

4. *(b)* Required number of tiles $= \dfrac{\text{Area of wall}}{\text{Area of 1 marble}}$

$$= \dfrac{1600 \times 1800}{40 \times 60} = 1200$$

5. *(a)* Let $l = 9x$ and $b = 4x$

Area of rectangle $= l \times b$

$$\Rightarrow \qquad 144 = 9x \times 4x \Rightarrow \ x^2 = \dfrac{144}{36} \Rightarrow x^2 = 4$$

$$\Rightarrow \qquad x = 2$$

∴ $l = 18$ cm and $b = 8$ cm

Hence, perimeter of rectangle $= 2(l + b)$

$$= 2(18 + 8) = 2 \times 26 = 52\,\text{cm}$$

6. *(c)* ∵ Diagonal $= 20$ cm (Given)

$$\text{Area of square} = \dfrac{(\text{Diagonal})^2}{2}$$

$$\therefore \qquad \text{Area} = \dfrac{20 \times 20}{2} = \dfrac{400}{2} = 200\,\text{m}^2$$

7. *(a)* In $\triangle ABC$, by Pythagoras theorem,

$$(AB)^2 = (AC)^2 - (BC)^2$$

$$\Rightarrow \qquad AB = \sqrt{(20)^2 - (9)^2} = \sqrt{319}$$

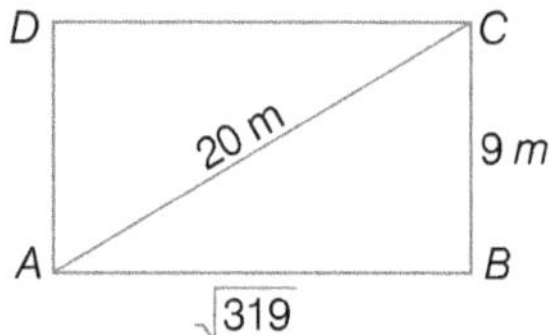

∴ Required area $=$ Length $\times$ Breadth $= 9\sqrt{319}$ sq m

8. *(c)* Dimensions of the box,

Length, $l = 10$ cm   Breadth, $b = 8$ cm

Height, $h = 6$ cm

∴ The maximum length of a pen that can be kept in

a rectangular box $= \sqrt{l^2 + b^2 + h^2}$

$$= \sqrt{10^2 + 8^2 + 6^2} = \sqrt{100 + 64 + 36}$$

$$= \sqrt{200} = 10\sqrt{2}\,\text{cm}$$

9. *(d)* ∵ $d = 15\sqrt{2}$ cm

$$\therefore \text{Area of square} = \dfrac{1}{2}d^2 = \dfrac{1}{2} \times (15\sqrt{2})^2$$

$$= 15 \times 15 = 225\,\text{sq.cm}$$

10. *(d)* Here, $a = 30$ cm, $b = 20$ cm, $c = 40$ cm

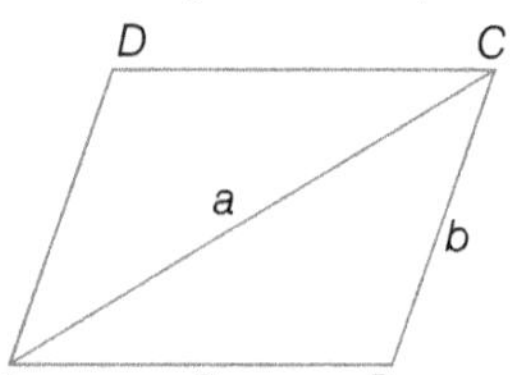

$$\Rightarrow s = \dfrac{a + b + c}{2} = \dfrac{30 + 20 + 40}{2} = 45\,\text{cm}$$

∴ Area of $\triangle ABC$

$$= \sqrt{s(s-a)\,(s-b)\,(s-c)}$$
$$= \sqrt{45 \times (45-30)\,(45-20)\,(45-40)}$$
$$= \sqrt{45 \times 15 \times 25 \times 5} = 75\sqrt{15}\ \text{cm}^2$$

Hence, area of parallelogram gm
$$ABCD = 2 \times \text{area}(\Delta ABC)$$
$$= 2 \times 75\sqrt{15} = 150\sqrt{15}\ \text{cm}^2$$

11. *(a)* Base of the parallelogram
$$AFCE = AF = \frac{1}{2}\ AB$$
$$\therefore \qquad AF = \frac{1}{2} \times 30\ \text{cm} = 15\ \text{cm}$$

and Height of the parallelogram, $AFCE = BC = 12\,\text{cm}$
$\therefore$ Area of parallelogram $AFCF = \text{Base} \times \text{Height}$
$$= (15 \times 12)\ \text{cm}^2$$
$$= 180\ \text{cm}^2$$

$\therefore$ Area of shaded region
$$= \text{ar}\ ABCD - \text{ar}\ AFCE$$
$$= (30 \times 12 - 180)$$
$$= 360 - 180 = 180\ \text{cm}^2$$

12. *(d)*

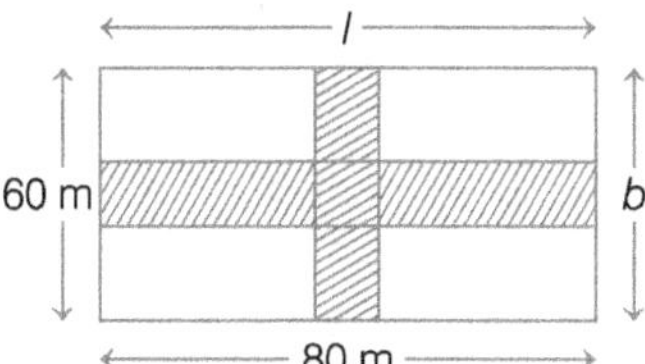

width of the road $= 10\ \text{cm}$
Area of roods $= 80 \times 10 + 60 \times 10 - 10 \times 10$
$$= 800 + 600 - 100 = 1300\ \text{sq m}$$

13. *(a)* $\because$ Area of equilateral triangle $= 4\sqrt{3}\ \text{cm}^2$
$$\Rightarrow\ \frac{\sqrt{3}}{4}\,a^2 = 4\sqrt{3}\ \Rightarrow\ a = 4\ \text{cm}\ [a \to \text{side}]$$
$\therefore$ Perimeter of the triangle $= 3 \times a = 3 \times 4 = 12\,\text{cm}$

14. *(b)* $\because b_1 = 15\,\text{cm}$ and $h_1 = 12\,\text{cm}$
$$\text{Area of Ist triangle} = \frac{1}{2} \times b_1 \times h_1 = \frac{1}{2} \times 15 \times 12$$
$$= 90\ \text{cm}^2$$
$\Rightarrow$ Area of 2nd triangle $= 2 \times 90 = 180\ \text{cm}^2$
$$\Rightarrow\ \frac{1}{2} \times b_2 \times h_2 = 180 \Rightarrow \frac{1}{2} \times 20 \times h_2 = 180$$
$$\Rightarrow\ h_2 = \frac{180}{10} = 18$$
Hence, height of another triangle $= 18\,\text{cm}$

15. *(b)* Let each equal sides of isosceles right angle triangle be x cm.

In ΔABC,

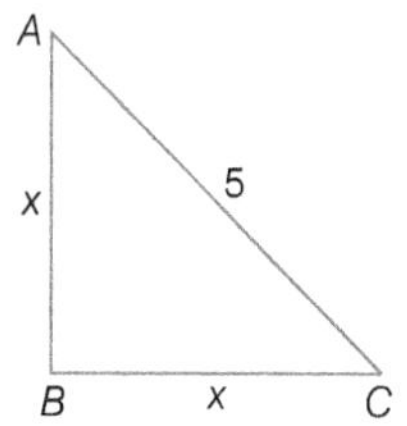

$$AB^2 + BC^2 = AC^2 \quad \Rightarrow \quad x^2 + x^2 = 25$$
$$\Rightarrow \qquad 2x^2 = 25 \quad \Rightarrow \quad x = \frac{5}{\sqrt{2}}$$

Hence, area of triangle $= \frac{1}{2} \times AB \times BC$
$$= \frac{1}{2} \times \frac{5}{\sqrt{2}} \times \frac{5}{\sqrt{2}} = \frac{25}{4} = 6.25\ \text{cm}^2$$

16. *(b)* Let r and a be the radius of a circle and side of a square respectively.
According to the question,
perimeter of circle = perimeter of square
$$\Rightarrow \qquad 2\pi r = 4a \ \Rightarrow\ a = \frac{\pi r}{2}$$
$\therefore$ Area of circle $= \pi r^2 = 3.14 r^2$

Area of square $= a^2 = \frac{\pi^2 r^2}{4} = 2.46\ r^2$

$\therefore$ Clearly the area of circle is larger than the area of square.

17. *(c)* Let the radius of the outer circle and the inner circle be R and r respectively.
Circumference of outer circle $= 2\pi R$
Circumference of inner circle $= 2\pi r$
According to the question,
$$2\pi R - 2\pi r = 132$$
$$\therefore \qquad (R - r) = \frac{132}{2\pi} = \frac{132 \times 7}{2 \times 22} = 21$$
$\therefore$ Width of the road $= 21\ \text{m}$

18. *(b)* Let r be the radius of the field.
Area of circular field $= 61600\ \text{m}^2$
$$\Rightarrow\ \pi r^2 = 61600$$
$$\Rightarrow\ r^2 = \frac{61600 \times 7}{22} \ \Rightarrow\ r^2 = 19600 \quad \therefore \quad r = 140\,\text{m}$$
$\therefore$ Circumference of the circular field $= 2\pi r$
$$= 2 \times \frac{22}{7} \times 140 = 880\ \text{m}$$
$\therefore$ Cost of fencing $= ₹\ (880 \times 10.6) = ₹\ 9328$

19. *(c)* According to the question,
Radius of the circle $= 28$ cm
Length of filament = Circumference of the circle $= 2\pi r$
$$= 2\pi \times 28 = 176\ \text{cm}$$

Let side of the square be 'a' cm.

Perimeter of square = Length of filament

$\therefore \quad 4a = 176 \Rightarrow a = \dfrac{176}{4} \Rightarrow a = 44\,\text{cm}$

20. *(c)* Let sides of square field be r m.

$\therefore$ Radius of circle $= r$ m

According to the question, $2\pi r - 4r = 32$

$\Rightarrow \qquad 2r(\pi - 2) = 32$

$\Rightarrow \qquad r\left(\dfrac{22 - 14}{7}\right) = 16 \Rightarrow r = \dfrac{16 \times 7}{8} = 14\,\text{m}$

Hence, perimeter of square field $= 4r$

$\qquad\qquad = 4 \times 14 = 56\,\text{m}$

21. *(c)* **I.** True.

As circumference $= 2 \times \pi \times r$

$\qquad 2 \times \dfrac{22}{7} \times r = 22\,\text{cm} \quad \Rightarrow \quad r = 3.5\,\text{cm}$

$\therefore$ Area $= \pi r^2 = \dfrac{22}{7} \times (3.5)^2 = \dfrac{77}{2} = 38.5\,\text{cm}^2$

II. True.

Let the side of 2 squares be x and y respectively.

$\therefore \qquad \dfrac{x^2}{y^2} = \dfrac{256}{324} = \dfrac{16 \times 16}{18 \times 18} \quad \Rightarrow \quad \dfrac{x}{y} = \dfrac{8}{9}$

Ratio of perimeters of squares $= \dfrac{4x}{4y} = \dfrac{x}{y} = \dfrac{8}{9} = \dfrac{16}{8}$

III. True. As perimeter of square $= 4a$ then Area $= a^2$

Now, perimeter of new square $= 2 \times 4a$

Then side $= 2a$

$\therefore$ Area $= (2a)^2 = 4a^2$

$\therefore$ Required Ratio $= a^2 : 4a^2 = 1 : 4$

22. *(a)* As 4 quadrants make a circle.

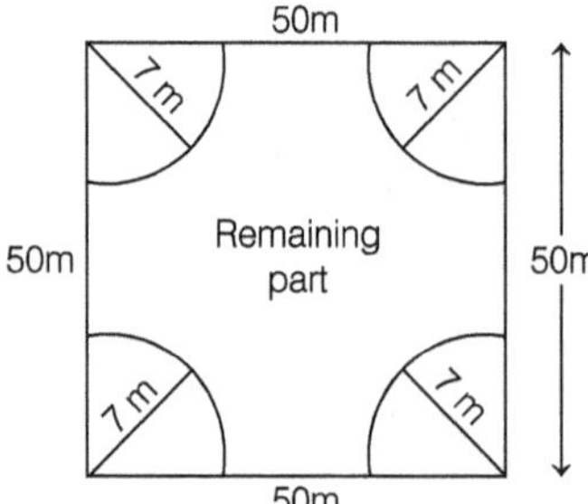

$\therefore$ Area of remaining part = Area of square – Area of

circle $= \left[(50)^2 - \left(\dfrac{22}{7}\right) \times 7 \times 7\right]$

$\qquad = [2500 - 154] = 2346\,\text{sq m}$

23. *(c)* Let, a_1 and a_2 are the sides of the squares.

then, $a_1 = \dfrac{68}{4} = 17\,\text{cm}$ and $a_2 = \dfrac{60}{4} = 15\,\text{cm}$

According to the question,

Area of the 3rd square $= [(17)^2 - (15)^2]$

$\qquad = (17 + 15)\,(17 - 15) = 32 \times 2 = 64\,\text{sq cm}$

Let a_3 be the side of the 3rd square.

According to the question,

$\qquad (a_3)^2 = 64\,\text{sq cm} \Rightarrow a_3 = \sqrt{64} = 8\,\text{cm}$

$\therefore$ Perimeter of the 3rd square

$\qquad = 4 \times a_3 = 4 \times 8 = 32\,\text{cm}$

24. *(a)* Let $AB = CA = a$ cm and base $= b$ cm

Now, area of $\Delta ABC = \dfrac{1}{2} \times b \times h$

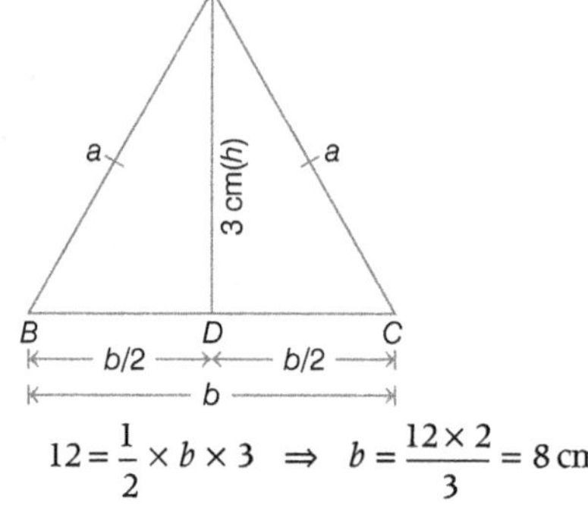

$\Rightarrow \qquad 12 = \dfrac{1}{2} \times b \times 3 \quad \Rightarrow \quad b = \dfrac{12 \times 2}{3} = 8\,\text{cm}$

Here, $\qquad BD = CD = \dfrac{b}{2} = \dfrac{8}{2} = 4\,\text{cm}$

In right angled ΔABD, by Pythagoras theorem,

$\qquad AB = \sqrt{BD^2 + AD^2}$

$\Rightarrow \qquad a = \sqrt{4^2 + 3^2} = \sqrt{16 + 9} = \sqrt{25} = 5\,\text{cm}$

Now, perimeter of the isosceles triangle

$\qquad = 2a + b = 2 \times 5 + 8 = 10 + 8 = 18\,\text{cm}$

25. *(d)* Let breadth of the rectangle be b.

Then, length $= (b + 3)$

According to the question,

$\qquad 2(b + b + 3) = 50 \quad \Rightarrow \quad 2b + 3 = 25$

$\Rightarrow \qquad 2b = 22 \quad \Rightarrow \quad b = \dfrac{22}{2} = 11\,\text{cm}$

$\therefore$ Breadth $= 11$ cm and length $= (11 + 3) = 14\,\text{cm}$

$\therefore$ Area of the circle = Area of the rectangle

$\Rightarrow \qquad \pi r^2 = 14 \times 11 \quad \Rightarrow \quad r^2 = \dfrac{14 \times 11 \times 7}{22} = 49$

$\therefore \qquad r = \sqrt{49} = 7\,\text{cm}$

$\therefore$ Diameter $= 2r = 2 \times 7 = 14\,\text{cm}$

26. *(a)* Let the side of the square be a.

$\therefore$ Area of the square $= a \times a = a^2$

Now, area of $\Delta AEF = $ (Area of square) $-$ (Area of

$\Delta ABE + $ Area of $\Delta CEF + $ Area of ΔADF)

$$= a^2 - \left(\frac{1}{2} \times a \times \frac{a}{2} + \frac{1}{2} \times \frac{a}{2} \times \frac{a}{2} + \frac{1}{2} \times a \times \frac{a}{2} \right)$$

$$= a^2 - \left(\frac{a^2}{4} + \frac{a^2}{8} + \frac{a^2}{4} \right) = a^2 - \frac{5a^2}{8} = \frac{3a^2}{8} \quad ...(ii)$$

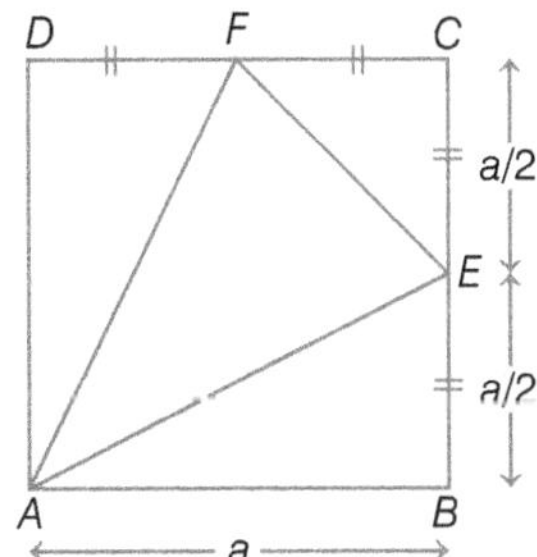

Area of $\triangle AEF$: Area of square $ABCD = \frac{3a^2}{8} : a^2 = 3 : 8$

27. *(d)* Diagonal of a square $= \sqrt{2} \times$ Side

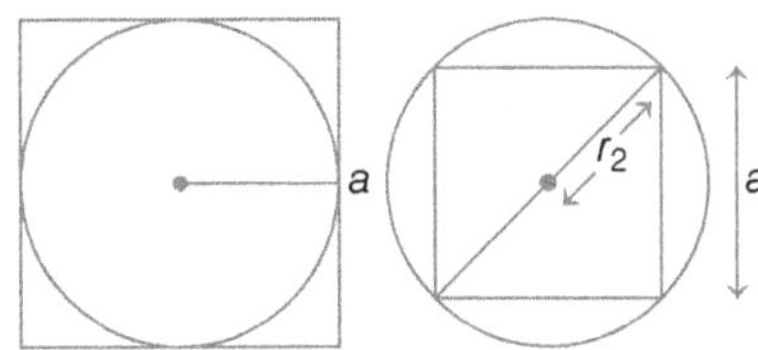

$\therefore$ Ratio of area of smaller circle to larger circle

$$= \frac{\pi r_1^2}{\pi r_2^2} = \frac{\pi \times \left(\dfrac{a}{2} \right)^2}{\pi \times \left(\dfrac{\sqrt{2}a}{2} \right)^2} \quad [\text{here, } a = \text{side of square}]$$

$$= \frac{1}{2} = 1 : 2$$

28. *(c)* Here, shaded part *ABCD* can be visualised as $\triangle ABD + \triangle BCD$.

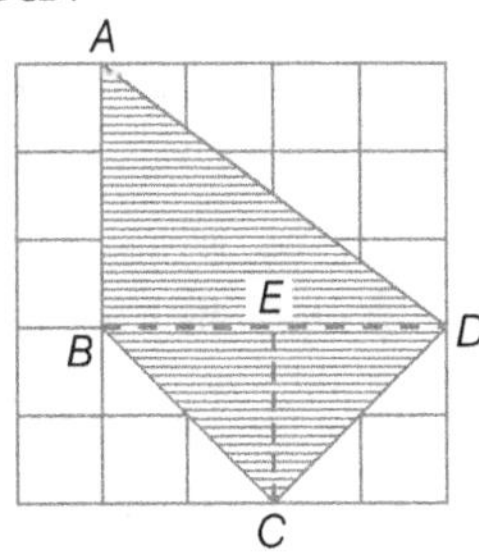

$\therefore$ Area of shaded region

$= $ Area of $\triangle ABD + $ Area of $\triangle BCD$

$$= \frac{1}{2} \times AB \times BD + \frac{1}{2} \times CE \times BD$$

$$= \frac{1}{2} \times 3 \times 4 + \frac{1}{2} \times 2 \times 4 = 6 + 4 = 10 \text{ sq cm}$$

Chapter 15. Data Handling

1. *(a)* Ordering the hourly wages from least to greatest, we get

₹ 725, ₹ 750, ₹ 850, ₹ 875, ₹ 925, ₹ 950

Range = Highest − Lowest = ₹ 950 − ₹ 725 = ₹ 225

2. *(c)* Given data 8, 11, 19, 14, 13, 18, 26, x, $2x$, 5

Sum of given data

$= 8 + 11 + 19 + 14 + 13 + 18 + 26 + x + 2x + 5$

$= 114 + 3x$

$\because$ Mean $= \dfrac{\text{Sum of observations}}{\text{Number of observations}}$

$\Rightarrow \quad 36 = \dfrac{114 + 3x}{10} \Rightarrow 36 \times 10 = 114 + 3x$

$\Rightarrow \quad 360 - 114 = 3x \Rightarrow 3x = 246 \Rightarrow x = \dfrac{246}{3} = 82$

3. *(a)* Mean $= \dfrac{0 + 1 + 2 + 3 + 4 + 5 + 6 + 7 + 8 + 9}{10}$

$\qquad = \dfrac{45}{10} = 4.5$

4. *(c)* $\because$ The average cost of 5 mangoes = ₹ 10

$\therefore$ Total cost of 5 mangoes $= 10 \times 5 = $ ₹ 50

$\because$ The average cost of 3 mangoes = ₹ 9

$\therefore$ Total cost of 3 mangoes = ₹ 27

Cost of the remaining 2 mangoes = 50 − 27 = ₹ 23

$\therefore$ Average of remaining 2 mangoes $= \dfrac{23}{2} = $ ₹ 11.5

5. *(b)* Total temperature on Wednesday, Thursday and Friday was $25 \times 3 = 75°$

Total temperature on Thursday, Friday and Saturday was $24 \times 3 = 72°$

Hence, the difference between the temperature on Wednesday and Saturday = 3°

If Saturday's temperature = 28°, then Wednesday's temperature = 28 + 3 = 31°

6. *(b)* The marks in the ascending order are

12, 17, 19, 27, 36, 38, 39, 42, 47, 48, 61, 65, 68, 78, 84.

$\qquad n = 15$ which is odd

$\therefore$ Median $= \left(\dfrac{15 + 1}{2} \right)$th term = 8th term = 42

7. *(d)* Given observation in ascending order

10, 12, 14, 15, 16, $(x + 2)$, 22, 24, 25, 29, 30

$n = 11$ (odd) $\quad \therefore$ median $= \dfrac{n + 1}{2}$th term

$\Rightarrow \quad 26 = $ 6th term $\Rightarrow 26 = x + 2 \Rightarrow x = 24$

8. *(a)* According to question,

The mode of the distribution is 30 as it has the maximum frequency.

9. *(b)* Ascending order of the given data without x

14, 25, 25, 25, 26, 28, 28, 28, 30, 30, 30, 40, 40, 40

There are frequencies of 25, 28, 30, 40 same.

$\because$ Mode $= 40$ $\therefore x = 40$

10. *(d)* Average sales of brand B

$= \dfrac{\text{Total sales of brand } B \text{ in 6 months from January to June}}{6}$

$= \dfrac{36 + 38 + 43 + 35 + 45 + 54}{6} = \dfrac{251}{6} = ₹\ 41.83 \text{ lakh}$

11. *(d)* Average cost $= \dfrac{82 + 45 + 75 + 20 + 38}{5} = 52$

12. *(b)* According to the question,

Total number of trials $= 100$, number of heads $= 59$

$\therefore$ Probability of getting a head

$= \dfrac{\text{Number of heads in trials}}{\text{Total number of trials}} = \dfrac{59}{100}$

13. *(c)* Frequency of getting an even number

$=$ Frequency of getting $2 +$ Frequency of getting 4

$+$ Frequency of getting $6 = 45 + 46 + 71 = 162$

$\therefore$ Probability of getting an even number

$= \dfrac{162}{300} = \dfrac{81}{150} = \dfrac{27}{50}$

14. *(a)* According to the question,

$P(\text{picking a white ball}) + P(\text{picking a green ball}) = 1$

$\dfrac{x}{2} + \dfrac{2}{3} = 1 \quad \Rightarrow \quad 3x + 4 = 6$

$\Rightarrow \quad 3x = 2 \Rightarrow x = \dfrac{2}{3}$

15. *(a)* Total number of Sample space $= 25 \times 25$

Favourable cases of their winning $= 25$

$\therefore$ Probability (they win a prize) $= \dfrac{25}{(25 \times 25)} = \dfrac{1}{25}$

$\therefore$ Probability (they will not win a prize)

$= 1 - \dfrac{1}{25} = \dfrac{24}{25}$

16. *(c)* $n(S) = \{(HHH), (HTH), (THH), (HHT), (THT), (TTH), (HTT), (TTT)\} = 2^3 = 8$

Let $E =$ Event of getting exactly 2 heads

$= \{(H, H, T), (H, T, H), (T, H, H)\} \Rightarrow n(E) = 3$

$\therefore$ Required probability $= \dfrac{n(E)}{n(S)} = \dfrac{3}{8}$

17. *(a)* The mean age of Ist 10 students $= 18\,\text{yr}$

$\therefore$ Their total age $= 10 \times 18 = 180\,\text{yr}$

Now, the mean age of the 12 students

$= 18 + 2 = 20\,\text{yr}$

$\therefore$ Their total age $= 12 \times 20 = 240\,\text{yr}$

The age of the 2 new students $= 240 - 180 = 60\,\text{yr}$

$\therefore$ The mean of the age of the 2 added students is

$= \dfrac{60}{2} = 30\,\text{yr}$

18. *(d)* According to the question,

$a = \dfrac{x + x + 1 + x + 2 + x + 3 + x + 4}{5}$

$\Rightarrow 5a = 5x + 10 \Rightarrow a = x + 2$

$\Rightarrow x = a - 2 \qquad\qquad \ldots \text{(i)}$

Required mean

$= \dfrac{x + 2 + x + 3 + \ldots\ldots\ldots\ldots + x + 10}{9}$

$= \dfrac{9x + 54}{9} = x + 6 = a - 2 + 6 = a + 4 \,[\text{from Eq. (i)}]$

19. *(d)* Total marks of remaining 100 students

$= 300 \times 60 - 100 \times 80 - 100 \times 50$

$= 18000 - 8000 - 5000 = 18000 - 13000 = 5000$

$\therefore$ Mean marks of remaining 100 students

$= \dfrac{5000}{100} = 50$

20. *(a)* Given, mean of 5 observations is 9.

$\therefore \dfrac{\text{Sum of 5 observations}}{\text{Number of observations}} = 9$

$\Rightarrow$ Sum of 5 observations $= 9 \times 5 = 45$

If 1 is subtracted from each observation, then

New means of 5 observations

$= \dfrac{\text{Sum of 5 observations} - 5}{5} = \dfrac{45 - 5}{5} = \dfrac{40}{5} = 8$

Median of 5 observations $= \left(\dfrac{5 + 1}{2}\right)$th term

$= 3\text{rd term} = 8$

If 1 is subtracted from each observation, then

New median $= 8 - 1 = 7$

Hence, the new mean and median are 8 and 7 respectively.

21. *(a)* Total number of boys in schools B and C together $= 350 + 300 = 650$

Total number of girls in schools B and C together $= 140 + 160 = 300$

$\therefore$ Required difference $= 650 - 300 = 350$

22. *(b)* Total number of students Studying in class X of school $E = 210 + 380 = 590$

According to the question,

Number of students Studying in class IX of the school $E = \dfrac{590 \times 80}{100} = 472$

23. *(c)* From graph, Total number of toys sold

$= 30 + 80 + 40 + 60 + 70 = 280$

$\therefore$ Total money earn $= 280 \times 40 = ₹\ 11200$

Practice Set 1

1. *(c)* Let the angle be x.

$\therefore$ Complementary angle $= 90° - x$

According to the question, $3x = 2(90° - x)$

$\Rightarrow \qquad 5x = 180° \Rightarrow x = 36°$

2. *(a)* Consider, $- [10 \times (-2) + (-25)] \div (-5)$

$= -[-20 - 25] \div (-5)$

$= -[-45] \div (-5) = 45 \div (-5) = -9$

3. *(d)* Given, $7y - 9 = -4 \Rightarrow 7y = -4 + 9$

$\Rightarrow \qquad 7y = 5 \Rightarrow y = \dfrac{5}{7}$

4. *(a)* The correct sequence of steps :

III. Each exterior angle $= \dfrac{360°}{n} = \dfrac{360°}{10°} \quad [\because n = 10]$

I. Each exterior angle $= 36°$

II. Each interior angle $= 180° - 36° = 144°$

5. *(a)* According to the question,

$$\left[\left\{(y^2)^{\frac{1}{m}}\right\}^{\frac{m}{2}}\right]^2 = y^{2 \times \frac{1}{m} \times \frac{m}{2} \times 2} = y^2$$

6. *(c)* Given figure

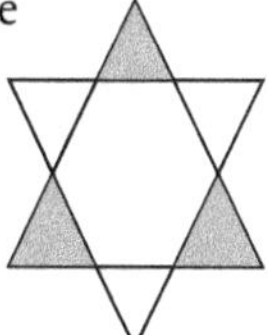

Order of rotational symmetry is 3.

7. *(d)* According to the question,

$$\text{SI} = \dfrac{P \times r \times t}{100} = \dfrac{3200 \times 9 \times 7}{100} = ₹\,2016$$

8. *(b)* Given, number of sweaters bought $= 4$

and cost of 1 sweater $= x$

$\therefore$ Cost of 4 sweaters $= 4x$

Now, number of skirts bought $= 1$

Cost of 1 skirt $= ₹\,20 \quad \therefore$ Total cost $= 4x + 20$

According to the question,

$$4x + 20 = 160$$

9. *(a)*

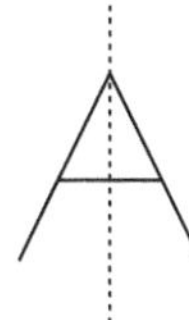

Letter A has only vertical line of symmetry.

10. *(b)*

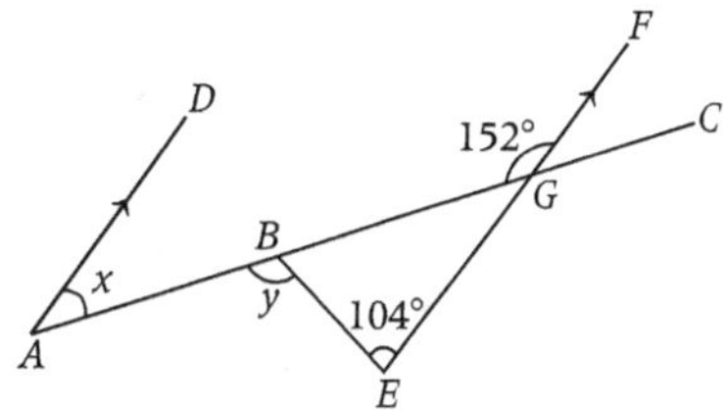

Now, $\qquad AD \parallel GF$

$\Rightarrow \angle x + 152° = 180°$ [interior angles on the same side of a transversal are supplementary]

$\therefore \qquad \angle x = 180° - 152° = 28°$

$\angle AGE = x = 280°$ [vertically opposite angles]

Now, in $\triangle BEG$,

$$\angle BEG + \angle BGE = \angle y$$

[exterior angle is equal to the sum of interior opposite angles]

$\therefore \qquad \angle y = 104° + 28° = 132°$

11. *(b)* According to the question,

Tom's percent $= \dfrac{553}{700} \times 100 = 79\%$

Abrahim's percent $= \dfrac{486}{600} \times 100 = 81\%$

$\therefore$ Abrahim's performance is better.

12. *(a)* Interest earned by Andrew $= \dfrac{5500 \times 2 \times 1}{100}$

$$= ₹\,110$$

and Interest earned by Anamika

$$= \dfrac{4800 \times 1 \times 2}{100} = 96$$

$\therefore$ Difference in interests $= ₹\,(110 - 96) = ₹\,14$

13. *(b)* According to the question,

$2[2a - 1 + a + 9] = 91 \Rightarrow 6a = 91 - 16$

$\therefore \qquad a = \dfrac{75}{6}$

$\therefore$ Length $= 2a - 1 = 2 \times \dfrac{75}{6} - 1 = 25 - 1 = 24\,\text{m}$

14. *(c)* Let $\dfrac{1}{3} + \dfrac{1}{5} = A$ and $\dfrac{1}{3} + \dfrac{1}{5} + \dfrac{1}{7} = B$

According to the question, we have

$(1 + A)\,B - (1 + B)\,A = B + AB - A - AB$

$= B - A = \left(\dfrac{1}{3} + \dfrac{1}{5} + \dfrac{1}{7}\right) - \left(\dfrac{1}{3} + \dfrac{1}{5}\right) = \dfrac{1}{7}$

15. *(b)* As, $\triangle ABC \cong \triangle XYZ$. Then, $\angle XYZ = \angle ABC$

$\therefore \qquad \angle Y = \angle B \Rightarrow \angle B = 36°$

and $\qquad \angle A = 180° - 90° - \angle B$

$= 180° - 90° - 36° = 54°$

16. *(b)*

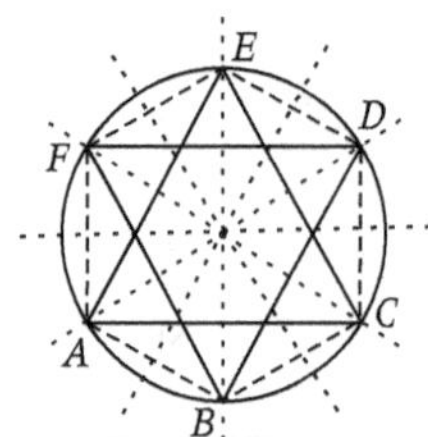

It has 6 lines of symmetry.

17. *(a)* 5 times a number $(n) = 5n$

7 more than 5 times a number $= 7 + 5n$

According to the 1st statement, $5n + 7 = 17$

18. *(a)* Dimension of the floor $= 20\,\text{m} \times 10\,\text{m}$

Area of the floor $= (20 \times 10)\,\text{m}^2 = 200\,\text{m}^2$

Length of each square marble $= 1\,\text{m}$

Then its area $= 1\,\text{m}^2$

Total number of blue and white color marbles

$= \text{Area of the floor/Area of each marble} = \dfrac{200}{1} = 200$

Number of blue color marbles required $= \dfrac{200}{2} = 100$

19. *(d)* $(p^x)^{zy} + (p^y)^{zx} + (p^z)^{xy} = p^{xyz} + p^{xyz} + p^{xyz}$

$\qquad\qquad = 3 \times p^{xyz} = 3 \times p^0 = 3 \times 1 = 3$

20. *(a)* Let the number of items purchased be X and $X + 18$.

Then, $X + 18 = \dfrac{75}{100}$ of total number of items

$$X + 18 = \left(\dfrac{75}{100}\right)(X + 18 + X)$$

$\Rightarrow \qquad X + 18 = \dfrac{3(2X + 18)}{4} \Rightarrow X + 18 = \dfrac{3(X + 9)}{2}$

$\Rightarrow \qquad 2X + 36 = 3X + 27 \Rightarrow X = 9$

Hence, the required number $= 9 + 9 + 18 = 36$

21. *(a)* Given that, $A : B : C = 5 : 6 : 7$

$$\therefore \left(\dfrac{A}{B}\right) : \left(\dfrac{B}{C}\right) : \left(\dfrac{C}{A}\right) = \left(\dfrac{5}{6}\right) : \left(\dfrac{6}{7}\right) : \left(\dfrac{7}{5}\right)$$

$$= \left(\dfrac{5 \times 7 \times 5}{6 \times 7 \times 5}\right) : \left(\dfrac{6 \times 5 \times 6}{7 \times 5 \times 6}\right) : \left(\dfrac{7 \times 6 \times 7}{5 \times 6 \times 7}\right) = 175 : 180 : 294$$

22. *(a)* Marya's salary $= ₹30000$

Money spent on rent $= \dfrac{20}{100} \times 30000 = ₹6000$

Remaining salary $= ₹(30000 - 6000) = ₹24000$

Money spent on other expenses $= \dfrac{80}{100} \times 24000$

$\qquad\qquad\qquad\qquad = ₹19200$

Remaining money or savings $= 24000 - 19200$

$\qquad\qquad\qquad = ₹4800$

23. *(c)* $\dfrac{17\frac{2}{3} + 21\frac{1}{2} - 9\frac{1}{3}}{79\frac{1}{2} - 49\frac{2}{3}} = \dfrac{\frac{53}{3} + \frac{43}{2} - \frac{28}{3}}{\frac{159}{2} - \frac{149}{3}} = \dfrac{\frac{25}{3} + \frac{43}{2}}{\frac{159}{2} - \frac{149}{3}}$

$= \dfrac{\dfrac{50 + 129}{6}}{\dfrac{477 - 298}{6}} = \dfrac{\frac{179}{6}}{\frac{179}{6}} = 1$

24. *(a)* Let CP be x.

$\therefore$ Marked price $= 20\%$ of $x + x$

$\qquad = \dfrac{20}{100} \times x + x = \dfrac{2x}{10} + x = 1.2x$

SP of product $= 90\%$ of $1.2x = 1.08x$

Profit $= 120$

$\therefore \qquad\qquad \text{CP} = \text{SP} - \text{Profit}$

$\Rightarrow \qquad x = 1.08x - 120 \Rightarrow 120 = 1.08x - x$

$\Rightarrow \qquad 120 = 0.08x \qquad \Rightarrow \quad x = 1500$

25. *(a)* $\dfrac{3x - 7 + 11x + 21}{2} = \dfrac{14x + 14}{2} = 7x + 7$

At $\qquad x = 4, 7x + 7 = 7 \times 4 + 7 = 28 + 7 = 35$

26. *(b)* Cost of laptop $= ₹\,27900$ [given]

Discount $= 10\%$

Let actual price of laptop be x.

Then, $\dfrac{90}{100} x = 27900 \Rightarrow x = \dfrac{27900 \times 100}{90} = ₹31000$

Further, reduction of $5\% = 31000 \times \dfrac{5}{100} = ₹1550$

$\therefore$ Net discounted price $= 27900 - 1550 = ₹26350$

27. *(b)* Let time be T.

$\therefore$ We have, $\quad \text{SI} = \dfrac{P \times R \times T}{100}$

$\Rightarrow \quad 10800 = \dfrac{30000 \times 12 \times T}{100} \quad \Rightarrow \quad T = \dfrac{108}{3 \times 12}$

$\Rightarrow \qquad T = 3\,\text{yr}$

28. *(a)* Let the CP of 1 skirt $= ₹\,x$

CP of 1 kurti $= ₹\,y$

According to the question,

$\qquad\qquad 2x + 3y = 2200 \qquad\qquad\qquad …(i)$

and $\qquad\quad 2y + 4x = 2400$

$\Rightarrow \qquad\quad 2x + y = 1200 \qquad\qquad\qquad …(ii)$

From Eqs. (i) and (ii), we get

$\qquad x = ₹\,350$ and $y = ₹\,500$

$\therefore$ Required Ratio $= \dfrac{500}{350} = 10 : 7$

29. *(d)* Consider, $\dfrac{(2x^3z^2)^6}{8x^3y^4z^2 \cdot x^{-4}z^3} = \dfrac{2^6 x^{18} z^{12}}{8x^{3-4} y^4 z^5}$

$\qquad\qquad\qquad\qquad\qquad [\because (a^m)^n = a^{m \cdot n}]$

$$= \frac{2^6 x^{18} z^{12}}{8x^{-1} y^4 z^5} = \frac{2^6 x^{19} z^7}{8y^4} \left[\because a^m \times a^n = a^{m+n}, \frac{a^m}{a^n} = a^{m-n} \right]$$

$$= \frac{8x^{19} z^7}{y^4}$$

30. *(b)* Let the number of 10 paise, 25 paise, 50 paise coins be $10x$, $8x$, $9x$ respectively.

According to the question

$$10x \times 0.10 + 8x \times 0.25 + 9x \times 0.50 = 20 + 40$$

$$\Rightarrow \quad x + 2x + 4.5x = 60$$

$$\Rightarrow \quad 7.5x = 60 \Rightarrow x = 8$$

$\therefore$ Number of 25 paise coins $= 8 \times 8 = 64$

31. *(c)* Let $0.35 + 0.58 = A$ and $0.35 + 0.58 + 0.78 = B$

We have, $(1 + A)B - (1 + B)A$

$$= B + AB - A - AB = B - A$$

$$= 0.35 + 0.58 + 0.78 - 0.35 - 0.58 = 0.78$$

32. *(c)* Total number of balls in the bag $= 3 + 4 + 5 = 12$

Required probability $= \dfrac{\text{Number of blue balls}}{\text{Number of total balls}}$

$$= \frac{3}{12} = \frac{1}{4}$$

33. *(b)* Rate $= \dfrac{\text{SI} \times 100}{P \times T} = \dfrac{2500 \times 100}{7500 \times 5} = 6\dfrac{2}{3}\%$

34. *(a)* The coefficient of x^2 in

$$\frac{-49}{87} Px^2 + z^2 yx \text{ is } -\frac{49}{87} \times P$$

35. *(c)* I. Number of lines of symmetry = 0

II. Number of lines of symmetry = 4

III. Number of lines of symmetry = 1

36. *(d)* A Pythagoras triple consists of 3 positive integers a, b, c such that $a^2 + b^2 = c^2$.

So, we can see, option (d) verify it.

$$(17)^2 = (15)^2 + (8)^2 = 225 + 64 \Rightarrow 289 = 289$$

37. *(a)* Both Statements I and II are correct.

(as per the definition)

38. *(a)*

A. Mode is 1 as 1 occurred more times than the other numbers.

B. Mode is 19 as 19 occurred more times than the other numbers.

C. Mode is 11 as 11 occurred more time than others.

D. Mode is 9 as 9 occurred more times than others.

39. *(a)* P $\rightarrow$ Let the side of the square $= a$

$\therefore$ Perimeter $= 4a \Rightarrow 320 = 4a$

$\therefore \qquad a = 80\,\text{m}$

Area $= a^2 = 80 \times 80 = 6400\,\text{m}^2$

Q $\rightarrow \because$ Perimeter of square $= 4a$

Area $= a^2$

Perimeter of new square $= 2 \times 4a = 4 \times (2a)$

$\therefore$ Area $= (2a)^2 = 4a^2$

$\therefore$ Required ratio $= a^2 : 4a^2 = 1 : 4$

R $\rightarrow$

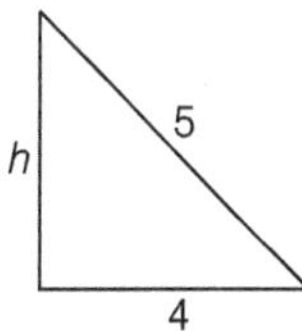

$$h^2 + 4^2 = 5^2 \Rightarrow h^2 = 25 - 16 = 9$$

$$\therefore \qquad h = 3$$

$\therefore$ Area $= \dfrac{1}{2} \times b \times h = \dfrac{1}{2} \times 4 \times 3 = 6\,\text{m}^2$

40. *(b)* I. False.

Sum of two rational numbers is always a rational number.

Example, $\dfrac{1}{2} + \dfrac{2}{3} = \dfrac{3+4}{6} = \dfrac{7}{6}$ is a rational number

II. True.

III. True.

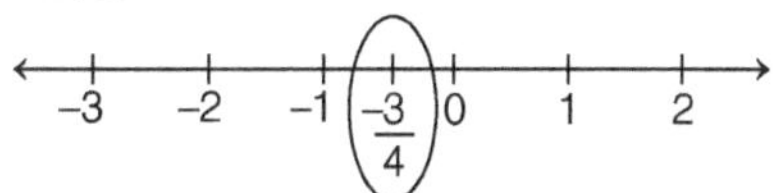

IV. False.

As $-\left(\dfrac{-3}{7} \right) = +\dfrac{3}{7}$ is a positive rational number.

41. *(b)* Let original length be l, original breadth be b and original height be h.

Original volume $= lbh$

Now, new length $= \dfrac{11}{10} l$

$$\left[\because \text{new length} = l + \frac{10}{100} l \right]$$

New breadth $= \dfrac{4}{5} b$ and new height $= \dfrac{11}{10} h$

New volume, $\dfrac{11}{10} l \times \dfrac{4}{5} b \times \dfrac{11}{10} h$

$$= \frac{484}{500} lbh$$

$$= 0.968\, lbh$$

$\therefore$ New volume as a percentage of original volume

$$= \frac{0.968\, lbh}{lbh} \times 100 = 96.8\%$$

42. *(d)* Option (a) has 3 folds of rotational i.e. $\dfrac{360°}{3} = 120°$

Option (b) has 5 folds of rotational i.e. $\dfrac{360°}{5} = 72°$

Option (c) has 4 folds of rotational i.e. $\dfrac{360°}{4} = 90°$

43. *(a)* Let SP be x. Profit = ₹1000

$\therefore \quad$ CP $= x - 1000$

New SP = 80% of $x = \dfrac{8}{10}x$ and loss = ₹600

$\therefore \qquad$ CP $= \dfrac{8}{10}x + 600$

So, we have

$$x - 1000 = \dfrac{8}{10}x + 600 \qquad [\because \text{CP is same}]$$

$\Rightarrow \qquad \dfrac{2}{10}x = 1600$

$\Rightarrow \qquad x = ₹\,8000$

$\therefore \qquad$ CP $= ₹\,(8000 - 1000) = ₹\,7000$

44. *(d)* Patient's total bill = ₹ 92000

Money back on 1st bill of ₹ 20000 $= \dfrac{90}{100} \times 20000$

$$= ₹18000$$

Money back on next of ₹ 40000 $= \dfrac{40000 \times 80}{100}$

$$= ₹32000$$

Remaining amount = 92000 − 20000 − 40000

$$= ₹\,32000$$

Money back on remaining amount $= \dfrac{32000 \times 40}{100}$

$$= ₹12800$$

$\therefore$ Total money received from insurance

$$= ₹\,18000 + ₹\,32000 + ₹\,12800 = ₹\,62800$$

45. *(c)* Consider $\dfrac{(2hj^2k^{-2} \cdot h^4 j^{-1} k^4)^0}{2h^{-3}j^{-4}k^{-2}}$

$$= \dfrac{1}{2h^{-3}j^{-4}k^{-2}} = \dfrac{h^3 j^4 k^2}{2} \quad \left[\because a^0 = 1 \text{ and } a^{-m} = \dfrac{1}{a^m}\right]$$

46. *(b)* Consider ΔDCB,

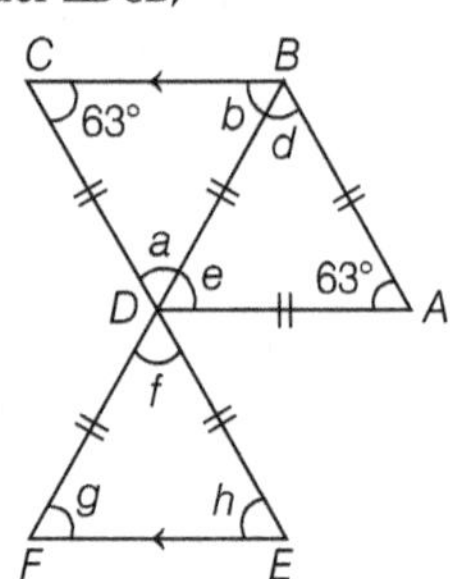

$$\angle a + \angle b + \angle DCB = 180°$$

$\Rightarrow \qquad \angle a + \angle b + 63° = 180°$

$\Rightarrow \qquad \angle a + \angle b = 117°$

Also, $\qquad\qquad \angle b = 63° \qquad [\because DC = DB]$

$\Rightarrow \qquad\qquad \angle a = 54°$

$$\angle FDE = \angle CDB = 54°$$

$$[\text{vertically opposite angles}]$$

$\therefore \qquad \angle CDB + \angle FDE = 54° + 54° = 108°$

47. *(a)* P : True

Angles multiples of 15° are 15°, 30°, 45°, 60°, 75°, 90° ...
These angles can be constructed using ruler and compass.

Q → True.

48. *(c)* Let the payment of Marie = ₹ X

John Paid $= X - X \times \dfrac{15}{100} = \dfrac{85X}{100} = \dfrac{17X}{20}$

Joseph Paid $= \dfrac{85X}{100} + \dfrac{85X}{100} \times \dfrac{25}{100}$

$$= \dfrac{85X}{100}\left(1 + \dfrac{25}{100}\right) = 85X \times \dfrac{125}{10000} = \dfrac{17X}{16}$$

According to the question,

$$X + \dfrac{17X}{20} + \dfrac{17X}{16} = 17475$$

$$\dfrac{(80X + 17 \times 4X + 17 \times 5X)}{80} = 17475$$

$$\dfrac{233X}{80} = 17475$$

$$X = 17475 \times \dfrac{80}{233} = 75 \times 80 = 6000$$

$$X = 6000$$

Hence, the amount paid by Marie is ₹ 6000.

49. *(b)* It is clear from the bar graph that, in 2016, the annual growth rate of total production is highest.

50. *(b)* For product P,

Total revenue for the period 2014-17

$$= 45 \times 9 + 25 \times 9 + 40 \times 9 + 35 \times 9$$

$$= 405 + 225 + 360 + 315 = 1305$$

For product Q,

Revenue $= 95 \times 4 + 40 \times 4 + 115 \times 4 + 60 \times 4$

$$= 380 + 160 + 460 + 240 = 1240$$

For product R,

Revenue $= 75 \times 13 + 95 \times 13 + 115 \times 13 + 65 \times 13$

$$= 975 + 1235 + 1495 + 845 = 4550$$

For product S,

Revenue $= 115 \times 3 + 155 \times 3 + 165 \times 3 + 140 \times 3$

$$= 345 + 465 + 495 + 420 = 1725$$

So, product Q fetches the lowest revenue.

Practice Set 2

1. *(d)* Consider, $\dfrac{(-2) \times 3 \times (-3) \times (-2)}{-1} = \dfrac{-36}{-1} = 36$

$\therefore$ Correct option is (d).

2. *(b)* According to the question, X is 20% more than Z, then $X = 120\%$ of $Z = \dfrac{120Z}{100} = \dfrac{6Z}{5}$

and Y is 50% more than Z

then $Y = 150\%$ of $Z = \dfrac{150Z}{100} = \dfrac{3Z}{2}$

$\therefore$ Required ratio $= \dfrac{X}{Y} = \dfrac{\dfrac{6Z}{5}}{\dfrac{3Z}{2}} = \dfrac{4}{5} = 4:5$

3. *(d)* According to the question,

$x + 2x + 3x = 120 \implies 6x = 120$

$\qquad\qquad\qquad x = 20$

$\therefore$ Here marks are 20, 40 and 60

4. *(a)* The size of greatest part $= \dfrac{5}{3+4+5} \times 6000$

$\qquad\qquad\qquad = 2500$ acres.

5. *(c)* In the given figure, ΔABD is an equilateral triangle.

$\therefore$ All angles are of measure $60°$.

In ΔBDC, $\angle BDC + \angle DCB + \angle DBC = 180°$

$\qquad\qquad\qquad\qquad$ [angle sum property]

$\implies \qquad 90° + 35° + \angle DBC = 180°$

$\implies \qquad\qquad\qquad \angle DBC = 180° - 125° = 55°$

Now, $\qquad\qquad\qquad \angle ABC = \angle ABD + \angle DBC$

$\qquad\qquad\qquad\qquad = 60° + 55° = 115°$

6. *(d)* Albert bought the refrigerator at ₹ 52000

Amount for repairing = ₹ 4000

Total cost price = ₹ 52000 + ₹ 4000 = ₹ 56000

Selling price = ₹ 47000

Therefore the amount of loss = CP – SP

$\qquad\qquad\qquad = 56000 - 47000 = ₹\ 9000$

Loss percent $= \dfrac{\text{Loss} \times 100}{\text{CP}} = 9000 \times \dfrac{100}{56000} = \dfrac{900}{56}$

$\qquad\qquad = \dfrac{225}{14}\% = 16\dfrac{1}{14}\%$

7. *(a)* We know that,

Net percent effect $= \left(x + y + \dfrac{xy}{100}\right)\%$

Given; Increased salary $= x = 50\%$

Decreased salary $= y = -50\%$

Putting the values

She loss $\% = \left(50 - 50 - \dfrac{50 \times 50}{100}\right) = -25\%$

or $\qquad 25\%$ loss

8. *(c)* Let CP of 1 book = ₹ 1

$\because$ CP of 32 books = SP of 24 books

$\therefore$ SP of 1 books $= \dfrac{32}{24} = \dfrac{4}{3}$

$\therefore$ profit percent $= \dfrac{\text{SP} - \text{CP}}{\text{CP}} \times 100 = \dfrac{\dfrac{4}{3} - 1}{1} \times 100 = \dfrac{100}{3}\%$

9. *(c)* Given expression is $P\%$ of $1864 + 60 = 618.2$

$\dfrac{1864 \times P}{100} + 60 = 618.2$

$\implies \dfrac{1864 \times P}{100} = 558.2 \implies P = \dfrac{5582}{10} \times \dfrac{100}{1864}$

$\implies \qquad\qquad P = 29.94$

10. *(a)* The given statement $= (-12 - 4) \times 3^2$

$\qquad\qquad\qquad\qquad = (-16) \times 9 = -144$

11. *(b)* 2 is opposite to 4.

12. *(c)* $\angle AOC + \angle BOC = 180°$ $\qquad$ [Linear pair]

$\implies \qquad 2x - 10° + 3x + 20° = 180°$

$\implies \qquad\qquad\qquad 5x + 10 = 180°$

$\implies \qquad\qquad\qquad 5x = 170°$

$\implies \qquad\qquad\qquad x = \dfrac{170°}{5} = 34°$

So, $(5x + 40)° = (5 \times 34 + 40)° = (170 + 40)° = 210°$

13. *(b)* Given, $S_n = \dfrac{n}{2}\{2a + (n-1)\,d\}$

Here, $n = 10$, $a = 6$ and $d = 4$

$\therefore S_{10} = \dfrac{10}{2}\{2 \times 6 + (10 - 1)4\} = 5\{12 + 36\} = 240$

14. *(a)* Prescription orders in India, for 2010

$\qquad\qquad = 3500000000000 = 3.5 \times 10^{12}$

Average price of each prescription = ₹ 65

$\therefore$ Total price $= ₹\ 65 \times 3.5 \times 10^{12} = 227.5 \times 10^{12}$

$\qquad\qquad = 2.275 \times 10^{14}$

15. *(c)* Given, $x = -2$, $y = 3$ and $z = -4$

$\therefore -4x + 5y + 2z = -4(-2) + 5(3) + 2(-4)$

$\qquad\qquad = 8 + 15 - 8 = 15$

16. *(b)* By the given statement in question,

Perimeter $= 2(2w) + 2(w) = 4w + 2w = 6w$

where, w is the width of the rectangle in inches.

17. *(a)* Commission received by travelling agent at rate = 4.5%

Amount of commission received = ₹ 31.5

We have, $\dfrac{4.5}{100} \times x = ₹\ 31.5$

$\therefore \quad x = \dfrac{31.5}{4.5} \times 100 = 700$

18. *(b)* Given, $C = \dfrac{AX}{X + 15}$

Here, $A = 50$ gm and $X = 10$ yr

$\therefore \quad C = \dfrac{50 \times 10}{10 + 15} = \dfrac{500}{25} = 20$ gm

19. *(d)* By folding the given pattern we get shape as in option (d).

20. *(a)* Consider, $63 - (-3)\ \{-3 - \overline{8 - 3}\} \div 3\{5 + (-3)\ (-1)\}$

$\quad = 63 + 3\ \{-3 - 5\} \div 3(5 + 3)\}$

$\quad = 63 + 3\ \{-8\} \div 3\ (8)$

$\quad = 63 - 24 + 24 = 63 - 1 = 62$

21. *(d)* Given, $\angle 1 = 32°$ and $\angle 2 + \angle 3 = 90°$

Also, $\angle 1 + \angle 2 = 90° \Rightarrow \angle 1 = \angle 3 = 32°$

We know that,

$\quad \angle 3 + \angle 4 = 90° \Rightarrow 32° + \angle 4 = 90°$

$\Rightarrow \quad \angle 4 = 90° - 32° = 58°$

22. *(c)* Write the data in ascending order,

1.7, 2.5, 3.9, 5.1, 6.3

$\therefore$ Range = Largest number − Smallest number

$\quad = 6.3 - 1.7 = 4.6$

23. *(a)* Amount of money Arvind has = ₹1500

Amount spent on buying 3 identical shirts

$\quad = 0.75 \times 1500 = ₹1125$

$\therefore$ Cost of 1 such shirt $= \dfrac{1125}{3} = 375$

Now, cost of 2 pairs of shoes $= 1500 - 1125 = ₹375$

$\therefore$ Cost of 1 shirt + 2 pairs of shoes $= 375 + 375$

$\quad = ₹750$

24. *(b)* Consider, $\dfrac{2x^2y^4 \cdot 4x^2y^4 \cdot 3x}{3x^{-3}y^2}$

$= \dfrac{8x^{2+2+1}y^{4+4}}{x^{-3}y^2} \qquad [\because a^m \times a^n = a^{m+n}]$

$= \dfrac{8x^5y^8}{x^{-3}y^2} = 8x^{5+3}y^{8-2} \qquad \left[\because \dfrac{a^m}{a^n} = a^{m-n} \right]$

$= 8x^8y^6$

25. *(b)* Let total number of fruits be x.

$\therefore$ Number of oranges $= \dfrac{2}{5}x$

Number of bananas $= \dfrac{3}{5}x$

Number of bananas added = 80

Number of oranges added $= \dfrac{1}{4} \times \left(80 + \dfrac{3}{5}x \right)$

$= 20 + \dfrac{3}{20}x$

Total fruits $= \dfrac{2}{5}x + 20 + \dfrac{3}{20}x + \dfrac{3}{5}x + 80$

$\Rightarrow 148 + x = x + 100 + \dfrac{3}{20}x$

$\Rightarrow \quad 48 = \dfrac{3}{20}x \quad \Rightarrow \quad x = 16 \times 20 \Rightarrow x = 320$

26. *(d)* $\dfrac{(16)^{2x+1}(64)^5}{(256)^2 \times 4} = (16)^{6x}$

$\Rightarrow \dfrac{(2)^{4(2x+1)} \cdot (2)^{6 \times 5}}{(2)^{8 \times 2} \times (2)^2} = (2)^{4 \times 6x}$

$\Rightarrow (2)^{8x+4+30-16-2} = (2)^{24x}$

$\Rightarrow \quad 8x + 16 = 24x \Rightarrow 16x = 16$

$\Rightarrow \quad x = 1$

27. *(c)* Mean $= \dfrac{\text{Sum of terms}}{\text{Number of terms}}$

$= (2 + 4 + 6 + 7 + 7 + 13 + 18 + 92)/8 = \dfrac{149}{8} = 18.625$

Here, $n = 8$

$\therefore$ Median $= \dfrac{\dfrac{n}{2}\text{th term} + \left(\dfrac{n}{2} + 1\right)\text{th term}}{2}$

$= \dfrac{\text{4th term} + \text{5th term}}{2} = \dfrac{7 + 7}{2} = 7$

$\therefore$ Required difference $= 18.625 - 7 = 11.625$

28. *(c)* Area of the floor $= (3 \times 12)\ \text{m}^2$

It is given that, 100 square marbles are needed to cover the floor of area $(3 \times 12)\ \text{m}^2$.

Area of each marble $= \dfrac{3 \times 12}{100}\text{m}^2 = \dfrac{36}{100}\text{m}^2 = 0.36\ \text{m}^2$

Since the marbles are in square shape, the length of each marble $= \sqrt{(0.36)}\ \text{m} = 0.6\ \text{m} = 60\ \text{cm}$

29. *(b)* In $\triangle AOB$ and $\triangle DOC$

$\quad \angle AOB = \angle DOC \qquad$ [vertically opposite angles]

$\quad\quad OA = OD$ (given)

$\quad\quad OB = OC$ (given)

$\therefore \quad\quad \triangle AOB \cong \triangle DOC$ (by SAS congruency)

30. *(d)* Consider, $\dfrac{25P - 12}{3}$

Given, $P = 6$

We have, $\dfrac{25 \times 6 - 12}{3} = \dfrac{138}{3} = 46$

31. *(d)* Age of Johanson = 5 yr

Age of Joseph = $(5 + n)$ yr

Age of Johanson, 3 yr later = $5 + 3 = 8$ yr

and age of Joseph, 3 yr later = $8 + n$

So, their total age, after 3 yr = $8 + 8 + n = 16 + n$

32. *(a)* Ratio of share is $3 : 5 : 8$ among A, B and C respectively.

$\therefore$ Share of $B = \dfrac{5}{16} \times 3200 = ₹\ 1000$

Share of $C = \dfrac{8}{16} \times 3200 = ₹\ 1600$

$\therefore$ Required difference = $1600 - 1000 = ₹\ 600$

33. *(a)* Let the sum of money = $₹\ P$

and Rate = $R\%$

According to the question,

$$\dfrac{P \times R \times 5}{100} = 3P - P \Rightarrow \dfrac{P \times R \times 5}{100} = 2P$$

$$R = 40\%$$

Again let the sum 5 times be in T yr.

Then, $\dfrac{P \times 40 \times t}{100} = 5P - P$

$$\dfrac{P \times 40 \times t}{100} = 4P \Rightarrow t = 10\ \text{yr}$$

34. *(d)* Let the fraction be x.

According to the question,

$$x + \dfrac{7}{x} = \dfrac{11}{2} \Rightarrow \dfrac{x^2 + 7}{x} = \dfrac{11}{2}$$

$$2x^2 + 14 = 11x$$

$$2x^2 - 11x + 14 = 0 \Rightarrow (2x - 7)(x - 2) = 0$$

$$\therefore \qquad x = \dfrac{7}{2}, \dfrac{2}{1}$$

But, $\dfrac{2}{1}$ is not in option. Option (d) is correct.

35. *(a)* Let r be the radius of circle.

Now, $P = \pi r^2$, $Q = 2\pi r$, $R = 2r$

$$\therefore \quad \dfrac{P}{QR} = \dfrac{\pi r^2}{2\pi r \times 2r} = \dfrac{1}{4} \quad \therefore \quad \dfrac{P}{QR} = 1 : 4$$

36. *(c)* Given, $AD = \dfrac{1}{2} BC$

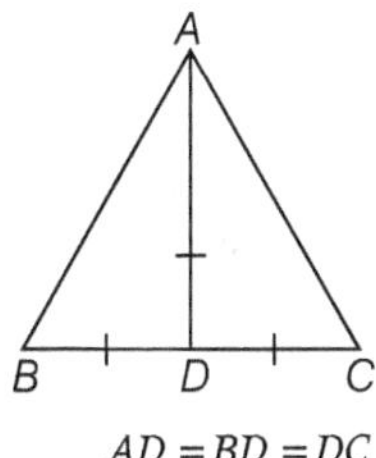

$$AD = BD = DC$$

In $\quad\ \triangle ABD, \angle ABD = \angle BAD \qquad \text{...(i)}$

[Sides opposite to equal angles are equal]

In $\triangle ADC,\qquad \angle ACD = \angle DAC \qquad \text{...(ii)}$

Now in $\triangle ABC$,

$$\angle ABC + \angle BAC + \angle ACB = 180°$$

$$\Rightarrow \angle BAD + \angle BAC + \angle DAC = 180°$$

[from Eqs. (i) and (ii)]

$$\Rightarrow \qquad 2\angle BAC = 180° \quad \therefore \quad \angle BAC = 90°$$

37. *(c)* **Assertion** 5 is a real number and can be written as $\dfrac{5}{1}$ that is, the ratio of 2 integers.

Hence, **5** is a rational number.

$\therefore$ Assertion statement is true.

Reason Square roots of all positive integers are not rational. Reason is not true.

38. *(d)* I. Supplement of $80° = 180° - 80° = 100°$

II. Complement of $80° = 90° - 80° = 10°$

III. Hypotenuse

IV. Rectangle

39. *(d)* **P.** Here, sample space of the experiment is

$$S = \{1, 2, 3, 4, 5, 6\}$$

Let E be the event of an even number is obtained

$$\therefore \quad E = \{2, 4, 6\} \quad \therefore \quad P(E) = \dfrac{n(E)}{n(S)} = \dfrac{3}{6} = \dfrac{1}{2}$$

Q. Total cases = $4 \times 4 \times 4 = 64$ ways.

Cases when men are going in different restaurants

$$= 4 \times 3 \times 2 = 24\ \text{ways}.$$

$\therefore$ Required probability = $\dfrac{24}{64} = \dfrac{3}{8}$

R. $\ \text{SI} = \dfrac{200 \times 5 \times 6}{100} = ₹\ 60$

S. Loss $\ \therefore$ The correct option is (d).

40. *(b)* **P.** False.

If perimeter of an equilateral triangle is 45 cm.

Then, $3a = 45 \Rightarrow a = \dfrac{45}{3} = 15\ \text{cm}$

$$\therefore \quad \text{Area} = \dfrac{\sqrt{3}}{4} a^2 = \dfrac{\sqrt{3}}{4} \times (15)^2 = \dfrac{225\sqrt{3}}{4}\ \text{cm}^2$$

Q. True. Here, Diagonal = 10 cm

$$\therefore \ \text{Area} = \dfrac{1}{2} \times (\text{Diagonal})^2 = \dfrac{1}{2} \times (10)^2 = 50\ \text{cm}^2$$

R. False. According to the question, $2\pi r - r = 37$

$$r(2\pi - 1) = 37 \Rightarrow r = \dfrac{37}{(2\pi - 1)}$$

$\therefore$ Circumference = $2\pi r = \dfrac{2\pi}{(2\pi - 1)} \times 37 \approx 44$

S. False. If $\angle ABC = 75°$ (given)

then $\angle XYZ = 75°$ (by CPCT)

41. *(c)* Let the cost of air conditioner be x.

Profit on sales of 1st type air conditioner = 20 %
Sales price of 1st type air conditioner = 30400
So, $\dfrac{120}{100} \times x = 30400 \Rightarrow x = \dfrac{30400 \times 100}{120} = 25333.33$

Loss on sales of 2nd type air conditioner = 25%
So, $\dfrac{75}{100} \times x = 30400 \Rightarrow x = \dfrac{30400 \times 100}{75} = 40533.33$

Total cost price = $25333.33 + 40533.33 = 65866.66$
Total sell = $2 \times 30400 = 60800$
Gain/Loss = $60800 - 65866.66$
$= -5066.66 \approx -5067$
Hence, loss on sale is ₹ 5067.

42. *(c)* $AD \parallel BC, AB \parallel CD$

then $\quad \angle A = \angle C, \angle B = \angle D \quad \therefore \quad \angle A = 78°$
In $\triangle ADX$, $AD = XD \quad \Rightarrow \quad \angle DAX = \angle DXA$

  [angles opposite to equal sides are also equal]
$\therefore \qquad \angle DXA = 78°$
Also, $\angle ADX + \angle DAX + \angle DXA = 180°$
$\Rightarrow n + 78° + 78° = 180° \quad \therefore \quad n = 24°$
Also, $AB \parallel CD$
$\therefore \qquad \angle ABC + \angle BCD = 180°$
$\therefore \qquad m + 68° + 78° = 180° \Rightarrow m = 34°$
[interior angles on the same side of transversal are
            supplementary]

43. *(a)* $\therefore$ Number of students who got grade B

$= 42 - 42\left(\dfrac{1}{2} + \dfrac{1}{3} + \dfrac{1}{7}\right)$

$= 42 - 42\left(\dfrac{21 + 14 + 6}{42}\right) = 42 - 41 = 1$

44. *(a)* Consider, $\dfrac{(2m^{-1}pq^0)^{-4} \cdot 2m^{-1}p^3}{2pq^2}$

$= \dfrac{2^{-4}\, m^4\, p^{-4} \cdot 2m^{-1}p^3}{2pq^2} \qquad [\because a^0 = 1]$

$= \dfrac{m^3}{2^4\, p^2\, q^2} = \dfrac{m^3}{16\, p^2\, q^2} \qquad \left[\because a^{-m} = \dfrac{1}{a^m}\right]$

45. *(b)* According to the question,
Ratio of their salary is 4 : 5
Let the original salary of Mukesh and Aparna be $4K$ and $5K$ respectively.
After increasing ₹ 6000, the ratio becomes 48 : 55
$\therefore \qquad \dfrac{4K + 6000}{5K + 6000} = \dfrac{48}{55}$

$220K + 330000 = 240K + 288000$
$\Rightarrow \qquad 20K = 42000 \Rightarrow K = 2100$
$\therefore$ Mukesh's salary $= 4K = 4 \times 2100 = ₹ 8400$

46. *(d)* Let the ratio of interest allowed by bank be R %.

According to the question,
$\dfrac{12000 \times 5 \times 10}{100} - \dfrac{12000 \times 3 \times R}{100} = 3320$

$\Rightarrow \qquad 6000 - 360R = 3320$

$\Rightarrow \qquad R = \dfrac{2680}{360} = 7\dfrac{4}{9}\%$

47. *(b)* In the given question, a radius of 3 m is divided in such a way that the radius of smaller semi-circle is 1 m and radius of bigger semi-circle is 2 m.

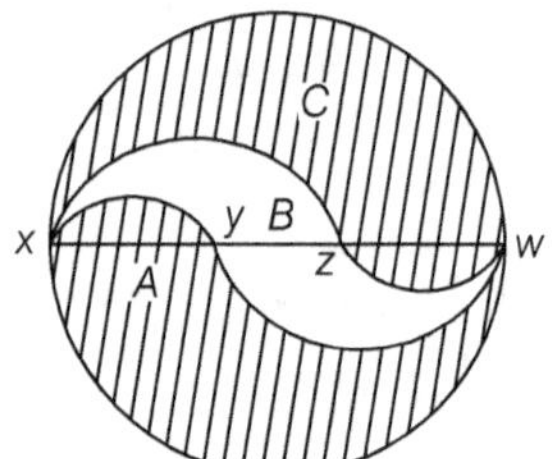

Area of shaded portion A = Area of semi-circle of radius 3 m – Area of semi-circle of radius 2 m + Area of semi-circle of radius 1 m

$= \dfrac{1}{2}\pi\,(3)^2 - \dfrac{1}{2}\pi\,(2)^2 + \dfrac{1}{2}\pi\,(1)^2$

$= \dfrac{1}{2}\pi\,(9 - 4 + 1) = 3\pi \text{ sq m}$

Area of portion $B = 2$ [Area of semi-circle of radius 2 m – Area of semi-circle of radius 1 m]

$= 2\left[\dfrac{1}{2}\pi(2)^2 - \dfrac{1}{2}\pi\,(1)^2\right] = 3\pi \text{ sq m}$

Area of shaded portion C = Area of portion A
Hence, the ratio of areas A, B and C is $1 : 1 : 1$.

48. *(c)* Number of seeds Sangeeta has = x

$\therefore$ Number of seeds Manisha has $= x + \dfrac{25x}{100} = \dfrac{125}{100}x$

Number of seeds given by Sangeeta to Manisha = 50

We have, $x - 50 = \dfrac{1}{2}\left(\dfrac{125}{100}x + 50\right)$

$\Rightarrow \qquad x - 50 = \dfrac{125}{200}x + 25$

$\Rightarrow \qquad x - \dfrac{125}{200}x = 75 \Rightarrow \dfrac{75}{200}x = 75 \Rightarrow x = 200$

49. *(d)*   **50.** *(a)*